S0-AYC-553

The Vietnam Conflict

War / Peace Bibliography Series

Richard Dean Burns, Editor

This Series has been developed
in cooperation with the
Center for the Study of Armament and Disarmament,
California State University, Los Angeles

Songs of Protest, War & Peace

A Bibliography & Discography
R. Serge Denisoff

Warfare in Primitive Societies

A Bibliography
William Tulio Divale

The Vietnam Conflict

Its Geographical Dimensions, Political Traumas, &
Military Developments
Milton Leitenberg & Richard Dean Burns

The Vietnam Conflict

Its Geographical Dimensions, Political Traumas, & Military Developments

Milton Leitenberg &
Richard Dean Burns
Compilers assisted by
Janice Roswell, Judith Roswell, & Lillemor Lindh

Santa Barbara, California
Oxford, England

Library of Congress Catalog Card Number 73-81980
ISBN Paperbound Edition 87436-120-6

American Bibliographical Center—Clio Press, Inc.
2040 Alameda Padre Serra
Santa Barbara, California

European Bibliographical Center—Clio Press
30 Cornmarket Street
Oxford OX1 3EY, England

Designed by Barbara Monahan
Composed by Camera-Ready Composition
Printed and bound by Consolidated Printers
in the United States of America

CONTENTS

FOREWORD

With this bibliographical series, the Center for the Study of Armament and Disarmament, California State University at Los Angeles, seeks to promote a wider understanding of martial violence and the alternatives to its employment. The Center, which was formed by concerned faculty and students in 1962-63, has as its primary objective the stimulation of intelligent discussion of war/peace issues. More precisely, the Center has undertaken two essential functions: (1) to collect and catalogue materials bearing on war/peace issues; and (2) to aid faculty, students and the public in their individual and collective probing of the historical, political, economic, philosophical, technical, and psychological facets of these fundamental problems.

This bibliographical series is, obviously, one tool with which we may more effectively approach our task. Each issue in this series is intended to provide a comprehensive "working," rather than definitive, bibliography on a relatively narrow theme within the spectrum of war/peace studies. While we hope this series will prove to be a useful tool, we also solicit your comments regarding its format, contents, and topics.

RICHARD DEAN BURNS
Series Editor

BRIEF CHRONOLOGY OF U.S. INVOLVEMENT WITH VIETNAM

208 B.C.E.	Founding of a Kingdom of Vietnam
939 C.E.	Direct Chinese Rule of Vietnam overthrown
1859-83	French consolidation of Indochina Empire; sporadic outbursts of Vietnamese anticolonial resistance
1885-95	Can Vuong "Protect the Monarch" movement led by Vietnamese mandarins against the French
1930-31	Serious nationalist uprisings; vigorously put down; communist party founded
1941	Japan invades French Indochina; U.S. OSS officers work with Viet Minh against the Japanese
1945	(August) Japan surrenders; Ho Chi Minh declares Vietnam independence; appeals for U.S. support
1946	French forces return; outbreak of 1st Indochina war
1949	(March) French establish Bao Dai government
1950	U.S. recognizes Bao Dai and begins sending supplies; Peking recognizes Ho government
1954	(April) U.S. seriously considers military intervention
	(May 8) French surrender Dien Bien Phu
	(May 8-July 11) Geneva Conference on Indochina
	(July 7) Ngo Dinh Diem appointed head of South Vietnam
1955	(February 19) U.S. forms SEATO with protocol covering Indochina
	(July 20) Talks begin for Vietnam elections; Diem rejects Hanoi's proposal for holding elections
1956	Last French troops leave; U.S. undertakes training and supplying of South Vietnamese army; elections to unify Vietnam not held
1957	(May 9) Diem visits U.S., addresses joint session of Congress

1960	(December 20) Formation of National Liberation Front of South Vietnam
1961	President Kennedy increases U.S. advisors to 18,000 and permits their entry into combat.
1962	Diem begins "strategic hamlet" program (July) U.S.-U.S.S.R. reach agreement on Laos neutralization
1963	(July) Buddhist uprisings against Diem (November 1) Diem overthrown and killed by military junta led by General Duong Van Minh (November-December) U Thant and Sihanouk of Cambodia propose talks for a peaceful settlement, coalition government, and neutralization
1964	(January) General Nguyen Khanh overthrows Minh junta (August) Gulf of Tonkin incident; Congress authorizes "all necessary measures"
1965	(February 7) U.S. begins bombing of North Vietnam (March 24-25) First Teach-In held at University of Michigan (June) Nguyen Cao Ky becomes Premier (November 4) U.S. forces reach 154,000 (December 24) U.S. begins a bombing pause; Hanoi calls for adhering to Geneva accords
1966	(March-June) Buddhist uprising against Ky (July 25) Ky urges invasion of North Vietnam (July 30) Large-scale Congressional protest begins (December 8) U.S. forces reach 362,000
1967	(April) Massive peace demonstrations throughout U.S. (September) Nguyen Van Thieu elected President of South Vietnam
1967-68	"Free-fire" zones created in South Vietnam; civilian casualties and refugee populations rise sharply
1968	(January-February) Tet offensive (March) President Johnson withdraws from Presidential race (October) President Johnson announces total bombing halt of North; U.S. steps up bombing in Laos
1969	(January) Four-party talks begin in Paris (May) President Nixon begins gradual withdrawal of 500,000-plus troops from Vietnam (September) Ho Chi Minh dies (November-December) Nixon announces "Vietnamization" program
1970	(March 18) Prince Sihanouk ousted from Cambodian government by Lon Nol

	(April 30) Nixon announces invasion of Cambodia
	(May) Nationwide protests against Cambodia invasion
	(June-July) Senate votes 81-0 to repeal Tonkin Gulf Resolution; seeks to legislate restriction on U.S. military actions in Southeast Asia
1971	(January 12) Nixon signs bill repealing Tonkin Gulf Resolution
	(February-March) U.S.-South Vietnam incursion into Laos
	(October 14) U.S. forces reduced to 206,000
1972	(March 30) Renewed North Vietnam attacks on South Vietnam
	(April 6) U.S. responds by renewing daily bombing of North Vietnam
	(May 9) Nixon orders mining of Haiphong and extends bombing of the North
	(October 26) Hanoi announces willingness to accept cease-fire and return U.S. POWs
	(December 16) Kissinger breaks off talks in Paris
	(December 18-30) Heavy U.S. bombing campaign around Hanoi and Haiphong
1973	(January 8) Paris talks renewed
	(January 24) Cease-fire initialed in Paris

INTRODUCTION

The Vietnam conflict has been underway for a very long time; it has encompassed perhaps three "wars." The First Indochina war (1946-54) found the Vietnamese struggling to eject the French from Indochina, a struggle which some Vietnamese like to point out had begun in the 1880s. The Second Indochina war (1961-68) found the United States, under the direction of Presidents John F. Kennedy and Lyndon B. Johnson, intervening in a "civil" contest between the two halves of Vietnam. The Third Vietnam war (1969-73), as its critics call it, developed under the leadership of President Richard Nixon and featured a dependence upon American technological weaponry, and particularly upon airpower.

Whether there have been two or three Vietnam "wars" is less significant than the fact that this conflict has touched the politics and emotions of peoples and governments around the world. And its effect upon the United States and Southeast Asia has been, understandably, traumatic.

The conflict's interminable duration and ever-mounting destructiveness have caused many Americans, especially the younger generations, to reevaluate the United States' cold war attitudes and policies, its emphasis of military over public priorities, its functioning (as opposed to ideal) political processes, and its moral conscience. In these Americans, the conflict has aroused a sense of dissatisfaction which, in turn, has manifested itself in emotional and political dissent, in passive and violent response. Yet, in other Americans, perhaps a majority, the response to the conflict has been a less dramatic but equally significant defense of the old order, of national honor, and of American commitment to anticommunism.

To those people living in Southeast Asia, the consequences of the fighting since 1965 have been often catastrophic. The United States determined early that it was going to use its technological advantage, rather than a heavy concentration of manpower, to bring its opponents to terms. This decision led inevitably to such vast destructiveness, not only in loss of life but in disruption of the countryside, that critics of American tactics have labeled these operations "ecocide."

From any vantage point, then, the Vietnam conflict has left a bewildering array of historical questions with vast ramifications for the present and future. For if the lessons of the past are to be truly meaningful, it is vital that the politics and military tactics be accurately portrayed and dispassionately criticized. This bibliography has assumed, as its primary purpose, the task of assisting in the illumination of these historical questions.

The remarks which follow are designed to focus on some of the issues which have received sharp criticism and which are delineated in the bibliography.

I

America's involvement in Indochina affairs began during World War Two when its agents sought to enlist the support of Vietnamese nationals, such as Ho Chi Minh, to harass the Japanese. Few people on this side of the Pacific knew or understood that Japan's invasion of Indochina had marked merely an interlude in an ongoing struggle by native forces to gain their independence from the French. Yet President Franklin D. Roosevelt, believing colonialism to be outmoded, argued against the reestablishment of the prewar empires in Asia upon conclusion of the war. He had little sympathy for French desires to regain control of their overseas territories and, on more than one occasion, urged that Indochina be given its independence.

What actually transpired in Indochina during the months after Japan's surrender is still a matter of historical contention, but it is clear now that it was a harbinger of things to come. During the war the Japanese had been too occupied with other matters to patrol outlying regions and, consequently, the Viet Minh were able to rally and organize nationalists of all political persuasions in anticipation of claiming independence when peace came. As the war ended, the Viet Minh quickly marched into Hanoi, created the Democratic Republic of Vietnam, and declared their independence. After a brief interlude, during which they recognized the Viet Minh regime, the French—with the assistance of British and Japanese forces—staged a coup and regained control of the major cities in Vietnam.

Although General Douglas MacArthur complained that the use of Japanese military forces to defeat our former allies was a disgraceful affair, the United States did nothing. The Pentagon Papers reveal that Ho Chi Minh tried to interest President Harry Truman in the plight of his new government during 1945-46, but that the Americans chose not to intervene at this time because of their desire to enlist France's support in revitalizing Europe and because of Ho's previous communist background.[1]

Following several abortive attempts at negotiations between the French and the Viet Minh, the French fleet in November 1946 bombarded the Vietnamese sections of Haiphong, killing some 6,000 unsuspecting citizens. The precedent for bloodiness came early in this war. The Viet Minh retaliated on December 20 with an attack upon French positions in Hanoi. When this action failed to dislodge the French, the native forces slipped away into the jungles and mountains to continue the struggle for independence.

The First Indochina war was underway. Although the United States proclaimed a "hands-off" attitude, it soon found itself indirectly involved. American military and economic aid being sent to France under NATO and various other European-oriented programs began, inevitably, to find its way to Southeast Asia. That Washington did not protest can be explained by two factors: first, the outbreak of the Korean war redirected American policymakers toward Asia and, second, the American people, becoming caught up in their anticommunism, accepted programs aimed at "containing" their foes everywhere with little critical examination. Thus, in 1950, Washington recognized Paris' puppet regime headed by Emperor-playboy Bao Dai and began to supply the French forces openly.

The Eisenhower administration, at the urging of Secretary of State John Foster Dulles, intensified support of French military efforts in Indochina. To prevent the collapse of French forces in early 1954, Washington officials, among them Vice President Richard Nixon, Dulles and military chiefs, pressed for direct American military intervention. Dwight Eisenhower resisted this effort primarily because he could not obtain British support for joint action, and the embittered French were forced to accept a cease-fire and acknowledge Vietnam independence in July at Geneva.

The forced French withdrawal from Indochina in 1955-56 left a big-power political vacuum which the United States promptly assumed for the West. From the records and memoirs of the mid-1950s it is clear that Dulles was instrumental in launching American efforts to abrogate the Geneva settlement; but the Kennedy administration also sanctioned these policies. These activities involved, in part, sabotage of North Vietnamese facilities, terrorization of North Vietnamese Catholics into fleeing to the South, establishment of an *Armie Clandestine* in Laos, and supply of illegal arms and advisors to South Vietnam. More significantly, Eisenhower endorsed President Diem's refusal to hold talks with Ho regarding reunification, including national elections.

[1]See the Senator Gravel Edition of *The Pentagon Papers*, 5 vols. (Boston: Beacon, 1971-72). For a review of this collection see Richard Dean Burns, "The Pentagon Papers: Review and Comment," *Southeast Asia Quarterly*, forthcoming.

It is worth noting here that the Eisenhower administration initiated the curious, ever-shifting public statements "justifying" America's involvement and interest in Indochina. On April 7, 1954, the President linked to Southeast Asia the "falling domino" principle, which had been used earlier by the Truman administration in regard to the Near East. He also stressed the importance of Indochina's "production of materials that the world needs," an infrequent official justification of American involvement, but one whose use its critics have exaggerated. Interestingly, Eisenhower also emphasized "the possibility that many human beings [might without U.S. action] pass under a dictatorship that is inimical to the free world."[2] If he meant what he said, then the war's critics cannot argue that the Thieu government does not meet Washington's standards. One further comment: the Pentagon Papers conveniently gathered together most of Washington's official statements on the "Justification of the War," and they appear in the back of each volume of the Senator Gravel edition.

The Second Indochina war began quietly enough with the decisions of the prounification forces to form the National Liberation Front and of President John F. Kennedy to ignore the restrictions imposed by the Geneva accords as the civil war went increasingly against Diem. As in the Truman years, the American decision to step up its participation seems to have been dictated more by global concerns—a desire to stand up to Russia and to demonstrate the administration's "credibility," a word which would appear more and more frequently—than by any specific American interests in Southeast Asia. And yet, as American military involvement increased, both Washington and South Vietnam Buddhists became disillusioned with the performance of President Diem and his family. On November 1, 1963, Diem was overthrown and assassinated in a palace coup; within the month President Kennedy also was dead.

As the Viet Cong (which the Viet Minh were now called) pressed toward victory in the South, it fell to President Lyndon B. Johnson to make the choice between withdrawing or augmenting American forces. The records indicate that there was little hesitation or discussion of alternatives associated with American withdrawal; he was determined that the United States would not be forced out of Southeast Asia. As soon as the elections of November 1964 had registered a landslide victory for the "moderate" Johnson against the "radical" Senator Barry Goldwater, the President expanded the United States' military operations to include a limited, controlled aerial bombing of the North. Although Marine Corps units were deployed to Vietnam in early 1965 as "defensive measures," it was not until Congressional endorsement was extended in the Tonkin Gulf

[2]Each volume of *The Pentagon Papers*, cited above, has an appended list of "official justifications" for American involvement in the Vietnam conflict.

resolution of August 1965 that Johnson greatly increased American military forces.

The Second Indochina war was now fully joined. Employing the policy of "graduated response," attributed to Presidential advisor W.W. Rostow, President Johnson sought to bring the Hanoi regime to the recognition that it could not reunify Vietnam by force and to accept the existence of South Vietnam as an independent nation. This program greatly miscalculated the determination of Ho's regime and the Southern Viet Cong to determine their country's destiny on their own terms.

So the war intensified and casualties mounted in a contest for which many Americans could not find a satisfactory achievable purpose. As the bloodshed increased, Johnson found himself coming under sharp attack from these domestic critics. Choosing to ignore the arguments of these "doves," the administration justified its policies on the grounds that the three previous presidents had pledged American aid to South Vietnam; that Vietnam represented a test case in America's opposition to the "new Communist strategy" of national liberation movements sponsored by Peiping; that this was a struggle for freedom against aggression by terror; that America's "credibility" was being tested; and that if South Vietnam fell to the communists, the rest of Southeast Asia would, like "falling dominoes," come under Peiping's domination. Perhaps the most curious theme to come from Washington was that the United States must make Hanoi abide by the Geneva Accords of 1954—the very agreements which Washington itself had consistently ignored!

The simplistic nature of the "official" justifications for the new war failed to convince many of its critics. They questioned whether Washington should try to "save" the Vietnamese people by virtually destroying their nation, whether Ho was really a puppet of international communism, as the Administration portrayed him to be, or whether America should assume the role of world policeman by intervening in such "domestic" quarrels. In early 1968, Senator Eugene McCarthy challenged the Johnson policies in the Democratic presidential primaries. After a poor showing in the initial test in New Hampshire, Johnson withdrew from the race. During his final months in office, Johnson halted the bombing of North Vietnam and began formal peace talks in Paris; but the presidential contest found an "interventionist" of 1954 moving into the White House—Richard M. Nixon.

Although Nixon had claimed during the campaign to possess a secret plan to end the war, it was soon apparent that the new administration was prepared only for more of the same—Vietnamization and increased use of American military technology. While retaining essentially the same American political objectives of 1965, Nixon sought to mollify domestic dissent by pulling out American ground forces and, subsequently, reducing American casualties. But in order to maintain a favorable military situation, the administration ordered a greatly increased use of bombing.

It was Nixon's reliance on aerial bombing to continue the war which caused critics to label his operations the "Third Indochina War." In four years, this bombing effort had more than doubled the death and destruction that had resulted from military activities during the Kennedy-Johnson years. At the same time, the Nixon administration expanded its bombing into Cambodia (26% of its territory has been under saturation bombing with 2,000,000 people killed, wounded or displaced) and intensified its bombing in Laos (over four times that of the previous years and eight times more than dropped on Japan in WW II). The vastly accelerated bombing of South Vietnam produced similar carnage; it is little wonder that Americans came to be considered the "new barbarians."

America's role in the Vietnam conflict appeared to have entered its final phase in 1972. The large-scale North Vietnamese invasion of the South, on March 30, resulted in renewed American bombing of the North and, on May 8, the mining of the harbor at Haiphong. Although the South Vietnamese military did not respond well to this new challenge, American airpower halted the North's drive and inflicted very heavy losses in men and material upon the invading forces. For reasons of its own, Hanoi announced on October 26 that it would adhere to a cease-fire, previously sketched out by negotiators, if the agreement was signed by October 31. Obviously, this move was timed to bring pressure upon Richard Nixon as the presidential election was to be held on November 7th. The American people were assured by Nixon that only a few "minor" details were left to be adjusted, but he insisted that he would not sign under pressure.

After receiving his popular "mandate" in the November election, Nixon sent his Special Advisor Henry Kissinger to Paris to complete negotiations with North Vietnam's Le Duc Tho. The secret Kissinger-Tho discussions collapsed on December 16, 1972, and Nixon ordered the bombing (December 18-30) of North Vietnam's industrial heartland; particularly hard hit were areas in and around Hanoi. On January 8, 1973, the Kissinger-Tho talks were resumed and on January 24 a cease-fire was initialed in Paris.

Historians will long analyze the sequence of events during this diplomatic interlude and will argue heatedly as to whether the December bombings were necessary, whether they actually caused Hanoi to alter its position, or whether public outcry—at home and abroad—softened Washington's demands. Regardless of which view of the diplomacy emerges as the accepted historical consensus, it was evident that few observers expected the Indochina struggle to halt simply because Kissinger and Tho had agreed upon a cease-fire.

II

America's military tactics and weapons policies have employed the conventional and the novel; they have also received nearly as much criticism as have the political maneuverings.[3] In the early 1960s, the nation's military program and strategic theories placed great emphasis upon the ability of its armed forces to contain "wars of national liberation," and to maintain a strategic nuclear deterrent. Many military and civilian officials relished the opportunity, in 1964-65, to demonstrate in Vietnam that they had the tactics and equipment necessary to beat down "brushfire wars." According to *Armed Forces Management* (November 1965), "Just as Vietnam has become a test-bed for the proof-testing and debugging of new hardware, new tactical concepts, new logistics systems, so is it a test of the validity of Defense's basic policy—not an exception to it."

That Vietnam became a proving ground is evidenced by the employment of new military tactics and weapons systems. These tactics included the extensive use of airborne (helicopter) troops on "search and destroy" missions, the designation for artillery and aircraft of widespread "free-fire zones," the intentional "population relocation" programs designed to clear free-fire zones, and the extensive use of air power in support and interdiction missions. American military forces became heavily engaged also in pacification programs designed to "win the hearts and minds" of the South Vietnamese peasants; unfortunately, this program's acronym (WHAM) was often too vividly demonstrated by operational tactics such as "search and destroy missions," B-52 "carpet bombing," and ground-strafing gunships.

Among the innovative weapons systems employed in Vietnam were new delivery systems for the application of CS gas and herbicides; light-gathering and heat-gathering devices for nighttime; ground-based, antipersonnel targeting; laser-guided and television-guided bombs; and ground-based sensors ("electronic battlefield") which detected personnel and motor traffic and telemetered this information through circling aircraft to ground-based computers which called in air strikes. The Air Force also made extensive use of special aircraft for airborne tactical air control and electronic countermeasures over the China Sea and North Vietnam. Even more bizarre and unprecedented was the use of meteorological warfare designed to cause an additional amount of rainfall. Other less dramatic devices such as lightships which lit up the night sky and "gunships" with multibarreled, rapid-fire machine guns (6,000 rpm per gun) also came into general use with awesome results.

The United States' virtually unimpeded use of airpower in Indochina has been one of this conflict's most striking and controversial features. Compared with America's World War II bombing effort of slightly over 2,000,000 tons in all theatres and its dropping of a little less than 1,000,000 tons during the Korean War, U.S. airplanes deposited on Indochina more than 7,000,000 tons of bombs

[3]For a documented development of these arguments, see Milton Leitenberg, "America in Vietnam: Statistics of a War," *Survival* 14:6 (1972), pp. 268-74.

between 1965 and October 1, 1972. (More than one-half of this total tonnage was dropped during the Nixon administration.) When all other forms of bombardment (artillery shelling, rocket attacks, etc.) are combined, the total tonnage expended on Vietnam is doubled.

The use by the United States of some 7,000 tons of CS gas raised serious legal questions and widespread diplomatic protest. Although the United States is not a signatory to the Geneva Protocol of 1925 prohibiting the use of gas warfare, American presidents beginning with Franklin Roosevelt have affirmed our intention to abide by it. Despite this position, Vietnam witnessed the first battlefield use of gas since Italy's Ethiopian campaign and Japan's assault on China in the late 1930s. Critics felt that renewed use of gas on the battlefield weakened the international restraints against the employment of more toxic chemical weapons in future wars. In response to strong opposition, particularly that marshaled in the United Nations General Assembly, Washington agreed to curtail its use of CS gas.

There are serious questions about the long-range effects of the use of herbicides and of the extensive bombing on Indochina's basic ecology. Although only very minor herbicidal operations had been carried out before as military operations (by the British in Malaya and the French in Algeria) and despite the fact that very little was known about the ultimate impact of such operations, the United States applied some 83,000 tons of herbicides in Vietnam. In food-denial and area-denial programs, herbicides were employed at strengths twelve to fifteen times that used in commercial agricultural operations. During the crop destruction program, from 1962 until the end of 1970, some ten percent of all the cultivated land in South Vietnam was "treated." Additionally, data from American sources indicates that 20,000 square kilometers (5½ million acres) of forest were in part destroyed by aerial spraying. This included the destruction of some 300,000 acres comprising one-half of the total coastal and delta mangrove forests, and 4,000,000 acres of mature upland forest, about one-fifth the total forest area of South Vietnam or roughly the size of Massachusetts. Additionally, specially designed bulldozers (called "Rome Plows") have been used to scrape other forest areas clear of vegetation. This program has bared the land at a rate of 1,000 acres a day; by mid-1971 some 750,000 acres were cleared, resulting in a denuded area roughly the size of the state of Rhode Island. Also, South Vietnam's ecological problems have been complicated by the heavy bombing, particularly by B-52s. It has been estimated that these activities have left some 23 million craters.

The total impact of this unprecedented disruption of Vietnam's basic ecology cannot be assessed at this time. It is possible that the clearing and the use of herbicides may bring about a drastic change in the basic soil structure; and that the cratering has disturbed the thin layer of top soil to such an extent that its return to fertility is questionable. It is little wonder, then, that American technology now also has to its credit the dubious distinction of inventing "ecocide."

Another product of these various military programs has been the violent displacement of large numbers of the Indochina population. Aerial bombing and the establishment of free-fire zones have accounted for the majority of these refugees. In all, about one-third of the South Vietnamese, Laotian and Cambodian populations have been classified as refugees: 6,000,000 South Vietnamese out of a population of 18,000,000; from 800,000 to over a million Laotians out of 2,000,000 to 3,000,000; and 1,600,000 to 2,000,000 Cambodians out of some 7,000,000. A return to economic normalcy will also be extremely difficult because rubber plantations and commercial forests have been destroyed in the South, as has been industry in the North; crater-pocked cropland poses a trying reclamation task in both the North and South. The destruction of physical structures, i.e., bridges, railroads, tunnels and buildings, has been extensive. Numerous towns in both North and South Vietnam have been leveled with hardly a wall left standing.

The social fabric of Indochina has also been badly mauled by the passing years of war. Efforts to extend the control of the Saigon government through the establishment of strategic hamlets, relocation programs and pacification programs have often had less than the desired military effect, and have added to the serious social disruption. This turmoil was augmented by the Viet Cong practice of selective assassination and by the American-sponsored "Operation Phoenix" which, as part of the pacification project, "neutralized" some 84,000 members of the suspected "VC infrastructure" in South Vietnam—21,000 of these individuals were killed outright during 1967 to 1971.

Most wars have had atrocities and, certainly, Vietnam is no exception. The United States has been charged with violating the Geneva convention (1925) on gas warfare because of its use of tear gas and herbicides; with ignoring the traditional immunities of noncombatants because of its "free-fire" zones and bombing tactics; and with ignoring the prisoner of war rules because of its not infrequent failure to stop the torture of POWs. American battlefield discipline apparently collapsed at My Lai and, so critics have claimed, many times elsewhere. The North Vietnamese and Viet Cong, too, have been charged with "war crimes" for their execution of civilians at Hue during the Tet offensive; for their practices of impressing civilians as supply-bearers; for their failure to follow POW rules; and for their employment of "blind" weapons (such as rockets) against urban noncombatants.

On balance, however, it would appear that the vastly greater amount of questionable conduct, in terms of injury and damage, must be lodged against the Americans. Depending upon the critic, this preponderance of charges against the U.S. stems from its sheer affluence in military fire power and from its inability to impose (or, indeed, to recognize the need for) restraint in applying its modern arsenal.

While the war initially found American combat soldiers performing with enthusiasm, the protracted field fighting, with its battlefield objectives becoming less clearly related to the conclusion of the war, had unexpected and decidedly adverse effects upon the Army. Morale gradually deteriorated until, eventually, some units would not obey orders to advance against the enemy. Racial disputes broke out between white and black servicemen, and, finally, assaults upon officers and noncommissioned officers, known as "fragging," became prevalent. The use of drugs by American troops also became common: marijuana use was widespread, nearly universal in rear areas, and the extensive use of heroin became a matter of grave concern to military leaders. The Army was much harder hit by the decline of morale than either the Air Force or Navy, yet senior officers in all of the services had become increasingly concerned about the war's drain on their service's vital human resources.

Critics of the war may not have evaluated fairly the problems encountered and met by the nation's armed services, but there can be little doubt that the Vietnam conflict will occupy a great deal of the armed services attention in the years to come. American military leaders have a vital, if staggering, task ahead of them in reevaluating the many facets of this lengthy contest; if this task is undertaken honestly and candidly, we all will benefit by their endeavors.

III

In retrospect, it is obvious that the Vietnam conflict became emotionally and intellectually entwined with the general social unrest which dominated the 1960s. This decade found ethnic minorities pressing for the redress of long-standing grievances, it saw the roles of traditional political and educational institutions undergoing serious challenge, and it witnessed a revolution in personal and community values. Clearly, America has been transformed, and the war certainly has played a role in the transformation.

Another real tragedy of the Vietnam conflict has been the gradual but distinct dehumanization which has taken place in America and among Americans. This is evident in the acceptance of military tactics and technology without paying any regard to the larger moral and ethical considerations. Thus, America lost a quality which had long set it apart from most other nations—its boundless optimism and idealism.

The Vietnam war toll, by any measure, has been staggering. Preliminary statistics place American casualties at 46,000 killed (with an additional 10,000 nonbattlefield deaths) and over 300,000 wounded; South Vietnamese losses were about 181,000 killed; and North Vietnamese and Viet Cong deaths were estimated to be 922,000. United States aircraft losses have been placed at 4,900 helicopters and 3,700 fixed-wing planes; nearly 1,100 of these latter were lost over North Vietnam. The cost to the American taxpayers has been some 140 billion dollars, and this figure will increase considerably when veterans' benefits are finally included.

All of this, and more, comprises the significance of the Vietnam conflict. Much has been written about the military, political and social effects of this most garish, most violent struggle; and much more will be written. At this point, however, only one thing is clear: the cease-fire terms do not reflect any deepening American understanding, after all of these years, regarding the essential nature of the Vietnam conflict. As a former State Department expert on the Far East put it: "By the evidence, the policymakers in Washington never really understood, from beginning to end, what the Indochinese revolution was all about—that it was inherently a *political*, not a military, struggle. Blinded by this error, the United States tried to dominate and suppress the Indochinese revolutionaries—and failed ingloriously. Whether it can repair its position in Asia will depend on whether it has learned the lesson of its eleven-year Indochinese war: Asia is not to be molded after American patterns."[4]

[4]O. Edmund Clubb, "The Cease-Fire," *Nation* 216:7 (Feb. 12, 1973), p. 201.

NOTE ON RESEARCH TOOLS

By scope and definition, a "working" bibliography is primarily designed to introduce its readers to the comprehensive, multifaceted nature of its topic. This, we believe, has been accomplished in our bibliographical survey of the many and varied issues raised by the Vietnam conflict.

The extended "Table of Contents" reflects a deliberate, frequently arbitrary, subdividing of general themes and, thus, provides the reader with an issue-oriented "subject index." The "Table of Contents" should be carefully reviewed; the readers who do not find what they are looking for in one section should be prepared to investigate another. If the reader is primarily interested in general overviews of the Vietnam conflict, he should go directly to Section III, "Selected Works." These books have been so labeled because they do provide broad coverage of the issues and because they do represent most of the varied viewpoints on the conflict.

There are several other tools and sources available to the readers who wish to search beyond the items listed in this bibliography. Section I, "General References," offers a selected list of bibliographies, guides, indexes, documentary collections, journals, atlases, and yearbooks which will allow the researcher to pursue a variety of topics in greater depth.

Finally, we wish to offer two other, more specific, recommendations to the serious researcher who desires references not cited below:

(a) Vietnamese sources, both North and South, are cited in bibliographies prepared for the annual September issue of the *Journal of Asian Studies*, 1966-. For the years prior to 1966, see the *Cumulative Bibliography of Asian Studies, 1941-1965: Author Bibliography*, 4 vols. (Boston: G. K. Hall, 1970) and *Cumulative Bibliography of Asian Studies, 1941-1965: Subject Bibliography*, 4 vols. (Boston: G. K. Hall, 1970).

(b) Finally, for the most complete, up-to-date guide to source materials, see John Brown Mason's *Research Resources: Annotated Guide to the Social Sciences,* 2 vols. (Santa Barbara, ABC-Clio Press, 1968, 1971). Volume 1 surveys international relations and recent history indexes, abstracts and periodicals. Volume 2 orders and arranges official publications, including U.S. government, United Nations, international organizations, and statistical sources. These two volumes are indispensable tools for the serious researcher.

The Vietnam Conflict

I / GENERAL REFERENCES

A / Bibliographies

1 Auvade, Robert. *Bibliographie critique des oeuvres parues sur l'Indochine française.* Paris: G-P Maisonneuve and Larose, 1965.

2 Birnbaum, Eleazar, comp. *Books on Asia from the Near East to the Far East.* Toronto: University of Toronto Press, 1971.

3 Council on Foreign Relations. *Foreign Affairs Bibliography: A Selected and Annotated List of Books on International Relations.* 4 Vols. New York: 1933-. (Supplemented by listings in *Foreign Affairs.*).

4 Gallo, P.J. "Understanding the Vietnam War: A Bibliographic Essay." *New University Thought* 6 (May/June 1968), pp. 29-34.

5 Hay, S.N., and M.M. Case. *Southeast Asian History: A Bibliographic Guide.* New York: Praeger, 1962.

6 Hobbs, Cecil, comp. *Southeast Asia: An Annotated Bibliography of Selected Reference Sources in Western Languages.* Washington, D.C.: Library of Congress, 1952, 1964.

7 Hobbs, Cecil C., et al., comps. *Indochina: A Bibliography of the Land and the People.* Washington, D.C.: Library of Congress, 1950.

8 Journal of Asian Studies. *Cumulative Bibliography of Asian Studies, 1941-1965: Author Bibliography.* 4 Vols. Boston: G.K. Hall, 1970.

9 ——. *Cumulative Bibliography of Asian Studies, 1941-1965: Subject Bibliography.* 4 Vols. Boston: G.K. Hall, 1970.

10 *Journal of Asian Studies.* Each September issue carries a bibliography of books and journal articles for Southeast Asian nations.

11 Jumper, Roy. *Bibliography on the Political and Administrative History of Vietnam, 1802-1962: Selected and Annotated.* Saigon: Michigan State University, Vietnam Advisory Group, 1962.

12 Keyes, Jane G., comp. *A Bibliography of North Vietnamese Publications in the Cornell University Library.* [Datapaper no. 47]. Ithaca: Southeast Asia Program, Cornell University, 1962.

13 ——. *A Bibliography of Western-Language Publications Concerning North Vietnam in the Cornell University Library.* [Datapaper no. 63, supplement to no. 47]. Ithaca: Southeast Asia Program, Cornell University, 1966.

14 Lafont, Pierre B. *Bibliographie du Laos.* Paris: École Française d'Extrême Orient, 1964.

15 Legler, A., and K. Hubinek. *Der Krieg in Vietnam: Bericht und Bibliographie bis Sept. 30, 1968.* (Schriftender Bibliothek für Zeitgeschichte, Weltkriegs-bücherei-Stuttgart, Heft 8). Frankfurt: Bernard and Graefe Verlag für Wehrwesen, 1969.

16 McKinstry, John. *Bibliography of Laos and Ethnically Related Areas.* [Laos Project Paper No. 22]. Los Angeles: Department of Anthropology, University of California, 1961.

17 ——. *Bibliography of Laos and Ethnically Related Areas to 1961.* Berkeley: University of California Press, 1962.

18 Michigan State University. Vietnam Project. *What to Read on Vietnam: A Selected Annotated Bibliography.* New York: Institute of Pacific Relations, 1959.

19 Morrison, Gayle. *A Guide to Books on Southeast Asian History (1961-66).* Santa Barbara, California: ABC-Clio Press, 1967.

20 Nguyen The Anh. *Bibliographie critique sur les relations entre Vietnam et l'Occident des origines à 1954.* New York: Adler, 1967.

21 Nunn, G. Raymond. *Asia: A Selected and Annotated Guide to Reference Works.* Cambridge, Massachusetts: M.I.T. Press, 1971.

22 ——, comp. *South and Southeast Asia: A Bibliography of Bibliographies.* Honolulu: East-West Center, University of Hawaii, 1966.

23 O'Brien, P.A., comp. *Vietnam.* [Bibliographic Series 4, No. 113]. Adelaide: State Library of South Australia, 1968.

24 Ramsey, R.W., comp. *Some Keys to the Vietnam Puzzle.* [Bibliography Series, no. 7]. Gainesville: University of Florida Libraries, 1968.

25 Republic of Vietnam. *Catalogue of Books, 1966.* Saigon: Ministry of Information, 1967.

26 Rubinstein, Alvin Z. *Soviet Works on Southeast Asia: A Bibliography of Non-Periodical Literature, 1947-1965.* Los Angeles: University of Southern California Press, 1967.

27 Tregonning, K.G. *Southeast Asia: A Critical Bibliography.* Tucson: University of Arizona, 1969.

28 United Nations. Dag Hammerskjöld Library. *International Law and the Vietnam Conflict: Selected References.* New York, 1969. (United Nations Documents LIB/BIBLIO/69/2).

29 United Nations. E.C.A.F.E. Mekong Documentation Centre. *Cambodia: A Select Bibliography.* Bangkok: 1967.

30 U.S. Military Assistance Institute Library. *Vietnam: A Selected Bibliography.* Arlington, Virginia: Military Assistance Institute Library, 1965.

B / Guides & Indexes

B.1 / Guides to Periodicals

31 *Air University Library Index to Military Periodicals.* Maxwell Air Force Base, Alabama: Air University Library, 1949-.

32 *America: History and Life; A Guide to Periodical Literature.* Santa Barbara, California: ABC-Clio Press, 1963-.

33 *Current Digest of the Soviet Press.* New York: Joint Committee on Slavic Studies, 1949-.

34 *Index to Foreign Legal Periodicals and Collections of Essays.* Chicago: William D. Murphy, 1960-.

35 *Index to Periodical Articles Related to Law.* Hackensack, New Jersey: Fred B. Rothman, 1958-.

36 *International Political Science Abstracts.* Oxford: Basil Blackwell, 1951-.

37 *Reader's Guide to Periodical Literature.* New York: H.W. Wilson, 1905-.

38 *Social Science and Humanities Index.* New York: H.W. Wilson, 1913-.

39 United Nations. Dag Hammarskjöld Library. *United Nations Documents Index.* New York: United Nations, 1950-.

B.2 / Indexes to Newspapers

40 *The Christian Science Monitor Index.* Corvallis, Oregon: Helen M. Cropsey, 1960-.

41 *The New York Times Index.* New York: The New York Times, 1913-.

42 *The Wall Street Journal Index.* New York: Dow Jones, 1958-.

43 *Index to The Times.* London: The Times, 1906-.

C / Documentary Collections

44 Cole, A.B., et al., eds. *Conflict in Indo China and International Repercussions: A Documentary History 1945-1955.* New York: Cornell University Press, 1956.

45 Council on Foreign Relations. *Documents on American Foreign Relations.* New York: Harpers, 1952-. (annual)

46 Gettleman, Marvin E., ed. *Vietnam: History, Documents and Opinions on a Major World Crisis.* New York: Fawcett World Library, 1965. (2d ed. New York: Mentor, 1970.)

47 Gr. Br. Foreign Office. *Documents Relating to British Involvement in the Indo-China Conflict, 1954-1965.* Miscellaneous No. 25, Cmd. 2834. London: H.M.S.O., 1965.

48 Maki, J.M., ed. *Conflict and Tension in the Far East: Key Documents 1894-1960.* Seattle: University of Washington Press, 1961.

49 *The Pentagon Papers; as published by The New York Times.* New York: Quadrangle Books, 1971.

50 *The Pentagon Papers. The Senator Gravel Edition.* 5 Vols with Index. Boston: Beacon, 1971-72.

51 [Pentagon Papers.] *United States-Vietnam Relations, 1945-1967.* 12 Bks. Washington, D.C.: U.S. Government Printing Office, 1971.

52 *Public Papers of the Presidents of the United States.* Washington, D.C.: U.S. Government Printing Office, 1945-; 1957-. (Truman, Eisenhower, Kennedy, Johnson, Nixon)

53 Royal Institute of International Affairs. *Documents on International Affairs, 1928-.* London: Oxford University Press, 1929-. (annual)

54 U.S. Department of State. *American Foreign Policy: Current Documents.* Washington, D.C.: U.S. Government Printing Office, 1957-. (annual)

55 ——. *American Foreign Policy, 1950-55: Basic Documents.* 2 Vols. Washington, D.C.: U.S. Government Printing Office, 1957.

D / Journals

D.1 / Official & Semiofficial Organs

56 *Current Notes on International Affairs.* Canberra, Australia: Department of External Affairs, 1936-.

57 *External Affairs.* Ottawa, Canada: Department of External Affairs, 1948-.

58 *External Affairs Review.* Wellington, New Zealand: Department of External Affairs, 1951-.

59 Foreign Broadcast Information Service (FBIS). *Daily Report.* Washington D.C.: Library of Congress, 1947-.

60 *Free China Review.* Taipei: Republic of China, 1951-.

61 *International Affairs: A Monthly Journal of Political Analysis.* Moscow: Izvestia Printing Office, 1955.

62 *Peking Review: A Magazine of Chinese News and Views.* Peking: People's Republic of China, 1958-.

63 *SEATO Record.* Bangkok, Thailand: SEATO Headquarters, 1962-.

64 *Soviet Documents: Current Statements, Speeches, Reports, and Editorials.* New York: Crosscurrent Press, 1963-.

65 U.S. Department of State. *The Department of State Bulletin.* Washington D.C.: U.S. Government Printing Office, 1939-.

66 *Vietnam.* Hanoi: Democratic Republic of Vietnam, 1957-. (monthly)

67 *Vietnam Courier.* Hanoi: Democratic Republic of Vietnam, 1963-. (weekly; monthly after June 1972)

68 *Vietnam Economic Report.* Saigon: Council on Foreign Relations, 1970-. (monthly)

69 *Vietnam Magazine.* Saigon: Vietnam Council on Foreign Relations, 1967-. (monthly)

70 *Vietnam Newsletter.* Saigon: Vietnam Council on Foreign Relations, 1968-. (weekly)

71 *Vietnam Perspectives.* New York: American Friends of Vietnam, Inc., 1965-. (irregular)

72 *Vietnam Review.* Washington, D.C.: Embassy of Vietnam, 1962-. (quarterly)

73 *Vietnamese Studies.* Hanoi: Democratic Republic of Vietnam, 1964-. (supersedes *Vietnam Advances.*)

D.2 / Private Journals

74 *Asia Recorder: A Weekly Digest of Outstanding Asian Events with Index.* New Delhi, India: Sankaran, 1955-.

75 *Asian Survey: A Monthly Review of Contemporary Asian Affairs.* Berkeley: University of California, 1961-.

76 *Australian Outlook.* Melbourne: Australian Institute of International Affairs, 1947-.

77 *China Mainland Review.* Hong Kong: University of Hong Kong, 1966-.

78 *China Quarterly.* London: Congress of Cultural Freedom, 1960-.

79 *Contemporary Japan: A Review of Far Eastern Affairs.* Tokyo: Foreign Affairs Association of Japan, 1932-.

80 *Eastern Economist.* New Delhi, India: 1943-.

81 *Facts on File: A Weekly News Guide, with Cumulative Index.* New York: Person's Index, 1940-.

82 *Kessing's Contemporary Archives.* Bristol: Kessing's Publications, 1931-. (a weekly diary)

83 *Pacific Affairs: An International Review of the Far East and Pacific Area.* Vancouver: University of British Columbia, 1928-.

84 *Pakistan Horizon.* Karachi: Pakistan Institute of International Affairs, 1948-.

85 *Vital Speeches of the Day.* Pelham, New York: City News Publishing Co., 1934-.

E / Atlases & Yearbooks

E.1 / Atlases

86 Hall, D.G.E. *Atlas of South East Asia.* New York: St. Martin's Press, 1964.

87 United Nations. *Atlas of Physical, Economic and Social Resources of the Lower Mekong Basin.* (Prepared for U.N. Economic Commission for Asia and the Far East.). Washington, D.C.: 1968.

E.2 / Yearbooks

88 Council on Foreign Relations. *The United States in World Affairs.* New York: Harpers, 1932-.

89 London Institute of World Affairs. *Year Book of World Affairs.* London: Stevens and Sons, 1947-.

90 *The New International Year Book: A Compendium of the World's Progress for the Year.* New York: Funk and Wagnalls, 1932-.

91 Royal Institute of International Affairs. *Survey of International Affairs.* London: Oxford University Press, 1925-.

92 United Nations. Statistical Office. *Statistical Year Book.* New York: United Nations, 1949-.

93 ——. *Yearbook of International Trade Statistics.* New York: United Nations, 1949-.

II / AREA DIMENSIONS

A / Southeast Asia

A.1 / General

94 Ball, W. MacMahon. *Nationalism and Communism in East Asia.* Melbourne: Melbourne University Press, 1952.

95 Bloodworth, Dennis. *An Eye for the Dragon: Southeast Asia Observed, 1954-1970.* New York: Farrar, Straus and Giroux, 1970.

96 Burling, Robbins. *Hill Farms and Padi Fields: Life in Mainland Southeast Asia.* Englewood Cliffs, New Jersey: Prentice-Hall, 1965.

97 Butwell, Richard A. *Southeast Asia Today—and Tomorrow: A Political Analysis.* New York: Praeger, 1964.

98 Cady, John Frank. *Southeast Asia: Its Historical Development.* New York: McGraw-Hill, 1964.

99 ——. *Thailand, Burma, Laos and Cambodia.* Englewood Cliffs, New Jersey: Prentice-Hall, 1966.

100 Coedes, George. *The Making of Southeast Asia.* Berkeley: University of California Press, 1966.

101 Crozier, B. *South-East Asia in Turmoil.* Baltimore: Penguin Books, 1965.

102 Dobby, E.H.G. *Southeast Asia.* London: University of London Press, 1950.

103 "The Economic Effects of the Vietnamese War in East and Southeast Asia." *Quarterly Economic Review* [QER Special number 3]. (Nov. 1968).

104 Elsbree, W.M. *Japan's Role in Southeast Asian Nationalist Movements.* Cambridge, Massachusetts: Harvard University Press, 1963.

105 Embree, J., and W.L. Thomas, Jr. *Ethnic Groups of Northern Southeast Asia.* New Haven: Yale University Press, 1950.

106 Fifield, Russell H. *The Diplomacy of Southeast Asia: 1945-1958.* New York: Harper, 1958.

107 Fischer, A. *South-East Asia: A Social, Economic, and Political Geography.* 2d ed. New York: E.P. Dutton, 1965.

108 Hall, D.G.E. *History of Southeast Asia.* New York: St. Martin's Press, 1955.

109 ——. *A History of Southeast Asia.* 3d ed. London: Macmillan, 1968.

110 Jacoby, E.H. *Agrarian Unrest in Southeast Asia.* New York: Columbia University Press, 1949.

111 Jumper, Roy, and Marjorie Weiner Normand. *Governments and Politics of Southeast Asia.* 2d ed. Ithaca: Cornell University Press, 1964.

112 Kahin, G. McT. *The Asian-African Conference, Bandung, Indonesia, April 1955.* Ithaca: Cornell University Press, 1956.

113 ——, and John W. Lewis. *Governments and Politics of Southeast Asia.* New York: Cornell University Press, 1964.

114 Kroef, J.M. van der. "The Gorton Manner: Australia, Southeast Asia, and the U.S." *Pacific Affairs* 42:3 (1969), pp. 311-333.

115 Kunstadter, Peter, ed. *Southeast Asian Tribes, Minorities, and Nations.* 3 Vols. Princeton: Princeton University Press, 1967.

116 Lyon, Peter. *War and Peace in Southeast Asia.* London: Oxford University Press, 1969.

117 Purcell, Victor. *The Chinese in Southeast Asia.* 2d ed. London: Oxford University Press, 1965.

118 Rose, Saul, ed. *Politics in Southern Asia.* New York: St. Martin's Press, 1963.

119 SarDesai, D.R. *Indian Foreign Policy in Cambodia, Laos and Vietnam 1947-1964.* Berkeley: University of California Press, 1969.

120 Schaaf, C.H., and R.H. Fifield. *The Lower Mekong: Challenge to Cooperation in Southeast Asia.* Princeton: Van Nostrand, 1963.

121 Schecter, J. *The New Face of Buddha: The Rise of Buddhism as a New Political Force in Southeast Asia.* New York: Coward, McCann, 1967.

122 Shaplen, Robert. *Time out of Hand: Revolution and Reaction in Southeast Asia.* New York: Harper and Row, 1969.

123 Smith, R.M. *Government and Politics of Southeast Asia.* Ithaca: Cornell University Press, 1964.

124 Thompson, V., and Richard Adloff. *The Left Wing in Southeast Asia.* New York: Sloane, 1950.

125 ——. *Minority Problems in Southeast Asia.* Stanford: Stanford University Press, 1955.

126 Trager, Frank N., ed. *Marxism in Southeast Asia: A Study of Four Countries.* Stanford: Stanford University Press, 1959.

127 Trumbull, Robert. *The Scrutable East: A Correspondent's Report on Southeast Asia.* New York: David McKay, 1964.

128 U.K. Central Office of Information. *Vietnam, Laos and Cambodia: Chronology of Events, 1945-68.* London: British Information Service, 1968.

129 Vandenbosch, A., and R. Butwell. *The Changing Face of Southeast Asia.* Lexington: University of Kentucky Press, 1966.

130 Warner, Denis. *Reporting Southeast Asia.* Sydney: Angus & Robertson, 1966.

A.2 / French Indochina (Historical)

131 Ajalbert, Jean. *Les Nuages sur l'Indochine.* Paris: Louis-Michaud, 1912.

132 Alberti, Jean B. *L'Indochine d'autrefois et d'aujourd'hui.* Paris: Société d'Éditions Géographiques, Maritimes et Coloniales, 1934.

133 Barthouet, Arnaud. *La Tragédie franco-indochinoise.* Paris: Delmas, 1948.

134 Bauchar, René (pseudonym of Jean Charbonneau). *Rafales sur l'Indochine.* Paris: Fournier, 1946.

135 Bernard, Paul. *Le Problème économique indochinois.* Paris: Nouvelles Éditions Latines, 1934.

136 Cady, John Frank. *The Roots of French Imperialism in Eastern Asia.* Ithaca: Cornell University Press, 1954.

137 Cultru, P. *Histoire de la Cochincine française des origines à 1883.* Paris: Challamel, 1910.

138 Cunningham, Alfred. *The French in Tonkin and South China.* London: Sampson Low, 1902.

139 Daufès, E. *La Garde indigène de l'Indochine de sa création à nos jours.* 2 Vols. Avignon: Seguin, 1933-34.

140 Gosselin, Charles. *L'Empire d'Annam.* Paris: Perrin, 1904.

141 Goudal, Jean. *Labor Conditions in Indochina.* Geneva: International Labour Office, 1938.

142 Lancaster, Donald. *The Emancipation of French Indochina.* London: Oxford University Press, 1961.

143 Marchand, Jean. *L'Indochine en guerre (1870-1954).* Paris: Pouzet, 1955.

144 Masson, André. *Histoire de l'Indochine.* Paris: Presses Universitaires de France, 1950.

145 Robequain, D. *The Economic Development of French Indochina.* London: Oxford University Press, 1944.

146 Roberts, Stephen H. *History of French Colonial Policy, 1870-1925.* 2 Vols. London: P.S. King, 1929.

147 Sarrault, Albert. *La Mise en valeur des colonies françaises.* Paris: Payot, 1923.

148 Thompson, Virginia. *French Indochina.* London: Allen and Unwin, 1937.

B / U.S. & Southeast Asia

B.1 / General

149 Bell, Coral. "Security in Asia: Reappraisals after Vietnam." *International Journal* 24:1 (1968), pp. 1-12.

150 Bell, David E. "Investment Opportunities in Southeast Asia." *Vital Speeches* 31 (Nov. 1, 1964), pp. 61-62.

151 Black, Eugene R. *Alternative in Southeast Asia.* [Foreword by Lyndon B. Johnson.] New York: Praeger, 1969.

152 Brand, H. "On 'Containment' in Asia." *Dissent* 14 (Mar/Apr 1967), pp. 140-144.

153 Chomsky, Noam. *At War with Asia.* New York: Random House, 1969.

154 Fifield, R.H. *Southeast Asia in United States Policy.* New York: Praeger, 1963.

155 Fleming, D.F. "Vietnam and After." *The Western Political Quarterly* 21 (Mar. 1968), pp. 141-151.

156 ——. "What Is Our Role in East Asia?" *The Western Political Quarterly* 18 (Mar. 1965), pp. 73-86.

157 Gurtov, M. *Southeast Asia after Withdrawal from Vietnam.* Santa Monica, California: Rand, P-4413, Aug. 1970.

158 Hunter, R.E., and P. Windsor. "Vietnam and United States Policy in Asia." *International Affairs* (Great Britain) 44:2 (1968), pp. 202-213.

159 Johnstone, W.C. "U.S. Policy in Southeast Asia: What's Ahead?" *Current History* 50 (Feb. 1966), pp. 106-111.

160 Jordan, Amos A. *Foreign Aid and the Defense of Southeast Asia.* New York: Praeger, 1962.

161 Kalb, Marvin, and Elie Abel. *Roots of Involvement: The U.S. in Asia, 1787-1971.* New York: Praeger, 1971.

162 Kirk, D. *Wider War: The Struggle for Cambodia, Thailand and Laos.* New York: Praeger, 1971.

163 Larson, Donald R., and Arthur Larson. *Vietnam and Beyond: A New American Foreign Policy and Program.* Durham, North Carolina: Duke University, Rule of Law Research Center, 1965.

164 Montgomery, J.D. *The Politics of Foreign Aid: American Experience in Southeast Asia.* New York: Praeger, 1962.

165 Nixon, Richard M. "Asia After Vietnam." *Foreign Affairs* 46:1 (1967), pp. 111-125.

166 Reischauer, Edwin O. *Beyond Vietnam: The United States and Asia.* New York: Vintage Books, 1968.

167 Roseman, Alvin. "Thailand, Laos and Cambodia: A Decade of Aid." *Current History* 49 (Nov. 1964), pp. 271-277, 306-307.

168 Sylvester, John F. *Eagle and the Dragon.* Philadelphia: Dorrance Co., 1965.

169 U.S. House of Representatives. Committee on Armed Services. *Report of Special Subcommittee Following Visit to Southeast Asia, April 7-19, 1966.* 89th Cong., 2d Sess., July 19, 1966.

170 U.S. House of Representatives. Committee on Foreign Affairs. Hearings; *The Future U.S. Role in Asia and in the Pacific.* 90th Cong., 2d Sess., Feb.-Apr. 1968.

171 ——. *Report of the Special Study Mission to East and Southeast Asia.* [House Rpt. 91-30] 91st Cong., 1st Sess. Mar. 6, 1969.

172 ——. Report; *United States Policy Toward Asia.* [May 19, 1966] 89th Cong., 2d Sess., 1966.

173 ——. *Special Study Mission to Southeast Asia and the Pacific: Report by Hon. Walter H. Judd, Minnesota, Chairman; Hon. Marguerite Stitt Church, Illinois; Hon. E. Ross Adair, Indiana; Hon. Clement J. Zablocki, Wisconsin.* [Jan. 29, 1954] 83d Cong., 2d Sess., 1954.

174 U.S. Senate. Committee on Foreign Relations. Hearings; *The Southeast Asia Collective Defense Treaty.* 83d Cong., 2d Sess., 1954.

175 ——. *Report on Indochina: Report of Senator Mike Mansfield on a Study Mission to Vietnam, Cambodia, Laos.* [Oct. 15, 1954] 83d Cong., 2d Sess., 1954.

176 ——. Report; *Vietnam, Cambodia and Laos: Report by Sen. Mike Mansfield.* [Oct. 6, 1955] 84th Cong., 1st Sess., 1955.

177 ——. Staff Report; *Thailand, Laos, and Cambodia: January 1972.* 92d Cong., 2d Sess., 1972.

178 Volsky, Dmitry. "U.S. Military Expansion in South-East Asia." *International Affairs* (Moscow) 2 (Feb. 1968), pp. 47-51.

B.2 / SEATO

179 Eckel, Paul E. "SEATO: An Ailing Alliance." *World Affairs* 134:2 (Fall 1971), pp. 97-114.

180 Greene, Fred. *U.S. Policy and the Security of Asia.* New York: McGraw-Hill, 1968.

181 Hasluck, Paul. "Vietnam and SEATO." *Current Notes on International Affairs* (Canberra) 37 (May 1966), pp. 257-260.

182 Joyce, J.A. "SEATO: False Alibi." *Christian Century* 84 (Nov. 8, 1967), pp. 1424-1429.

183 Leifer, M. "Cambodia and SEATO." *International Journal* 17 (1962), pp. 122-132.

184 Lyon, Peter. "SEATO in Perspective." *The Yearbook of World Affairs, 1965.* London: Stevens, 1965, pp. 113-136.

185 Magnien, M. "Une Opération montée par l' O.T.A.S.E., au Laos." *Cahiers du Communisme* 35 (1959), pp. 919-923.

186 McCloud, D.G. "United States Policies Toward Regional Organizations in Southeast Asia." *World Affairs* 133:2 (1970), pp. 133-145.

187 Modelski, G.A. "Indochina and SEATO." *Australian Outlook* 13 (March 1959), pp. 27-54.

188 Modelski, George A., ed. *SEATO: Six Studies.* Melbourne: F.W. Cheshire, 1962.

189 Nairn, Ronald C. "SEATO: A Critique." *Pacific Affairs* 41 (Spring 1968), pp. 5-18.

190 Neuchterlein, Donald E. "Thailand and SEATO: A Ten-year Appraisal." *Asian Survey* 4 (Dec. 1964), pp. 1174-1181.

191 "Southeast Asia Collective Defense Treaty, Signed at Manila, on 8 September 1954." *United Nations Treaty Series,* Vol. 209, pp. 28-36.

192 Trager, Frank N. "The United States, SEATO and the Defense of Southeast Asia." *United Asia* (India) 17:4 (1965), pp. 278-286.

C / China, Russia, & Southeast Asia

193 Barnett, A. Doak, ed. *Communist Strategies in Asia: A Comparative Analysis of Governments and Parties.* New York: Praeger, 1963.

194 Beloff, Max. *Soviet Policy in the Far East, 1944-1951.* London: Oxford University Press, 1953.

195 Brimmell, J.H. *Communism in Southeast Asia: A Political Analysis.* New York: Oxford University Press, 1959.

196 Butwell, Richard. "Communist Liaison in Southeast Asia." *United Asia* 6 (June 1954), pp. 146-151.

197 Candlin, A.H.S. "The Communist Threat to South and Southeast Asia." *Brassey's, 1964* (1964), pp. 83-95.

198 Chen, King C. *Vietnam and China, 1938-1954.* Princeton: Princeton University Press, 1969.

199 Clubb, Oliver Edmund. *The United States and the Sino-Soviet Bloc in Southeast Asia.* Washington, D.C.: Brookings Institution, 1962.

200 Dai, Shen-Yu. "Peking and Indochina's Destiny." *The Western Political Quarterly* 7 (Sept. 1954), pp. 346-368.

201 ——. *Peking, Moscow, and the Communist Parties of Colonial Asia.* Cambridge, Massachusetts: Center for International Studies, M.I.T., 1954.

202 Fairbairn, Geoffrey. *Revolutionary Warfare and Communist Strategy: The Threat to Southeast Asia.* London: Faber, 1968.

203 Fall, Bernard B. "Red China's Aims in South Asia." *Current History* 53 (Sept. 1962), pp. 136-181.

204 Girling, J.L.S. *People's War: Conditions and Consequences in China and Southeast Asia.* New York: Praeger, 1969.

205 Hinton, Harold. *Communist China in World Politics.* Boston: Houghton, Mifflin, 1966.

206 McLane, C. *Soviet Strategies in Southeast Asia: An Exploration of Eastern Policy Under Lenin and Stalin.* Princeton: Princeton University Press, 1966.

207 Pye, Lucian W. *Guerrilla Communism in Malaya: Its Social and Political Meaning.* Princeton: Princeton University Press, 1956.

208 Scalapino, Robert A., ed. *The Communist Revolution in Asia: Tactics, Goals and Achievements.* Englewood Cliffs, New Jersey: Prentice-Hall, 1965.

209 Thomas, J.R. "Soviet Russia and Southeast Asia." *Current History* 55 (Nov. 1968), pp. 575-580.

D / Cambodia

D.1 / General

210 Adloff, R., and V. Thompson. "Cambodia Moves Toward Independence." *Far Eastern Survey* 22 (Aug. 1953), pp. 105-111.

211 Armstrong, John P. *Sihanouk Speaks.* New York: Walker, 1964.

212 Barnes, William S. "United States Recognition Policy and Cambodia." *Boston University Law Review* 50 (1970), pp. 117-129.

213 Burchett, Wilfred G. *Mekong Upstream: A Visit to Laos and Cambodia.* Berlin: Seven Seas Publishers, 1959.

214 Chandler, David P. "Cambodia's Strategy of Survival." *Current History* 58 (Dec. 1969), pp. 344-348.

215 ——. "Changing Cambodia." *Current History* 59 (Dec. 1970), pp. 333-338.

216 Field, Michael. "Cambodia Between East and West." *New Leader* 43 (Jan. 4, 1960), pp. 18-20.

217 Ghosh, Manomohan. *A History of Cambodia: From the Earliest Time to the End of the French.* Saigon: J.K. Gupta, 1960.

218 Government of Cambodia. *Documents on Vietcong and North Vietnamese Aggression Against Cambodia* (1970). Phnom Penh: Ministry of Information, 1970.

219 Gr. Br. Secretary of State for Foreign Affairs. *Recent Diplomatic Exchanges concerning the Proposal for an International Conference on the Neutrality and Territorial Integrity of Cambodia.* Cmnd. 2678. London: H.M.S.O., 1965.

220 Laurent, Maurice. *L'Armée au Cambodge et dans les pays en voie de développment du Sud-est Asiatique.* Paris: Presses Universitaires de France, 1968.

221 Leifer, Michael. "Cambodia and Her Neighbours." *Pacific Affairs* 34 (1961-62), pp. 361-374.

222 ——. "Cambodia: The Politics of Accommodation." *Asian Survey* 4 (1964), pp. 674-679.

223 ——. *Cambodia: The Search for Security.* New York: Praeger, 1967.

224 ——. "Rebellion or Subversion in Cambodia?" *Current History* 56 (Feb. 1969), pp. 88-93, 112-113.

225 Munson, Frederick P. *Area Handbook for Cambodia.* Washington, D.C.: U.S. Government Printing Office, 1968.

226 Poole, Peter A. *Cambodia's Quest for Survival.* New York: American-Asian Educational Exchange, 1969.

227 Preschez, Phillippe. *Essai sur la démocratique du Cambodge.* Paris: Fondation Nationale des Sciences Politiques, Centre d'Études des Relations Internationales, 1961.

228 Reddi, V.M. "Cambodian Neutralism." *International Studies* 2 (Oct. 1960), pp. 190-205.

229 Sihanouk, Norodom. "Aspects of Cambodian Neutrality." *Free World Review* 4 (Summer 1958), pp. 11-12.

230 ——. "Cambodia Neutral: The Dictate of Necessity." *Foreign Affairs* 36:4 (1958), pp. 582-586.

231 ——. "The Future of Cambodia." *Foreign Affairs* 49 (Oct. 1970), pp. 1-10.

232 ——. "My Overthrow and Resistance." *Ramparts* 11:1 (July 1972), pp. 19-23, 42-47.

233 Simon, Jean-Pierre. "Cambodia: Pursuit of Crisis," *Asian Survey* 5:5 (1965), pp. 49-53.

234 Smith, Roger M. *Cambodia's Foreign Policy.* Ithaca: Cornell University Press, 1965.

235 ——. "Cambodia's Neutrality and the Laotian Crisis." *Asian Survey* 1:5 (1961), pp. 17-24.

236 Szaz, Z.M. "Cambodia's Foreign Policy." *Far Eastern Survey* 24 (Oct. 1955), pp. 151-158.

237 Taussig, H.C. "Neutral Cambodia." *Eastern World* 11 (Sept. 1957), pp. 32-35.

238 U.S. Agency for International Development. *The American Aid Program in Cambodia: A Decade of Cooperation, 1951-61.* Washington, D.C.: U.S. Government Printing Office, 1961.

239 U.S. International Cooperation Administration. *Cambodia: Fact Sheet, Mutual Security in Action.* Department of State Publication 6931. Far Eastern Series 85. Washington, D.C.: U.S. Government Printing Office, 1960.

240 Williams, Maslyn. *The Land in Between: The Cambodian Dilemma.* New York: Morrow, 1970.

241 Willmott, W.E. *The Chinese in Cambodia.* Vancouver: University of British Columbia, 1967.

D.2 / U.S. "Invasion" (1970)

242 Case, W. "Beyond Vietnam to Indo-China: The Legal Implications of the United States' Incursions into Cambodia and Laos." *Journal of International Law* 3 (Spring 1971), pp. 163ff.

243 Falk, R. A., et al. "Symposium on the United States Action in Cambodia." *American Journal of International Law* 65 (Jan. 1971). (special issue)

244 Grant, Jonathan S., comp. *Cambodia: The Widening War in Indochina.* New York: Washington Square Press, 1971.

245 Kaiser, Robert. "Getting into the Enemy's System: The Cambodian Operation as Limited Tactic." *Interplay* 3:10 (1970), pp. 26-28.

246 Kalicki, J.H. "Sino-American Relations after Cambodia." *World Today* (Great Britain) 26:9 (1970), pp. 383-393.

247 Lacouture, Jean. "From the Vietnam War to an Indochina War." *Foreign Affairs* 48:4 (1970), pp. 617-628.

248 Lowenfeld, A.F., et al. "Hammarskjöld Forum: Expansion of the Vietnam War into Cambodia—the Legal Issues." *New York Law Review* 45:1 (June 1970), pp. 625-678.

249 Nixon, Richard Milhous. *The Cambodia Strike: Defensive Action for Peace.* (A Report to the Nation, Apr. 30, 1970.) Washington, D.C.: U.S. Government Printing Office, 1970.

250 Stevenson, John R. "United States Military Action in Cambodia: Questions of International Law." *U.S. Department of State Bulletin* (June 22, 1970), pp. 765-770.

251 U.S. Senate. Committee on Foreign Relations. Staff Report; *Cambodia: May 1970.* Washington, D.C.: U.S. Government Printing Office, June 7, 1970.

252 U.S. Senate. Committee on Foreign Relations. Staff Report; *Cambodia: December 1970.* Washington, D.C.: U.S. Government Printing Office, Dec. 16, 1970.

253 Young, Kenneth T. "Thailand and the Cambodian Conflict." *Current History* 59 (Dec. 1970), pp. 351-355.

E / Laos

E.1 / General

254 Adams, Nina S., and Alfred W. McCoy, eds. *Laos: War and Revolution.* New York: Harper and Row, 1970.

255 Berval, R., et al. *Kingdom of Laos: The Land of the Million Elephants and the White Parasol.* Saigon: France-Asie, 1959.

256 Burchett, W. *Mekong Upstream.* Berlin: Seven Seas Publishers, 1959.

257 Fredman, H.B. *The Role of the Chinese in Lao Society.* Santa Monica, California: Rand, P-2161, 1961.

258 Gr. Br. Central Office of Information. Reference Division. *Laos.* London: H.M.S.O., 1970.

259 Halpern, J.M. *Government, Politics and Social Structure in Laos.* New Haven: Yale University Press, 1964.

260 Lebar, F.M., and A. Suddard, eds. *Laos: Its People, Its Society, Its Culture.* rev. ed. New Haven: Human Relations Area Files, 1967.

261 LeBoulanger, Paul. *Histoire du Laos français: Essai d'une étude chronologique des principautés laotiennes.* Franborough, England: Gregg, 1969.

262 Leerburger, F.J. "Laos: Case Study of U.S. Foreign Aid." *Foreign Policy Bulletin* 38:5 (1959), pp. 61-63.

263 Manich, M.L. *History of Laos.* Bangkok: Chalermnit Press, 1967.

264 Rose, S., ed. *Politics in Southern Asia: Independence and Political Rivalry in Laos 1945-1961.* London: Macmillan, 1963.

265 Sasorith, Katay. *Le Laos.* Paris: Berger-Levrault, 1953.

266 Sisouk, Na Champassak. *Storm over Laos: A Contemporary History.* New York: Praeger, 1961.

267 Souvanna Phouma, Prince. "Laos: le fond du problème." *France-Asie* 17 (1961), pp. 1824-1826.

268 Toye, Hugh. *Laos: Buffer State or Battleground?* New York: Oxford University Press, 1968.

269 U.S. General Accounting Office. Report; *Examination of Economics and Technical Assistance Program for Laos.* [for Fiscal Years 1955-57] Washington, D.C.: U.S. Government Printing Office, 1958.

270 ——. Report; *Follow-up Review of Economic and Technical Assistance Program for Laos.* Washington, D.C.: U.S. Government Printing Office, 1959.

271 U.S. House of Representatives. Committee on Foreign Affairs. Hearings; *Mutual Security Program in Laos.* [May 7-8, 1958] 85th Cong., 2d Sess., 1958.

272 U.S. House of Representatives. Committee on Government Operations. Hearings; *United States Aid Operations in Laos.* [Mar. 11 and June 1, 1959] 86th Cong., 1st Sess., 1959.

273 "Who's Who in Laos." *World Today* 16 (Sept. 1960) pp. 365-367.

E.2 / Pathet Lao

274 Adloff, R., and V. Thompson. "Laos: Background of Invasion." *Far Eastern Survey* 22 (May 1953), pp. 62-66.

275 Black, E.F. "Laos: A Case Study of Communist Strategy." *Military Review* 44 (Dec. 1964), pp. 49-59.

276 Caply, Michael. *Guérilla au Laos.* Paris: Presses de la Cité, 1966.

277 Fall, Bernard. "The Pathet Lao: A 'Liberation' Movement." In R. Scalapino, ed. *The Communist Revolution in Asia.* Englewood Cliffs, New Jersey: Prentice-Hall, 1965.

278 Hafner, J.A. "The Pathet Lao and Change in Traditional Economics of the Mao and Kha, 1958-1961." *Papers of Michigan Academy of Science, Arts, and Letters* 50 (1965), pp. 431-436.

279 Halpern, A.M., and H.B. Fredman. *Communist Strategy in Laos.* Santa Monica, California: Rand, RM-2561, June 1960.

280 Jonas, A., and G. Tanham. "Laos: A Phase in Cyclic Regional Revolution." *Orbis* 5 (Spring 1961), pp. 64-73.

281 Langer, P.F., and J.J. Zasloff. *North Vietnam and the Pathet Lao: Partners in the Struggle for Laos.* Cambridge, Massachusetts: Harvard University Press, 1970.

282 ——. *The Northern Vietnamese Military Adviser in Laos: A First Hand Account.* Santa Monica, California: Rand, RM-5688-ARPA, June 1968.

283 Langer, Paul F. *Comments on Bernard Fall's "The Pathet Lao: A 'Liberation' Party."* Santa Monica, California: Rand, P-3751, Feb. 1969.

284 ——. *The Soviet Union, China and the Pathet Lao: Analysis and Chronology.* Santa Monica, California: Rand, P-4765, Jan. 1972.

285 "Laos and the Communists." *World Today* 15 (Sept. 1959), pp. 333-341.

286 Morley, Lorna. "Menaced Laos." *Editorial Research Reports* 2 (Sept. 23, 1959), pp. 717-734.

287 Phoumi, Vongvichit. *Laos and the Victorious Struggle of the Lao People against U.S. Neo-Colonialism.* Hanoi: Neo Lao Haksat Publications, 1969.

288 Scalapino, R., and B. Fall, eds. *The Communist Revolution in Asia: The Pathet Lao: A Liberation Movement.* Englewood Cliffs, New Jersey: Prentice-Hall, 1965.

E.3 / Neutralization, 1960-62

289 Black, Col. E.F. "Laos: A Case Study of Communist Strategy." *Military Review* 44:12 (Dec. 1964), pp. 49-59.

290 Burnham, James. "Laos and Containment: With Editorial Comment." *National Review* 10 (Apr. 8, 1961), pp. 207-213.

291 Cousins, Norman. "Report from Laos." *Saturday Review* 44 (Feb. 18, 1961), pp. 12-18.

292 Czyzak, John J., and Carl F. Salans. "The International Conference on Laos and the Geneva Agreement of 1962." *Journal of Southeast Asian History* 7:2 (1966), pp. 27-47.

293 Dommen, Arthur J. *Conflict in Laos: The Politics of Neutralization.* New York: Praeger, 1964 (rev. 1971).

294 Fall, Bernard B. *Anatomy of a Crisis: The Laotian Crisis of 1960-1961.* New York: Doubleday, 1969.

295 ——. "The International Relations of Laos." *Pacific Affairs* 30 (Mar. 1957), pp. 22-34.

296 Goldbloom, M.J. "Our Strange Game in Laos." *Progressive* 23 (Dec. 1959), pp. 22-25.

297 Gr. Br. Secretary of State for Foreign Affairs. *Declaration and Protocol on the Neutrality of Laos, Geneva, July 23, 1962.* Treaty Series No. 27 (1963), Cmnd. 2025. London: H.M.S.O., 1963.

298 ——. *International Conference on the Settlement of the Laotian Question.* Cmnd. 1828. London: H.M.S.O., 1962.

299 Gross, Leo. "The Question of Laos and the Double Veto in the Security Council." *American Journal of International Law* 54 (Jan. 1960), pp. 118-131.

300 Henderson, William, and F.N. Trager. "Showdown at Geneva: Cease-fire in Laos." *New Leader* 44:21 (1961), pp. 9-11.

301 ——. "Laos: The Vientiane Agreement." *Journal of Southeast Asian History* 8:2 (Sept. 1967), pp. 257-267.

302 Hill, Kenneth L. "President Kennedy and the Neutralization of Laos." *Review of Politics* 31 (July 1969), pp. 353-369.

303 Kellogg, M.K. "The Laos Question: Double What Veto? *Virginia Law Review* 45 (Dec. 1959), pp. 1352-1360.

304 Lall, Arthur S. *How Communist China Negotiates.* New York: Columbia University Press, 1968.

305 Langer, Paul F. "Laos: Preparing for a Settlement in Vietnam." *Asian Survey* 9:1 (Jan. 1969), pp. 69-74.

306 Lee, Chae-Jin. "Communist China and the Geneva Conference on Laos: A Reappraisal." *Asian Survey* 7 (July 1969), pp. 522-539.

307 Magnien, M. "Adventure américaine au Laos." *Cahiers du Communisme* 37 (1961), pp. 179-184.

308 Ministry of Foreign Affairs. Laos. *North Vietnamese Interference in Laos.* Vientiane: 1965.

309 ——. *White Book on Violations of the Geneva Accords of 1962.* Vientiane: 1966.

310 ——. *White Book on Violations of the Geneva Accords of 1962.* Vientiane: 1968.

311 ——. *White Book on Violations of the Geneva Accords of 1962.* Vientiane: 1970.

312 Modelski, George. *International Conference on the Settlement of the Laotian Questions, 1961-62.* Vancouver: University of British Columbia Press, 1962.

313 Morley, Lorna. "Menaced Laos." *Editorial Research Reports* (Sept. 23, 1959), pp. 717-734.

314 Perazic, Elizabeth. "Little Laos Next Door to Red China." *National Geographic* 117 (Jan. 1960), pp. 46-69.

315 Ritvo, Herbert. "A Neutral Laos: The Danger." *New Leader* 44:15 (1961), p. 6.

316 Trager, F.N. "Dilemma in Laos." *America* 105:15 (1961), pp. 506-511.

317 U.S. Department of State. *The Situation in Laos.* Washington, D.C.: U.S. Government Printing Office, 1959.

318 "U.S. Reviews North Vietnamese Violations of Agreement on Laos." *U.S. Department of State Bulletin* 58 (June 24, 1968), pp. 817-820.

319 Warner, Denis. "Crisis in Laos: Sham Battle in a Real War." *Reporter* 21 (Nov. 12, 1959), pp. 25-27.

320 ——. "The Loss of Laos." *Reporter* 25:1 (1961), pp. 21-24.

E.4 / Laos & American War Activities

321 Abrams, Arnold. "The Once-hidden War; Escalation in Laos." *New Leader* 53 (Feb. 16, 1970), pp. 8-10.

322 Branfman, Fred. "Laos: No Place to Hide?" *Bulletin of the Concerned Asian Scholars* 2 (Fall 1970), pp. 15-46.

323 ——, comp. *Voices from the Plain of Jars: Life Under an Air War.* New York: Harper, 1972.

324 Burchett, Wilfred G. *The Furtive War: The United States in Vietnam and Laos.* New York: International Publishers, 1963.

325 ——. *The Second Indo-China War: Cambodia and Laos.* New York: International Publishers, 1970.

326 Campbell, A. "In Hot Pursuit; Reactions to U.S. Pursuit of North Vietnamese Inside Borders." *New Republic* 158 (Jan. 13, 1968), pp. 19-21.

327 "Concern Grows over U.S. Commitment in Laos." *Congressional Quarterly Weekly Report* 27 (Oct. 24, 1972), pp. 2069-2074.

328 Duskin, Edgar W. "Laos." *Military Review* 48 (Mar. 1968), pp. 3-10.

329 Everingham, John. "Let Them Eat Bombs." *Washington Monthly* (Sept. 1972), pp. 10-16.

330 Fredman, H.B. *Laos in Strategic Prospective.* Santa Monica, California: Rand, P-2330, June 1961.

331 Grant, Z. "Report from Laos, the Hidden War." *New Republic* 158 (Apr. 20, 1968), pp. 17-19.

332 Haney, Walt. "The Pentagon Papers and the United States Involvement in Laos." In *The Senator Gravel Edition: The Pentagon Papers, Critical Essays.* Vol. 5. Boston: Beacon, 1972.

333 Hersh, S.M. "How We Ran the Secret Air War in Laos." *New York Times Magazine* (Oct. 29, 1972), pp. 18-19.

334 Kann, P.S. "The Secret War: U.S. Role in Laos is Big but Another Vietnam Isn't Likely to Develop." *Wall Street Journal* (Dec. 18, 1969).

335 Langer, P.F. *Laos: Search for Peace in the Midst of War.* Santa Monica, California: Rand, P-3748, Dec. 1967.

336 Langland, S.G. "Laos Factor in a Vietnam Equation." *International Affairs* (London) 45 (Oct. 1969), pp. 631-647.

337 Mainwald, Helga. "Verstarkten U.S.A.–Aggression in Sudostasien: Laos [On the Intensified U.S. Aggression in Southeast Asia: Laos]." *Dokumentation der Zeit* (West Germany) 22:14 (1970) pp. 23-28.

338 Rusk, D. "Why Laos is Critically Important." *U.S. Department of State Bulletin* 51 (July 6, 1964), pp. 3-5.

339 Schancke, Don. *Mister Pop.* New York: McKay, 1970.

340 Shaplen, Robert. "Our Involvement in Laos." *Foreign Affairs* 48:3 (1970), pp. 478-493.

341 Simmons, E.H.S. "Laos and the War in Vietnam." *World Today* 22 (May 1966), pp. 199-206.

342 Starner, Frances. "Flight of the CIA." *Far Eastern Economic Review* 78:41 (Oct. 7, 1972), pp. 23-26.

343 Stevenson, Charles. *The End of Nowhere: American Policy toward Laos since 1954.* Boston: Beacon, 1972.

344 Trager, F.N. "Importance of Laos in Southeast Asia." *Current History* 46 (Feb. 1964), pp. 107-111.

345 U.S. Senate. Committee on Foreign Relations. Hearings; *United States Security Agreements and Commitments Abroad: Kingdom of Laos.* [Oct. 20-22, 28, 1969] 91st Cong., 1st Sess., 1970.

346 ——. Report; *Laos: April 1970.* 92d Cong., 1st Sess., 1971.

347 Urrows, Elizabeth. "Recurring Problems in Laos." *Current History* 57:340 (1969), pp. 361-363, 367.

348 Zasloff, Joseph. "Laos: The Forgotten World Widens." *Asian Survey* 10:1 (Jan. 1970), pp. 65-72.

F / Thailand

F.1 / General

349 Aertker, S.R., et al. "Communist Terrorist Camp: Thailand-Malaysian Frontier." *Military Review* 46 (June 1966), pp. 39-46.

350 American University. *Area Handbook for Thailand.* Washington, D.C.: U.S. Government Printing Office, 1963.

351 Ayal, Eliezer B. "Private Enterprise and Economic Progress in Thailand." *Journal of Asian Studies* 26 (Nov. 1966), pp. 5-14.

352 Blanchard, Wendell. *Thailand: Its People, Its Society, Its Culture.* New Haven: Human Relations Area Files, 1958.

353 Busch, Noel F. *Thailand: An Introduction to Modern Siam.* Princeton: Van Nostrand, 1959.

354 Darling, Frank C. "Modern Politics in Thailand." *Review of Politics* 24 (Apr. 1962), pp. 163-182.

355 Insor, D. *Thailand: A Political, Social, and Economic Analysis.* New York: Praeger, 1963.

356 Martin, James. V., Jr. "Thai-American Relations in World War II." *Journal of American Studies* 22 (Aug. 1963), pp. 451-467.

357 Muscat, Robert J. *Development Strategy in Thailand; A Study of Economic Growth.* New York: Praeger, 1966.

358 Neuchterlein, Donald E. "Thailand After Sarit." *Asian Survey* 4 (May 1964), pp. 842-850.

359 Poole, Peter A. *The Vietnamese in Thailand.* Ithaca: Cornell University Press, 1970.

360 Riggs, Fred W. *Thailand: The Modernization of a Bureaucratic Policy.* Honolulu: East-West Center Press, 1966.

361 Siffin, William J. *The Thai Bureaucracy: Institutional Change and Development.* Honolulu: East-West Center Press, 1966.

362 Sutton, Joseph L., ed. *Problems of Politics and Administration in Thailand.* Institute of Training for Public Service, Indiana University, 1962.

363 U.S. Department of State. *Background Notes: Thailand.* Washington, D.C.: U.S. Government Printing Office, 1966.

364 Wilson, David A. "China, Thailand and the Spirit of Bandung." *The China Quarterly* 30, 31 (Apr-June 1967 and July-Sept 1967), pp. 149-169, 96-127.

365 ——. *Politics in Thailand.* Ithaca: Cornell University Press, 1962.

366 ——. "Thailand–Scandal and Progress." *Asian Survey* 5 (Feb. 1965), pp. 108-112.

F.2 / Thailand & Vietnam War

367 Butwell, Richard. "Thailand after Vietnam." *Current History* 57:340 (1969), pp. 339-343, 368-369.

368 Casella, Allessandro. "United States-Thai Relations." *World Today* (Great Britain) 26:3 (1970), pp. 118-125.

369 Darling, Frank C. "American Policy in Thailand." *Western Political Quarterly* 15 (Mar. 1962), pp. 93-110.

370 ——. *The United States in Thailand.* Ithaca: Cornell University Press, 1966.

371 Fulham, Parke. "A Land at Peace? Country's Internal Situation and Its Foreign Relations." *Far Eastern Economic Review* 51 (Feb. 10, 1966), pp. 235-236.

372 Gordon, Bernard K. "Thailand: Its Meaning for the U.S." *Current History* 52 (Jan. 1967), pp. 16-21, 53-54.

373 Hanna, Willard A. "Thailand's Strategic Northeast: Defense and Development." *American Universities Field Staff Reports Service: Southeast Asia Series* 14 (1966).

374 Humphrey, Hubert H. "Vice President Reviews Asian Problems with Thai Premier: Joint Communiqué." *U.S. Department of State Bulletin* 54 (Mar. 14, 1966), pp. 396-397.

375 Karnow, Stanley. "The Looking Glass War: Insurgency in Thailand." *Far Eastern Review* 58 (Dec. 21, 1967), pp. 539-542.

376 Kuebler, Jeanne. "Thailand: New Red Target." *Editorial Research Reports* (Sept. 15, 1965), pp. 665-682.

377 Lomax, Louis E. *Thailand: The War That Is, The War That Will Be.* New York: Vintage, 1967.

378 Martin, Graham. "Thailand and Southeast Asia." *U.S. Department of State Bulletin* 66 (Feb. 6, 1967), pp. 193-199.

379 Murphy, Charles J.V. "Thailand's Fight to the Finish." *Fortune* 72 (Oct. 1964), pp. 122-127, 266-274.

380 Nairn, Ronald C. *International Aid to Thailand: The New Colonialism?* New Haven: Yale University Press, 1966.

381 Nuechterlein, Donald E. *Thailand and the Struggle for Southeast Asia.* Ithaca: Cornell University Press, 1965.

382 ——. "Thailand: Year of Danger and of Hope." *Asian Survey* 6 (Feb. 1966), pp. 119-124.

383 Parker, M. "Americans in Thailand: Counterinsurgency Activities of Armed Forces, USIS and AID." *Atlantic Monthly* 218 (Dec. 1966), pp. 51-58.

384 Shaplen, Robert. "Letter from Bangkok." *New Yorker* 43 (Mar. 18, 1967), pp. 135-172.

385 "Symposium on Northeast Thailand." *Asian Survey* 6 (July 1966), pp. 349-380.

386 U.S. Department of State. *Agreement Respecting Military Assistance between the Government of the United States of America and the*

Government of Thailand. Signed at Bangkok, October 17, 1950. (Treaties and Other International Acts Series 2434.) Washington, D.C.: U.S. Government Printing Office, 1953.

387 U.S. Senate. Committee on Foreign Relations. Hearings; *United States Security Agreements and Commitments Abroad: Kingdom of Thailand.* [Nov. 10-14, 1969] 91st Cong., 1st Sess., 1970.

388 Van der Kroef, Justus M. "Thailand between Two Millstones." *Contemporary Review* 209 (July 1966), pp. 20-24.

389 Wei-jiun, Chow. "Chinese Communists Trying to Turn Thailand into Second Vietnam: Activities of the Thai Communist 'Liberation Army' and Its 'Ten Policy' Statement." *Asian Outlook* 4 (Mar. 1969), pp. 23-44.

390 Wilson, David A. *The United States and the Future of Thailand.* New York: Praeger, 1970.

391 Wit, Daniel. *Thailand: Another Vietnam?* New York: Scribner's, 1968.

III / VIETNAM: HISTORY & POLITICS

A / Vietnam: General

392 Bain, Chester A. *Vietnam: The Roots of the Conflict.* Englewood Cliffs, New Jersey: Prentice-Hall, 1967.

393 Blanchet, M.T. *La Naissance de l'état associé du Vietnam.* Paris: Genin, 1954.

394 Buell, Hal. *Vietnam: Land of Many Dragons.* New York: Dodd, 1968.

395 Cairns, James Ford. *The Eagle and the Lotus: Western Intervention in Vietnam, 1847-1968.* Melbourne: Lansdowne Press, 1969.

396 Cannon, Terry. *Vietnam: A Thousand Years of Struggle.* San Francisco: Peoples' Press, 1969.

397 Chesneaux, Jean. *Contribution à l'histoire de la nation vietnamienne.* Paris: Éditions Sociales, 1955.

398 ——. *La Culture et les hommes: contribution à l'histoire de la nation vietnamienne.* Paris: Éditions Sociales, 1965.

399 ——. *Le Vietnam études de politique et d'histoire.* Paris: Maspero, 1968.

400 Crawford, Ann (Caddell). *Customs and Culture of Vietnam.* Illustrations by Han Dinh Cam. Rutland, Vermont: C.E. Tuttle, 1966.

401 Deschamp, Hubert, and Paul Chavet, eds. *Gallieni, pacificateur.* Paris: Presses Universitaires de France, 1949.

402 Despuech, Jacques. *Le Trafic des piastres.* Paris: Éditions des Deux Rives, 1953.

403 Do Van Minh. *Vietnam: Where East and West Meet.* 2d rev. ed. New York: Paragon Book Reprint Corp., 1968.

404 Duncanson, D.J. *Government and Revolution in Vietnam.* Oxford: Oxford University Press, 1968.

405 Fall, Bernard B. *The Two Viet-Nams.* New York: Praeger, 1963.

406 Hammer, Ellen Joy. *Vietnam: Yesterday and Today.* New York: Rinehart and Winston, 1966.

407 Isoart, P. *Le Phénomène national vietnamien de l'indépendance unitaire à l'indépendance fractionnée.* Paris: Librarie Générale de Droit et de Jurisprudence, 1961.

408 ——. *Le Vietnam.* Paris: Armand Colin, 1970.

409 Jumper, Roy, and Nguyen Thi Hue. *Notes on the Political and Administrative History of Viet Nam, 1802-1962.* Saigon: Michigan State University Vietnam Advisory Group, 1962.

410 Laurent, Arthur. *La Banque de l'Indochine et la piastre.* Paris: Éditions des Deux-Rives, 1954.

411 Le Thanh Khoi. *Le Viet-Nam: histoire et civilisation.* Paris: Éditions de Minuit, 1955.

412 Leifer, Michael. "DeGaulle and Vietnam: A Conception of Political Pathology." *International Journal* (Toronto) 23 (Spring 1969), pp. 221-233.

413 Levy, Roger. *L'Indochine et ses traites.* Paris: Paul Hartmann, 1947.

414 Marr, David G. *Vietnamese Anticolonialism.* Berkeley: University of California Press, 1971.

415 Masson, André. *Histoire du Vietnam.* Paris: Presses Universitaires de France, 1960.

416 McAleavy, Henry. *Black Flags in Vietnam: The Story of a Chinese Intervention.* New York: Macmillan, 1968.

417 McAlister, John T. *Vietnam: The Origins of Revolution, 1885-1946.* Washington, D.C.: American University, Center for Research in Social Systems, 1968.

418 McAlister, John T., Jr., and Paul Mus. *The Vietnamese and Their Revolution.* New York: Harper and Row, 1970.

419 Montaigu, Fernand de. *La Colonisation française dans l'est de la Cochinchine.* Limoges: Perrette, 1929.

420 Mus, Paul. "The Role of the Village in Vietnamese Politics." *Pacific Affairs* 22 (Sept. 1949), pp. 265-272.

421 ——. *Viet-Nam: sociologie d'une guerre.* Paris: Éditions du Seuil, 1950.

422 Newman, B. *Background to Vietnam.* London: R. Hale, 1965.

423 Nghiem Dang. *Vietnam: Politics and Public Administration.* Honolulu: East-West Center Press, 1966.

424 Nguyen Phut Tan. *A Modern History of Vietnam, 1802-1954.* Saigon: Khai-Trr, 1964.

425 Nguyen Thai Binh. *Vietnam: The Problem and a Solution.* Paris: Vietnam Democratic Party, 1962.

426 Nguyen Van Thai, and Nguyen Van Mung. *A Short History of Vietnam.* Saigon: The Times Publishing Co., 1958.

427 Robaud, Louis. *Viet-Nam: la tragédie indochinoise.* Paris: Valois, 1931.

428 Rouyer, Charles E. *Histoire militaire et politique de l'Annam et du Tonkin depuis 1799.* Paris: Lavauzelle, 1906.

429 Sheehan, Susan. *Ten Vietnamese.* New York: Knopf, 1967.

430 Smith, Ralph Bernard. *Vietnam and the West.* London: Heinemann Educational, 1968.

431 Thich Nhat Hanh. *Vietnam: Lotus in a Sea of Fire.* New York: Hill and Wang, 1967.

432 Tran Van Tung. *Viet-nam.* New York: Praeger, 1959.

433 Truong Buu Lam. *Patterns of Vietnamese Response to Foreign Intervention: 1858-1900.* New Haven: Southeast Asia Studies, Yale University, 1967.

B / Struggle: Revolution & Independence

B.1 / Second World War, 1940-46.

434 *Breaking Our Chains: Documents on the Vietnamese Revolution of August, 1945.* Hanoi: Foreign Languages Publishing House, 1960.

435 Chen, King C. "The Chinese Occupation of Vietnam, 1945-46." *France-Asie/Asia* 196 (1969), pp. 3-28.

436 Decoux, Jean. *À la Barre de l'Indochine: histoire de mon gouvernement général, 1940-45.* Paris: Librairie Plon, 1952.

437 Devillers, Philippe. "Vietnamese Nationalism and French Policies." In William L. Holland, ed., *Asian Nationalism and the West.* New York: Macmillan, 1953.

438 Drachman, Edward R. *United States Policy toward Vietnam, 1940-1945.* Cranbury, New Jersey: Fairleigh Dickinson University Press, 1970.

439 Ducoroy, Maurice. *Ma Trahison en Indochine.* Paris: Les Éditions Internationales, 1949.

440 Garrett, C.W. "In Search of Grandeur: France and Vietnam, 1940-1946." *Review of Politics* 29 (July 1967), pp. 303-323.

441 Gaudel, André. *L'Indochine française en face du Japon.* Paris: Susse, 1947.

442 Gaultier, Marcel. *Prisons japonais.* Monte Carlo: Regain, 1950.

443 Hertrich, Jean-Michael. *Doc-Lap! L'indépendance ou la mort.* Paris: Vigneau, 1946.

444 Hess, Gary R. "Franklin Roosevelt and Indochina." *Journal of American History* (Sept. 1972), pp. 353-368.

445 Isaacs, Harold R. *New Cycle in Asia.* New York: Macmillan, 1947, pp. 156-175.

446 ——. *No Peace for Asia.* New York: Macmillan, 1947, pp. 134-176.

447 LeBourgeois, Jacques. *Saigon sans la France: des japonais au Viet-Minh.* Paris: Librairie Plon, 1949.

448 Martin, Françoise. *Heures tragiques au Tonkin: 9 mars 1945-18 mars 1946.* Paris: Berger-Levraut, 1948.

449 McAlister, John T., Jr. *Vietnam: The Origins of Revolution.* New York: Knopf, 1969.

450 McMahon, Maj. J.F. "Vietnam: Our World War II Legacy." *Air University Review* 19:5 (1968), pp. 59-66.

451 Mordant, General. *Au Service de la France en Indochine: 1941-1945.* Saigon: Imprimerie Française d'Outre-Mer, 1950.

452 Sabattier, G. *Le Destin de l'Indochine: souvenir et documents, 1941-1951.* Paris: Librairie Plon, 1952.

453 Sainteny, Jean. *Histoire d'une paix manquée.* Paris: Amiot Dumont, 1953.

454 U.S. Senate. Committee on Foreign Relations. Staff Study No. 2: *The United States and Vietnam: 1944-1947.* [Based on the Pentagon Papers] [Apr. 3, 1972] 92d Cong., 2d Sess., 1972.

B.2 / First Indochina War

455 Anley, Henry. *In Order to Die.* London: Burke, 1955.

456 Blanchet, André. *Au Pays des ballila jaunes; relations d'un correspondant de guerre en Indochine.* Saint-Étienne: Éditions Dorian, 1947.

457 Bodard, Lucien. *La Guerre d'Indochine: l'enlisement.* Paris: Gallimard, 1963.

458 ——. *La Guerre d'Indochine: l'humiliation.* Paris: Gallimard, 1965.

459 ——. *The Quicksand War: Prelude to Vietnam.* Boston: Little, Brown, 1967.

460 Buu Loc. "Aspects of the Vietnamese Problem." *Pacific Affairs* 25 (Sept. 1952), pp. 235-247.

461 Catroux, Georges. *Deux actes du drame indochinois: Hanoi, juin 1940; Dien Bien Phu, mars-mai 1954.* Paris: Librairie Plon, 1959.

462 Chassin, L.M. *Aviation Indochine.* Paris: Amiot Dumont, 1954.

463 Chezel, Guy de. *Parchute en Indochine.* Paris: Sirenes, 1947.

464 Dannaud, J.P. *Guerre morte.* Paris: George Lang, 1954.

465 Darcourt, Pierre. *De Lattre au Viet-Nam: une année de victoire.* Paris: La Table Ronde, 1965.

466 Demariaux, Jean-Claude. *Les Secrets des Îles Poulo-Condore: le grand bagne indochinois.* Paris: J. Payronnet, 1956.

467 Deutscher, Isaac. "How the Russians Bet a Little in Asia to Win a Lot in Europe." *Reporter* 2 (Sept. 23, 1954), pp. 19-22.

468 Devillers, Philippe. *Histoire du Vietnam de 1940 à 1952.* Paris: Éditions du Seuil, 1952.

469 Dinfreville, Jacques (pseudonym). *L'Opération Indochine.* Paris: Les Éditions Internationales, 1953.

470 Ély, Paul. *Memoires: l'Indochine dans la tourmente.* Paris: Librairie Plon, 1964.

471 Fall, Bernard B. "Indochina: The Last Year of the War—Communist Organization and Tactics." *Military Review* 36 (Oct. 1956), pp. 48-56.

472 ——. "The Last Year of the War—The Navarre Plan." *Military Review* 36 (Dec. 1956), pp. 48-56.

473 ——. *Political Development of Viet-Nam, V-J Day to the General Cease-Fire.* Ann Arbor, Michigan: University Microfilms, 1966.

474 ——. *Street without Joy: Insurgency in Indochina.* 4th ed. London: Pall Mall Press, 1965.

475 Ferrandi, Jean. *Les Officers français face au Vietminh, 1945-1954.* Paris: Fayard, 1966.

476 Goeldhieux, Claude. *Quinze mois prisonnier chez les Viets.* Paris: Armand Colin, 1960.

477 Graham, Andrew. *Interval in Indochina.* New York: St. Martin's Press, 1956.

478 Halle, Gunther. *Legion Étrangère.* East Berlin: Volk und Welt, 1952.

479 Hammer, Ellen J. *The Struggle for Indochina.* Stanford: Stanford University Press, 1956.

480 Institute Franco-Suisse d'Études Coloniales. *France and Viet-Nam: The Franco-Vietnamese Conflict According to Official Documents.* Geneva: Éditions du Milieu du Monde, 1947.

481 Katzenbach, E.L., Jr. "Indo-China: A Military-Political Appreciation." *World Politics* 4 (Jan. 1952), pp. 186-218.

482 Leroy, Jean. *Un Homme dans la rizière.* Paris: Éditions de Paris, 1955.

483 Mordal, Jacques. *Marine Indochine.* Paris: Amiot Dumont, 1953.

484 Navarre, Gen. Henri. *Agonie de l'Indochine, 1953-1954.* Paris: Librairie Plon, 1956.

485 Ngo Van Chien. *Journal d'un combattant Viet-Minh.* Paris: Éditions du Seuil, 1955.

486 O'Ballance, Edgar. *The Indo-China War, 1945-54: A Study in Guerilla Warfare.* London: Faber, 1964.

487 Paret, Peter. *French Revolutionary Warfare from Indochina to Algeria: The Analysis of a Political and Military.* New York: Praeger, 1964.

488 Riessen, René. *Jungle Mission.* New York: Crowell, 1957.

489 ——. *Le Silence du ciel.* Paris: Éditions de la Pensée Moderne, 1956.

490 Salisbury-Jones, Sir Guy. *So Full a Glory.* London: Weidenfeld & Nicholson, 1954.

491 Starobin, Joseph. *Eyewitness in Indo-China.* New York: Cameron and Kahn, 1954.

492 U.S. Department of State. *Indochina: The War in Viet-Nam, Cambodia, and Laos.* Washington, D.C.: Department of State Publication 5092. Far Eastern Series 58, 1953.

493 Vermeersch, Jeannette. *Paix immédiate au Viet-Nam discours prononcé à l'assemblée nationale le 27 janvier 1950 par Jeannette Vermeersch suivi d'une déclaration de Maurice Thorez.* Paris: Parti Communiste Français, 1950.

B.3 / Dien Bien Phu

494 Backlund, Donald R. "Stalingrad and Dien Bien Phu: Two Cases of Failure in Strategic Resupply." *Aerospace Historian* (Summer-Fall 1970), pp. 60-68.

495 Dejean, Maurice. "The Meaning of Dien Bien Phu." *U.S. Naval Institute Proceedings* 80 (July 1954), pp. 717-725.

496 Fall, Bernard B. *Hell in a Very Small Place: The Siege of Dien Bien Phu.* New York: Lippincott, 1967.

497 Grauwin, Paul. *Doctor at Dien Bien Phu.* New York: John Day, 1955.

498 Laniel, Joseph. *Le Drame indochinois: de Dien-Bien-Phu au pari de Genève.* Paris: Librairie Plon, 1957.

499 Long, W.F. "The Spectre of Dien Bien Phu." *Military Review* 46:10 (1966), pp. 35-39.

500 Renald, Jean. *L'Enfer de Dien Bien Phu.* Paris: Flammarion, 1954.

501 Roy, Jules. *The Battle of Dien Bien Phu.* Trans. by Robert Baldish. New York: Harper and Row, 1963.

502 Simcock, William. "Dien Bien Phu: Yesterday's Battlefield." *Canadian Army Journal* 12 (July 1958), pp. 35-46.

503 Stanley, G.F.C. "Dien Bien Phu in Retrospect." *International Journal* 10 (1954-55), pp. 38-50.

504 Vo Nguyen Giap. *Dien Bien Phu.* Hanoi: Éditions en Langues Étrangères, 1959.

B.4 / Geneva Accords

505 Democratic Republic of Vietnam. *Documents relatifs à l'exécution des accords de Genève concernant le Viet-Nam.* Hanoi: Ministry of Foreign Affairs, 1956.

506 Eden, Anthony. *Full Circle: The Memoirs of Rt. Hon. Sir Anthony Eden.* London: Cassell, 1960.

507 *Facts and Dates on the Problem of the Reunification of Viet-Nam.* Hanoi: Foreign Languages Publishing House, 1956.

508 Fall, Bernard B. "The Cease-Fire in Indochina: An Appraisal." *Far Eastern Survey* (Sept. 1954), pp. 135-139 and (Oct. 1954), pp. 152-155.

509 Frederic-Dupont. *Mission de la France en Asie.* Paris: Éditions France-Empire, 1956.

510 Guillain, Robert. *La Fin des illusions; notes d'Indochine, février-juillet 1954.* Paris: Centre d'Études de Politique Étrangère, 1954.

511 Hannon, J.S., Jr. "A Political Settlement for Vietnam: The 1954 Geneva Conference and Its Current Implications." *Virginia Journal of International Law* 8 (1967), pp. 20-65.

512 Karpikhim, A. "The U.S.A. Sabotages the Geneva Agreements on Indochina." *International Affairs* (Moscow) 8 (1959), pp. 57-62.

513 Lacouture, Jean, and Philippe Devillers. *End of a War: Indochina 1954.* New York: Praeger, 1969.

514 Lancaster, Donald. *The Emancipation of French Indochina.* London: Oxford University Press, 1961.

515 *On the Reestablishment of Normal Relations between the Northern and Southern Zones of Vietnam.* Hanoi: Foreign Languages Publishing House, 1955.

516 Randle, Robert F. *Geneva 1954: The Settlement of the Indochinese War.* Princeton: Princeton University Press, 1969.

517 Republic of Vietnam. *The Problem of Reunification of Vietnam.* Saigon: Ministry of Information, 1958.

518 ——. *Violations of the Geneva Agreements by the Viet-Minh Communists.* Saigon: 1959.

519 Ton That Thien. "The Geneva Agreements and Peace Prospects in Vietnam." *India Quarterly* 12 (Oct-Dec 1956), pp. 375-388.

520 Weinstein, F.B. *Vietnam's Upheld Elections: The Failure to Carry Out the 1956 Reunification Elections and the Effect on Hanoi's Present Outlook.* Ithaca: Southeast Asia Program, Department of Asian Studies, Cornell University, 1966.

B.5 / International Control Commission

521 Australia. Department of External Affairs. "Special Report of the International Control Commission in Vietnam." *Current Notes on International Affairs* 33:6 (1962), pp. 25-35.

522 Hannon, J.S., Jr. "The International Control Commission Experience and the Role of an Improved International Supervisory Body in the Vietnam Settlement." *Virginia Journal of International Law* 9 (1968), pp. 20-65.

523 Holmes, J. "Techniques of Peacekeeping in Asia." In A. Buchan, ed. *China and the Peace of Asia.* New York: Praeger, 1965.

524 Maneli, Mieczyslav. *War of the Vanquished: A Polish Diplomat in Vietnam.* New York: Harper and Row, 1971.

525 Martin, Paul. *Canada and the Quest for Peace.* New York: Columbia University Press, 1967.

526 Murti, B.S.N. *Vietnam Divided: The Unfinished Struggle.* New York: Asia Publishing House, 1964.

527 Naravane, A.S. "The International Commission for Vietnam." *Journal of the United Service Institution of India* 94 (Apr. 1964), pp. 159-167.

528 Thee, Marek. *Notes of a Witness: Laos and the Second Indochinese War.* New York: Vintage, 1973.

529 Wainhouse, David. *International Peace Observation: A History and Forecast.* Baltimore: Johns Hopkins Press, 1966.

B.5a / Official Reports

530 International Commission for Supervision and Control in Cambodia. *1st Progress Report, December 31, 1954.* Cmnd. 9458. London: H.M.S.O., 1955.

531 ——. *2d Progress Report, January 1-March 31, 1955.* Cmnd. 9534. London: H.M.S.O., 1955.

532 ——. *3d Interim Report, April 1-July 28, 1955.* Cmnd. 9579. London: H.M.S.O., 1955.

533 ——. *4th Interim Report, July 29-September 30, 1955.* Cmnd. 9671. London: H.M.S.O., 1955.

534 ——. *5th Interim Report, October 1, 1955-December 31, 1956.* Cmnd. 253. London: H.M.S.O., 1957.

535 ——. *6th Interim Report, 1957.* Cmnd. 526. London: H.M.S.O., 1958.

536 ——. *7th Interim Report, 1958.* Cmnd. 887. London: H.M.S.O., 1959.

537 ——. *Report of the I.C.C. on the Aggressions against Cambodia by the American-South-Vietnamese Forces.* Phnom Penh: Ministere des Affaires Étrangères, 1964.

538 International Commission for Supervision and Control in Laos. *1st Interim Report, January 15, 1955.* Cmnd. 9455. London: H.M.S.O., 1955.

539 ——. *2d Interim Report, January 1-June 30, 1955.* Cmnd. 9630. London: H.M.S.O., 1955.

540 ——. *3d Interim Report, July 1, 1955-May 16, 1957.* Cmnd. 314. London: H.M.S.O., 1957.

541 ——. *4th Interim Report, May 17, 1957-May 31, 1958.* Cmnd. 541. London: H.M.S.O., 1958.

542 International Commission for Supervision and Control in Vietnam. *1st and 2d Interim Reports, August 11-December 10, 1954.* Cmnd. 9461. London: H.M.S.O., 1955.

543 ——. *3d Interim Report, February 11-April 10, 1955.* Cmnd. 9499. London: H.M.S.O., 1955.

544 ——. *4th Interim Report, April 11-August 10, 1955.* Cmnd. 9654. London: H.M.S.O., 1955.

545 ——. *5th Interim Report, August 11-December 10, 1955.* Cmnd. 9706. London: H.M.S.O., 1956.

546 ——. *6th Interim Report, December 11, 1955-July 31, 1956.* Cmnd. 31. London: H.M.S.O., 1956.

547 ——. *7th Interim Report, August 1, 1956-April 30, 1957.* Cmnd. 335. London: H.M.S.O., 1957.

548 ——. *8th Interim Report, May 1, 1957-April 30, 1958.* Cmnd. 509. London: H.M.S.O., 1958.

549 ——. *9th Interim Report, May 1, 1958-January 31, 1959.* Cmnd. 972. London: H.M.S.O., 1959.

550 ——. *10th Interim Report, February 1, 1959-January 31, 1960.* Cmnd. 1040. London: H.M.S.O., 1960.

551 ——. *11th Interim Report, February 1, 1960-February 28, 1961.* Cmnd. 1551. London: H.M.S.O., 1961.

552 ——. *Special Report, June 2, 1962.* Cmnd. 1775. London: H.M.S.O., 1962.

553 ——. *Special Report, February 13, 1965.* Cmnd. 2609. London: H.M.S.O., 1965.

554 ——. *Special Report, February 27, 1965.* Cmnd. 2634. London: H.M.S.O., 1965.

C / South Vietnam

C.1 / General

555 Adair, Dick. *Dick Adair's Saigon: A Vietnam Sketchbook.* Philadelphia: John Westherhill, 1971.

556 American University. *Area Handbook for South Vietnam.* 2d ed. Washington, D.C.: U.S. Government Printing Office, 1967.

557 Barber, C.H. "Business Boom in Saigon." *Far Eastern Economic Review* 51 (Mar. 10, 1966), pp. 443-444, 447.

558 Berregan, Darrell. "The Ordeal of South Vietnam." *Reporter* 14 (Sept. 20, 1956), pp. 29-33.

559 Brelis, Dean. *Face of South Vietnam.* New York: Houghton, Mifflin, 1967.

560 Buttinger, Joseph. "The Ethnic Minorities in the Republic of Vietnam." In Wesley R. Fishel, ed. *Problems of Freedom: South Vietnam Since Independence.* Chicago: Free Press of Glencoe, 1961.

561 Buu Hoan. "Vietnam: Economic Consequences of the Geneva Peace." *Far Eastern Economic Review* (Dec. 11, 1958), pp. 753-757.

562 Carver, George A., Jr. "The Real Revolution in South Vietnam." *Foreign Affairs* 43:3 (Apr. 1965), pp. 387-408.

563 Celerier, Pierre. *Menaces sur le Viet-Nam.* Saigon: Imprimerie d'Extrême Orient (IDEO), 1950.

564 Chaffard, Georges. *Indochine: dix ans d'indépendance.* Paris: Calmann-Levy, 1964.

565 Child, Frank C. *Essays on Economic Growth, Capital Formation, and Public Policy in Viet-Nam.* Saigon: Michigan State University Viet-Nam Advisory Group, 1961.

566 ——. "Vietnam: The Eleventh Hour." *New Republic* (Dec. 4, 1961), pp. 14-16.

567 Coffey, Raymond. "Vietnam's Not-so-Free Press." *Saturday Review* (Oct. 14, 1967), pp. 122-123, 131.

568 Corley, Francis J. "Freedom in Indo-China: A Review Article." *Pacific Affairs* 34 (1961), pp. 378-380.

569 ——. "The President in the Constitution of the Republic of Vietnam." *Pacific Affairs* 34 (1961), pp. 165-174.

570 ——. "Progress in Vietnam." *America* 99 (May 10, 1958), pp. 191-193.

571 ——. "Vietnam since Geneva." *Thought* (Fordham Univ. Q.) 33 (1958-59), pp. 515-568.

572 Dorsey, John T., Jr. "South Vietnam in Perspective." *Far Eastern Survey* 27 (Dec. 1958), pp. 177-182.

573 Drinan, R.F. "Political Freedom in Vietnam." *America* 120 (Aug. 1969), pp. 821-831.

574 Faltermeyer, E.K. "The Surprising Assets of South Vietnam's Economy." *Fortune* 73 (Mar. 1966), pp. 110-121.

575 Finkle, J.L., and Tran Van Dinh. *Provincial Government in Viet Nam: A Study of Vinh Long Province.* Saigon: Michigan State University Vietnam Advisory Group, 1961.

576 Fishel, W.R. "Free Vietnam Since Geneva: Factors in the Rollback of Communism without War." *Yale Review* 49 (Sept. 1959), pp. 68-79.

577 ——, ed. *Problems of Freedom: South Vietnam Since Independence.* Chicago: Free Press of Glencoe, 1961.

578 Fitzgerald, Frances. "The Tragedy of Saigon." *Atlantic Monthly* 218 (Dec. 1966), pp. 59-67.

579 Gittinger, J. Price. *Studies on Land Tenure in Vietnam: Terminal Report.* Saigon: United States Operations Mission to Vietnam, 1959.

580 Goodrich, Carter. *Toward the Economic Development of Viet Nam.* New York: United Nations, 1956.

581 Grant, J.A.C. "The Vietnam Constitution of 1956." *American Political Science Review* 56 (June 1958), pp. 437-463.

582 Hallinan, T. *Economic Prospects of the Republic of Vietnam.* Santa Monica, California: Rand, P-4224, Nov. 1969.

583 Henderson, William. "South Vietnam Finds Itself." *Foreign Affairs* 35 (Jan. 1957), pp. 283-294.

584 Hendry, James Bausch. *The Small World of Khanh Hau.* Chicago: Aldine, 1964.

585 Hickey, Gerald C. *Village in Vietnam.* New Haven: Yale University Press, 1964.

586 Honey, P.J. "The Problem of Democracy in Vietnam." *World Today* (Feb. 1960), pp. 71-79.

587 Jumper, Roy. "Mandarin Bureaucracy and Politics in South Vietnam." *Pacific Affairs* 30 (Mar. 1957), pp. 44-58.

588 ——. "Sects and Communism in South Vietnam." *Orbis* 3 (Spring 1959), pp. 85-96.

589 Ladejinsky, W. "Vietnam: The First Five Years." *Reporter* 21 (Dec. 24, 1959), pp. 20-23.

590 Millet, Stanley. "Terror in Vietnam: An American's Ordeal at the Hands of Our 'Friends.' " *Harper's* (Sept. 1962), pp. 31-39.

591 Morrock, Richard. "Agrarian 'Reform' in South Vietnam." *Monthly Review* 16 (Nov. 1964), pp. 442-446.

592 Musolf, Lloyd D. "Public Enterprise and Development Perspectives in South Vietnam." *Asian Survey* 3:8 (Aug. 1963), pp. 357-372.

593 Nghiem Dang. *Viet-Nam: Politics and Public Administration.* Honolulu: East-West Center Press, 1966.

594 Nguyen Cong Vien. *Seeking the Truth: The Inside Story of Viet Nam after the French Defeat.* New York: Vantage, 1967.

595 Nguyen Kien. *Le Sud-Vietnam depuis Dien-Bien-Phu.* Paris: Maspero, 1963.

596 Nguyen Ngoc Bich. "Vietnam: An Independent Viewpoint." *China Quarterly* 9 (Jan/Mar 1962), pp. 105-111.

597 Nguyen Thai. *Is South Vietnam Viable?* Manila: Carmelo and Bauermann, 1962.

598 Nicolaus, Martin. "The Professor, the Policeman and the Peasant." *Viet-Report* 2 (Feb/Apr 1966).

599 O'Daniel, John W. *The Nation That Refused to Starve: The Challenge of the New Vietnam.* New York: Coward, McCann, 1960.

600 Purnell, K.H. "Vietnam Elections: Marching Out the Horses." *Nation* 205 (Sept. 25, 1967), pp. 267-269.

601 "Republic of Viet-Nam: Elections." *Current Notes on International Affairs* (Australia) 38 (Sept. 1967), pp. 349-370.

602 Richer, Edward. "Peace Activism in Vietnam." *Studies on the Left* 6 (Jan/Feb 1966), pp. 54-63.

603 Rose, Dale L. *The Vietnamese Civil Service System.* Saigon: Michigan State University Vietnam Advisory Group, 1961.

604 Schrock, J.L. *Minority Groups in the Republic of Vietnam.* Washington, D.C.: American University, 1966.

605 Scigliano, Robert. "The Electoral Process in South Vietnam: Politics in an Underdeveloped State." *Midwest Journal of Political Science* 4 (May 1960), pp. 138-161.

606 ——. "Political Parties in South Vietnam under the Republic." *Pacific Affairs* 33 (June 1960), pp. 327-346.

607 ——. *South Vietnam: Nation Under Stress.* Boston: Houghton, Mifflin, 1963.

608 Serong, F.P. *The Future of South Vietnam.* New York: National Strategy Information Center, 1971.

609 Smith, Desmond. "Saigon: Drowning in Dollars." *Nation* 203 (Dec. 5, 1966), pp. 602-605.

610 Smuckler, Ralph H., et al. *Report on the Police of Vietnam.* Saigon: Michigan State University Vietnam Advisory Group, 1955.

611 Tanham, G.K. "The Communist Challenge in the Provinces." *Vietnam Perspectives* 1:2 (1965), pp. 4-18.

612 Tolischus, O.D. "Elections in Vietnam." *New Leader* 48:16 (1965), pp. 8-9.

613 Trued, M.N. "South Vietnam's Industrial Development Center." *Pacific Affairs* 33 (Sept. 1960), pp. 250-267.

614 U.S. House of Representatives. Committee on Government Operations. Report No. 1142; *Land Reform in Vietnam.* [20th Rpt.] 90th Cong., 2d Sess., 1968.

615 U.S. Military Assistance Command, Vietnam. Office of the Staff Judge Advocate. *The Constitution of Vietnam: An Analysis and Comparison.* Saigon: 1967.

616 *Who's Who of the Republic of South Viet Nam.* Saigon: Gai Phong Editions, 1969.

617 Woodruff, Lloyd W. *Local Administration in Vietnam.* Saigon: Michigan State University Vietnam Advisory Group, 1961.

618 Young, Kenneth T. "United States Policy and Vietnamese Political Viability, 1954-67." *Asian Survey* 7 (Aug. 1967), pp. 507-514.

619 Young, S.M. "The New 'Democracy' in Vietnam." *Progressive* 31 (July 1967), pp. 10-11.

C.2 / U.S. Aid Projects

620 *Aid to Vietnam.* New York: American Friends of Vietnam, 1959.

621 Barrows, Leland. "American Economic Aid to Vietnam." *Viet My* 1 (1956), pp. 29-40.

622 Bennet, John T. *Political Implications of Economic Change: South Vietnam. SEADAG Papers on Development and Development Policy Problems, No. 19.* New York: The Asia Society, 1967.

623 Bresse, Gerald. *The Great City and Economic Development in Southeast Asia. SEADAG Papers on Problems of Development in Southeast Asia, No. 29.* New York: The Asia Society, 1968.

624 Brown, Lester R. *Seeds of Change: The Green Revolution and Development in the 1970's.* New York: Praeger, 1970.

625 Fishel, W.R. "American Aid to Vietnam." *Current History* 49 (Nov. 1965), pp. 294-299.

626 Gaud, W.S. "AID Report on Viet-Nam Commodity Programs." *U.S. Department of State Bulletin* 56 (Feb. 6, 1967), pp. 200-216.

627 Genin, P. "L'Aide américaine au Sud-Vietnam." *Le Cahiers de la République* 6:30 (1961), pp. 51-56.

628 Grant, James P. "AID's Proposed Program for Viet-Nam in Fiscal Year 1969." *U.S. Department of State Bulletin* 58 (May 6, 1968), pp. 594-598.

629 Hendry, J.B. "American Aid in Vietnam: The View from a Village." *Pacific Affairs* 33 (Dec. 1960), pp. 387-391.

630 Holbik, Karel. "U.S. Aid to Vietnam." *Inter Economics* 7 (July 1968), pp. 242-246.

631 Hope, Samuel R. "Vietnam Christian Service." *Journal of Presbyterian History* 47:2 (1969), pp. 103-123.

632 Hotham, David. "U.S. Aid to Vietnam—A Balance Sheet." *Reporter* (Sept. 16, 1957), pp. 30-33.

633 Joint Development Group. *The Postwar Development of the Republic of Vietnam: Policies and Programs.* New York: Praeger, 1970.

634 Moseley, G.V.H., III. "U.S. Aid to Indo-China." *New Leader* 41 (Feb. 24, 1958), pp. 13-14.

635 Roseman, Alvin. "United States Economic Commitments in Southeast Asia." *Current History* 54 (Jan. 1968), pp. 7-14.

636 Scigliano, R., and G.H. Fox. *Technical Assistance in Vietnam: The Michigan State University Experience.* New York: Praeger, 1965.

637 Smith, R.L. "The Lessons of Vietnam: A Study of Problems Faced by U.S. Aid Programs." *Challenge* 8 (Nov. 1959), pp. 7-12.

638 Tanham, George K., et al. *War without Guns, American Civilians in Rural Vietnam.* New York: Praeger, 1966.

639 Taylor, M.C. "South Vietnam: Lavish Aid, Limited Progress." *Pacific Affairs* 34 (1961), pp. 242-256.

640 United Nations. Economic Survey Mission to the Republic of Viet-Nam. Report; *Toward the Economic Development of the Republic of Vietnam.* (FAO Rpt. No. 539) New York: 1959.

641 U.S. Department of State. Office of Media Service. *Quiet Warriors: Supporting Social Revolution in Viet-Nam.* [Department of State Publication 8041, Far Eastern Series 140] Washington, D.C.: U.S. Government Printing Office, 1966.

642 U.S. General Accounting Office. Report; *Economic and Technical Assistance Program for Vietnam.* [For fiscal years 1955-57] Washington, D.C.: U.S. Government Printing Office, 1958.

643 U.S. House of Representatives. Committee on Government Operations. Hearings; *U.S. Assistance Programs in Vietnam.* [July 15-21, Aug. 2, 1971] 92d Cong., 1st Sess., 1971.

644 ——. Report; *A Review of the Inequitable Monetary Rate of Exchange in Vietnam.* [Report 91-1228] [June 25, 1970] 91st Cong., 2d Sess., 1970.

645 U.S. Senate. Committee on Foreign Relations. Hearings; *Supplemental Foreign Assistance Fiscal Year 1966—Vietnam.* 89th Cong., 2d Sess., 1966.

646 ——. Report; *United States Aid Program in Vietnam.* 86th Cong., 2d Sess., 1960.

C.3 / Religion & Politics (Buddhist)

647 Fairbanks, H.G. "Diem and the Buddhists." *Commonwealth* 78 (July 26, 1963), pp. 452-454.

648 Gheddo, Piero. *The Cross and the Bo-Tree: Catholics and Buddhists in Vietnam.* Trans. by Charles Underhill Quinn. New York: Sheed and Ward, 1970.

649 Hope, Marjorie. "Vietnam Perspectives: The Buddhist Way: Guns, Butter, or Chinh Nghia?" *War/Peace* 6 (Aug/Sept 1966), pp. 14-16.

650 Howe, Irving. "The Buddhist Revolt in Vietnam." *Dissent* 13 (May/June 1966), pp. 227-229.

651 Joiner, C.A. "South Vietnam's Buddhist Crisis: Organization for Charity, Dissidence, and Unity." *Asian Survey* 4:7 (July 1964), pp. 915-928.

652 Nakamura, Hajime. "The Buddhist Protest." *Japan Quarterly* 13 (Oct/Dec 1966), pp. 439-443.

653 Morgan, K.W. "The Buddhists: The Problem and the Promise." *Asia* 4 (Winter 1966), pp. 503-518.

654 Roberts, Adam. "Buddhism and Politics in South Vietnam." *World Today* 21 (June 1965), pp. 240-250.

655 ——. "The Buddhists, the War and the Vietcong." *World Today* 22 (May 1966), pp. 214-222.

656 Scigliano, Robert. "Vietnam: Politics and Religion." *Asian Survey* 4 (Jan. 1964), pp. 666-673.

657 Warner, Denis. "The Divided Buddhists of South Vietnam." *Reporter* 34 (June 16, 1966), pp. 22-24.

658 ——. "Vietnam's Militant Buddhists." *Reporter* 31 (Dec. 3, 1964), pp. 29-31.

659 Wulff, Erich. "The Buddhist Revolt: Diem's New Opponents Deserve U.S. Support." *New Republic* (Aug. 31, 1963), pp. 11-14.

C.4 / Ngo Dinh Diem/Madame Nhu

660 Borin, V.L. "Who Killed Diem and Why." *National Review* 16 (June 2, 1964), pp. 441-446.

661 Bouscaren, Anthony T. *The Last of the Mandarins: Diem of Vietnam.* Pittsburgh: Duquesne University Press, 1965.

662 Henderson, W., and W.R. Fishel. "The Foreign Policy of Ngo Din Diem." *Vietnam Perspectives* 2:1 (1966) pp. 3-30.

663 Huynh Sanh Thong. "Greatest Little Man in Asia." *Nation* 192 (Feb. 18, 1961), pp. 140-142.

664 Karnow, Stanley. "Diem Defeats His Own Best Troops." *Reporter* 24:2 (1961), pp. 24-29.

665 ——. "The Edge of Chaos." *Saturday Evening Post* (Sept. 28, 1963), pp. 27-36.

666 ——. "The Fall of the House of Ngo Dinh." *Saturday Evening Post* 236:45 (Dec. 21, 1963), pp. 75-79.

667 Luce, Clare Boothe. "The Lady is for Burning: The Seven Deadly Sins of Madame Nhu." *National Review* (Nov. 5, 1963), pp. 395-399.

668 "Ngo Dinh Diem, President of the Republic of Vietnam." *Far Eastern Economic Review* 26 (May 28, 1959), pp. 744-746.

669 Nguyen Minh Vy. "L'Inamovible famille Diem." *Democratic Nouvelle* 10 (Oct. 1963), pp. 14-19.

670 Oosten, Fernand. "Ngo Dinh Diem, der Viet Cong und die Amerikaner." *Aussenpolitik* 14 (Sept. 1963), pp. 624-633.

671 Shaplen, Robert. "A Reporter in Vietnam: Diem." *New Yorker* (Sept. 22, 1962), pp. 103-131.

672 Sharron, Marc. "The Fall of the House of Ngo: A Case Review." *Institute of Applied Psychology Review* 4 (Summer 1964), pp. 83-92.

673 Sparks, Will. "A New Role for Mme. Nhu." *New Leader* 46 (Nov. 25, 1963), pp. 8-10.

674 U.S. Senate. Committee on Foreign Relations. Staff Study No. 3: *U.S. Involvement in Overthrow of Diem, 1963.* [Based on the Pentagon Papers] [July 20, 1972] 92d Cong., 2d Sess., 1972.

675 Warner, Denis. "Agony in Saigon: the Lady and the Cadaver." *Reporter* 29:6 (1963), pp. 39-42.

676 ——. *The Last Confucian.* New York: Macmillan, 1963.

677 West, M.L. "The Tragedy of Diem and the Paradox of Asia." *America* 112 (Mar. 13, 1965), pp. 352-356.

C.5 / Ky/Thieu

678 "Thieu: An Interview with Oriana Fallaci." *New Republic* (Jan. 20, 1973), pp. 16-25.

679 Ton That Thien. "Ky's Election Victory." *Far Eastern Economic Review* 53 (Sept. 22, 1966), pp. 561-563.

680 Tran Van Dinh. "Thieu and Ky: The Rivalry of Puppets." *Nation* 206 (Jan. 29, 1968), pp. 136-139.

681 ——. "The Ky Question." *New Republic* 156 (Jan. 21, 1967), pp. 21-23.

682 ——. "Ky vs. Buddhists: Round 2." *New Republic* 15 (May 13, 1967), pp. 15-19.

D / North Vietnam

D.1 / General

683 Burchett, Wilfred G. *North of the 17th Parallel.* Hanoi: Red River Publishing House, 1957.

684 ——. *Vietnam North.* New York: International Publishers, 1966.

685 Chaliand, Gerard. *The Peasants of North Vietnam.* Baltimore: Penguin Books, 1969.

686 *The Democratic Republic of Viet Nam.* Hanoi: Foreign Languages Publishing House, 1960.

687 *Documents of the Third National Congress of the Viet Nam Workers' Party.* 4 Vols. Hanoi: Foreign Languages Publishing House, 1960.

688 Fall, Bernard B. "North Vietnam: A Profile." *Problems of Communism* 14 (July-Aug 1965), pp. 24ff.

689 ——. "North Viet-Nam's Constitution and Government." *Pacific Affairs* 33 (Sept. 1960), pp. 282-290.

690 ——. *The Viet-Minh Regime.* Ithaca: Cornell University Southeast Asia Program and the Institute of Pacific Relations, 1956.

691 ——. *Le Viet-Minh: la république démocratique du Viet-Nam 1945-1960.* Paris: A Colin, 1960.

692 Gerassi, John. *North Vietnam: A Documentary.* London: Allen and Unwin, 1968.

693 Gittinger, J. Price. "Communist Land Policy in North Viet Nam." *Far Eastern Survey* 27 (Aug. 1959), pp. 113-126.

694 Gurtov, M. *Indochina in North Vietnamese Strategy.* Santa Monica, California: Rand, P-4605, March 1971.

695 Hoang Van Chi. *From Colonialism to Communism: A Case History of North Vietnam.* New York: Praeger, 1964.

696 Honey, P.J. "North Vietnam's Party Congress." *China Quarterly* (Oct-Dec 1960), pp. 66-75.

697 ——, ed. *North Vietnam Today: Profile of a Communist Satellite.* New York: Praeger, 1962.

698 Kellen, K. *1971 and Beyond: The View from Hanoi.* Santa Monica, California: Rand, P-4634-1, June 1971.

699 Lacouture, Jean. "Inside North Vietnam." *New Republic* (May 21, 1962), pp. 17-20.

700 McCarthy, Mary. *Hanoi*. New York: Harcourt, Brace and World, 1968.

701 Porter, D. Gareth. *The Myth of the Bloodbath: North Vietnam's Land Reform Reconsidered.* (Interim Rpt. No. 2) Ithaca: Cornell University, International Relations of East Asia Project, 1972.

702 Raffaeli, J. *Hanoi, capitale de la survie.* Paris: Grasset, 1967.

703 Shadbad, Theodore, "Economic Developments in North Vietnam." *Pacific Affairs* 31 (Mar. 1958), pp. 36-53.

704 Tongas, Gérard. *J'ai vécu dans l'enfer communiste au Nord Viet-Nam et j'ai choisi la liberté.* Paris: Nouvelles Éditions Debresse, 1960.

705 Van Dyke, Jon M. *North Vietnam's Strategy for Survival.* Palo Alto, California: Pacific Books, 1972.

706 Zorza, Victor. "In Hanoi, the Doves Have Beaten the Hawks." *Atlas* 19:6 (1970), pp. 15-20.

D.2 / Ho Chi Minh

707 Azeau, H. *Ho Chi Minh: dernière chance.* Paris: Flammarion, 1969.

708 Durdin, Peggy, "Uncle Ho's Disciplined Joy." *New Yorker* 31 (Dec. 17, 1955), pp. 140-147.

709 Fall, B.B., ed. *Ho Chi Minh on Revolution: Selected Writings, 1920-1964.* New York: Praeger, 1967.

710 Halberstam, David. *Ho.* New York: Random House, 1965.

711 Ho Chi Minh. *Action et révolution 1920-1967.* Ed. by C. Capitan-Peter. Paris: Union Générale d'Éditions, 1968.

712 Ho Chi Minh. *Against U.S. Aggression for National Salvation.* Hanoi: Foreign Languages Publishing House, 1967.

713 ——. *Selected Works.* 3 Vols. Hanoi: Foreign Languages Publishing House, 1960-61.

714 Lacouture, Jean. *Ho Chi Minh: A Political Biography.* New York: Random House, 1968.

715 Pasquel-Rageau, C. *Ho Chi Minh.* Paris: Éditions Universitaires, 1970.

716 Rageau, Christine. "Ho Chi Minh et l'internationale communiste." *Partisans* 48 (June/Aug 1969), pp. 44-55.

717 Sainteny, Jean. *Face à Ho Chi Minh.* Paris: Seghers, 1970.

718 Schurmann, Franz. "Eulogy to Ho Chi Minh." *Ramparts* 8 (Nov. 1969), pp. 52-60.

719 Shaplen, Robert. "The Enigma of Ho Chi Minh." *Reporter* 12 (Jan. 27, 1955), pp. 11-19.

720 Stuhlmann, Manfred. *Ho Chi Minh: ein Leben für Vietnam.* Berlin: Dietz Verlag, 1960.

721 Sully, François. "Life Under Uncle Ho." *Newsweek* 6:1 (Aug. 27, 1962), pp. 34-38.

722 Woodis, J., ed. *Ho Chi Minh: Selected Articles and Speeches, 1920-1967.* New York: International Publishers, 1970.

D.3 / Vo Nguyen Giap

723 O'Neill, R.J. *The Strategy of General Giap since 1964.* Canberra Papers on Strategy and Defense No. 6, Australian National University, 1969.

724 O'Neill, Robert J. *General Giap, Politician and Strategist.* New York: Praeger, 1969.

725 Vo Nguyen Giap. *Banner of People's War: The Party's Military Line.* Preface by Jean Lacouture. New York: Praeger, 1970.

726 ——. *Big Victory, Great Task: North Vietnam's Minister of Defense Assesses the Course of the War.* New York: Praeger, 1968.

727 ——. *Once Again We Will Win.* Hanoi: Foreign Languages Publishing House, 1960.

728 ——. *People's War, People's Army: The Viet Cong Insurrection Manual for Underdeveloped Countries.* New York: Praeger, 1962.

729 ——. *The South Vietnam People Will Win.* Hanoi: Foreign Languages Publishing House, 1965.

D.4 / Relations With Communist World

730 Attwood, William. "Why Vietnam Worries the Russians." *Look* 31 (July 11, 1967), pp. 23-25.

731 Ballis, W.B. "Relations Between the U.S.S.R. and Vietnam." *Studies on the Soviet Union* 6:2 (1966), pp. 43-56.

732 Cameron, Allen W. "The Soviet Union and Vietnam: The Origins of Involvement." In W. Raymond Duncan, ed., *Soviet Policy in Developing Countries.* Waltham, Massachusetts: Ginn-Blaisdell, 1970.

733 Chen, King. "North Vietnam in the Sino-Soviet Dispute, 1962-64." *Asian Survey* 4 (Sept. 1964), pp. 1023-1036.

734 Dallin, Alexander. "Moscow and Vietnam." *New Leader* 48:10 (1965), pp. 5-8.

735 Donnell, J.C., and M. Gurtov. *North Vietnam: Left of Moscow Right of Peking.* Santa Monica, California: Rand, P-3794, Feb. 1968.

736 Glaubitz, Joachim. "Relations Between Communist China and Vietnam." *Studies on the Soviet Union* 6:2 (1966), pp. 57-67.

737 Honey, Patrick Joseph. *Communism in North Vietnam: Its Role in the Sino-Soviet Dispute.* Cambridge, Massachusetts: M.I.T. Press, 1963.

738 Kux, Ernst. "Ho Chi Minh Between Moscow and Peking." *Swiss Review of World Affairs* 14 (Apr. 1964), pp. 11-14.

739 London, Kurt L. "Vietnam: A Sino-Soviet Dilemma." *Russian Review* 26 (Jan. 1967), pp. 26-37.

740 McGovern, Raymond L. "Moscow and Hanoi." *Problems of Communism* 14 (May-June 1967), pp. 68ff.

741 McLane, C.B. "The Russians and Vietnam: Strategies of Indirection." *International Journal* (Toronto) 24 (Winter 1968/69), pp. 47-64.

742 Morris, Roger. "Russia's Stake in Vietnam." *New Republic* 152:7 (1965), pp. 13-15.

743 Nguyen Thai. "The Two Vietnams and China." *The Harvard Review* 2 (Fall-Winter 1963), pp. 26-32.

744 O'Ballance, Edgar. "Sino-Soviet Influence on the War in Vietnam." *Contemporary Review* 210 (Feb. 1967), pp. 70-76.

745 Ojha, I.C. "China and North Vietnam: The Limits of the Alliance." *Current History* 54 (1968), pp. 42-47.

746 Parry, Albert. "Soviet Aid to Vietnam." *Reporter* 36:1 (1967), pp. 28-32.

747 Rupen, R.A. "Vietnam and the Sino-Soviet Dispute: A Summary." *Studies on the Soviet Union* 6:2 (1966), pp. 99-118.

748 ——, and R. Farrell, eds. *Symposium on Vietnam and the Sino-Soviet Dispute, 1966; Munich.* New York: Praeger, 1967.

749 Tai Sung An. "The Sino-Soviet Dispute and Vietnam." *Orbis* 9 (Summer 1965), pp. 426-436.

750 Woodside, Alexander. "Peking and Hanoi: Anatomy of a Revolutionary Partnership." *International Journal* (Toronto) (Winter 1968-69).

751 Zagoria, Donald S. *The Viet-Nam Triangle: Moscow, Peking, Hanoi.* New York: Pegasus, 1968.

E / Struggle Renewed

E.1 / General

752 *American Imperialism's Intervention in Vietnam.* Hanoi: Foreign Languages Publishing House, 1955.

753 Fishel, W.R. "Communist Terror in South Vietnam: The Diem Regime Has Undertaken Bold Measures." *New Leader* 43 (July 4, 1960), pp. 14-15.

754 Honey, P.J. "The Foreign Policy of North Vietnam." *Public Policy* 16 (1967), pp. 160-180.

755 Pham Van Dong. "The Foreign Policy of the Democratic Republic of Vietnam." *International Affairs* (Moscow) 7 (July 1958), pp. 19-22.

756 Republic of Vietnam. *Communist Aggression in the Republic of Viet-Nam.* Saigon: 1964.

757 Spitz, Allan. "The North Vietnamese Regime: Expansion versus Consolidation." *Asian Studies* 8:1 (1970), pp. 25-37.

758 Steiner, H.A. "Viet-Nam: Civil War Again?" *New Republic* 133 (July 18, 1955), pp. 11-13.

759 Swearingen, R., and Hammond Rolph. *Communism in Vietnam: A Documentary Study.* Chicago: American Bar Association, 1967.

760 Tanham, George K. *Communist Revolutionary Warfare: The Vietminh in Indo China.* rev. ed. New York: Praeger, 1967.

761 Truong Chinh. *Primer for Revolt: The Communist Takeover in Vietnam.* New York: Praeger, 1963.

762 ——. *The Resistance Will Win.* Hanoi: Foreign Languages Publishing House, 1966.

763 White, P.T., and W.E. Garrett. "South Viet Nam Fights the Red Tide." *National Geographic* 120 (Oct. 1961), pp. 445-489.

E.2 / National Liberation Movement

764 Arnett, Peter. "The National Liberation Front." *Current History* 56 (Feb. 1960), pp. 82-87, 116.

765 Davis, L.L., and A. Adams. "The NLF: South Vietnam's Other Government." *Minority of One* 10 (Oct. 1968), pp. 12-16.

766 Fishel, W.R. "The National Liberation Front." *Vietnam Perspectives* 1:1 (1965), pp. 8-16.

767 Heneghan, G.M. *Nationalism, Communism, and The National Liberation Front of Vietnam: Dilemma for American Foreign Policy.* Unpublished PhD thesis, Stanford University, 1970.

768 Hodges, Donald C. *NLF: National Liberation Fronts, 1960/1970.* New York: Morrow, 1972.

769 Lamont, N.S. "On Communist Organization and Strategy in South Vietnam." *Public and International Affairs* 3 (Spring 1965), pp. 32-50.

770 Minear, Richard. "Douglas Pike and the NLF." *Bulletin of Concerned Asian Scholars* 2:1 (1969), pp. 44-47.

771 Munk, Michael. "Why the Vietnamese Support the NLF." *New Politics* 4 (Spring 1965), pp. 18-25.

772 Pike, Douglas. "How Strong Is the NLF?" *Reporter* 34 (Feb. 24, 1966), pp. 20-24.

773 ——. *Viet Cong: The Organization and Techniques of the National Liberation Front.* Cambridge, Massachusetts: M.I.T. Press, 1966.

774 "Program of the National Liberation Front." *New World Review* 36 (Winter 1968), pp. 102-115.

775 Seldon, Mark. "The National Liberation Front and the Transformation of the Vietnamese Society." *Bulletin of Concerned Asian Scholars* 2:1 (1969), pp. 34-43.

776 Vuglen, S.M. *National Liberation Movements: Communist Conspiracy or Political Realities?* Flanders, New Jersey: O'Hare Books, 1968.

777 Warner, Denis. "The NLF's New Program." *Reporter* 37:5 (1967), pp. 23-30.

E.3 / Viet Cong

778 Berman, Paul. *The Liberation Armed Forces of the NLF: Compliance and Cohesion in a Revolutionary Army.* Unpublished PhD thesis, M.I.T., 1970.

779 Betts, R.H. *Viet Cong Village Control: Some Observations on the Origin and Dynamics of Modern Revolutionary War.* Cambridge, Massachusetts: Center for International Studies, M.I.T., Aug. 8, 1969.

780 Bo Ngoai Giao. *Infiltration d'éléments armés communists et introduction clandestine d'armes du Nord au Sud Vietnam.* Saigon: Ministère des Affaires Étrangères, République du Vietnam, 1967.

781 Carver, George A., Jr. "The Faceless Viet Cong." *Foreign Affairs* 44 (Apr. 1960), pp. 347-372.

782 Cole, R.W., III. "Portrait of an Enemy." *Armor* 76:4 (1967), pp. 13-16.

783 Conley, M.C. *The Communist Insurgent Infrastructure in South Vietnam: A Study of Organization and Strategy.* Washington, D.C.: Department of the Army (Pamphlet No. 550-106), 1967.

784 ——. "Communist Thought and Viet Cong Tactics." *Asian Studies* 8 (Mar. 1968), pp. 206-222.

785 Davison, E.P. *Some Observations on Viet Cong Operations in the Villages.* Santa Monica, California: Rand, RM-5267/2-ISA/ARPA, May 1968.

786 Denton, F.H. *Volunteers of the Viet Cong.* Santa Monica, California: Rand, RM-5647-ISA/ARPA, Sept. 1968.

787 Duiker, William J. "Revolutionary Youth League: Cradle of Communism in Vietnam." *China Quarterly* (July-Sept 1972), pp. 475-499.

788 Duncanson, Dennis J. "The Vitality of the Viet Cong." *Survival* 9 (Jan. 1967), pp. 14-18.

789 Elliott, D.W.P., and M. Elliott. *Documents of an Elite Viet Cong Delta Unit: The Demolition Platoon of the 514th Battalion—Part One: Unit Composition and Personnel.* Santa Monica, California: Rand, RM-5848-ISA/ARPA, May 1969.

790 ——. *Documents of an Elite Viet Cong Delta Unit: The Demolition Platoon of the 514th Battalion—Part Two: Party Organization.* Santa Monica, California: Rand, RM-5849-ISA/ARPA, May 1969.

791 ——. *Documents of an Elite Viet Cong Delta Unit: The Demolition Platoon of the 514th Battalion—Part Three: Military Organization and Activities.* Santa Monica, California: Rand, RM-5850-ISA/ARPA, May 1969.

792 ——. *Documents of an Elite Viet Cong Delta Unit: The Demolition Platoon of the 514th Battalion—Part Four: Political Indoctrination and Military Training.* Santa Monica, California: Rand, RM-5851-ISA/ARPA, May 1969.

793 ——. *Documents of an Elite Viet Cong Delta Unit: The Demolition Platoon of the 514th Battalion—Part Five: Personal Letters.* Santa Monica, California: Rand, RM-5852-ISA/ARPA, May 1969.

794 Gignon, F. *Les Américains face au Viet-Cong.* Paris: Flammarion, 1965.

795 Gramont, Sanche de. "Under Viet Cong Control." *Saturday Evening Post* 239 (Jan. 29, 1960), pp. 27-33, 82.

796 Gration, P.C. "Development of Viet Minh Political Power." *Army Journal* (July 1972), pp. 3-16.

797 Grose, Peter. "Vietcong's 'Shadow Government.'" *New York Times Magazine* (Jan. 24, 1965), pp. 10-11, 64-67.

798 Hosmer, S.T. *Viet Cong Repression and Its Implications for the Future.* Santa Monica, California: Rand, R-475/1-ARPA, 1970.

799 Kelly, Gail. "Origins and Aims of the Viet Cong." *New Politics* 5 (Winter 1966), pp. 5-16.

800 Knoebl, K. *Victor Charlie: The Face of War in Vietnam.* London: Pall Mall Press, 1967.

801 Ladd, J.F. "Viet Cong Portrait." *Military Review* 44:7 (1964), pp. 67-80.

802 Leites, N. *The Viet Cong Style of Politics.* Santa Monica, California: Rand, RM-5487-1ISA/ARPA, May 1969.

803 Paignez, Y. *Le Viet-Minh et la guerre psychologique.* Paris: 1955.

804 Patton, Lt. Col. George S. "Why They Fight." *Military Review* 45:12 (1965), pp. 16-23.

805 Pike, Douglas. "Mystique of the Viet Cong." *Army* 17:6 (1967), pp. 25-33.

806 ——. *War, Peace, and the Viet Cong.* Cambridge, Massachusetts: M.I.T. Press, 1969.

807 Rolph, Hammond. "Viet Cong Documents on the War." *Communist Affairs* 5 (Sept/Oct 1967), pp. 18-26; (Nov/Dec 1967), pp. 22-34.

808 Samson, Jack. "Viet Cong Tactics: 'Ten against One.'" *Military Review* 47 (Jan. 1967), pp. 89-93.

809 Schesch, Adam. "Who Are the 'Vietcong'?" *Progressive* 32 (Sept. 1968), pp. 35-39.

810 Sheehan, Susan. "The Enemy." *New Yorker* 42 (Sept. 10, 1966), pp. 62-100.

811 "The Viet Cong: Politics at Gunpoint." *Communist Affairs* 4 (July/Aug 1966), pp. 3-13.

812 Warnenska, Monika. "Dans la jungle avec les partisans." *Nouvelle Revue Internationale* 9 (Jan. 1966), pp. 202-209.

813 Weiss, J.H. "How Hanoi Controls the Vietcong." *Reporter* 38 (Jan. 11, 1968), pp. 27-28.

814 Weller, Jac. "Viet Cong Arms and Men." *Ordnance* 50 (May-June 1966), pp. 602-610.

815 Zasloff, J.J. *Political Motivation of the Viet Cong: The Vietminh.* Santa Monica, California: Rand, KRM-4703/2-ISA/ARPA, May 1968.

IV / U.S. INVOLVEMENT

A / General

A.1 / Documents

816 Cameron, Allan W., comp. *Vietnam Crisis: A Documentary History, 1940-1956.* Ithaca: Cornell University Press, 1971.

817 U.S. Department of State. *Aggression from the North. The Record of North Vietnam's Campaign to Conquer South Vietnam.* Washington, D.C.: U.S. Government Printing Office, 1965.

818 ——. *A Threat to Peace: North Vietnam's Efforts to Conquer South Vietnam.* Department of State Publication 7308. Far Eastern Series 110. Washington, D.C.: U.S. Government Printing Office, 1961.

819 U.S. House of Representatives. Committee on Armed Services. Special Subcommittee on National Defense Posture. *Review of the Vietnam Conflict and Its Impact on U.S. Military Commitments Abroad.* 90th Cong. 2d Sess., Aug. 24, 1968.

820 U.S. House of Representatives. Committee on Foreign Affairs. Subcommittee on Asian and Pacific Affairs. Hearings; *Legislation on the Indochina War, June 22-July 12, 1971.* 92d Cong., 1st Sess., 1971.

821 U.S. Senate. Committee on Foreign Relations. *Background Information Relating to Southeast Asia and Vietnam.* 89th Cong., 1st Sess., Jan. 15, 1965.

822 ——. *Background Information Relating to Southeast Asia and Vietnam.* 89th Cong., 2d Sess., Mar. 1966.

823 ——. *Background Information Relating to Southeast Asia and Vietnam.* 90th Cong., 1st Sess., July 1967.

824 ——. *Background Information Relating to Southeast Asia and Vietnam.* 90th Cong., 2d Sess., Mar. 1968.

825 ——. *Background Information Relating to Southeast Asia and Vietnam.* 91st Cong., 1st Sess., Mar. 1969.

826 ——. *Background Information Relating to Southeast Asia and Vietnam.* 91st Cong., 2d Sess., June 1970.

827 ——. Hearings; *Briefing on Vietnam, Nov. 18-19, 1969* [by Sec. of State Rogers and Sec. of Defense M. Laird] 91st Cong., 1st Sess., 1969.

828 ——. Hearings; *Present Situation in Vietnam.* 90th Cong., 2d Sess., Mar. 29, 1968.

829 ——. Hearings; *Situation in Vietnam, July 30-31, 1959.* 68th Cong., 1st Sess., 1959.

830 ——. Hearings; *Vietnam Policy Proposals, Feb. 3-5, March 16, 1970.* 91st Cong., 2d Sess., 1970.

831 ——. Report; *Impact of the Vietnam War.* [Prepared by the Library of Congress, June 30, 1971.] 92d Cong., 1st Sess., 1971.

832 ——. Staff Report; *Vietnam: December 1969.* [Feb. 2, 1970] 91st Cong., 2d Sess., 1970.

833 ——. *Vietnam Commitments, 1961.* [Staff Study based on the Pentagon Papers, March 20, 1972.] 92d Cong., 2d Sess., 1972.

A.2 / Books (Overviews)

834 Austin, Anthony. *The President's War.* Philadelphia: Lippincott, 1971.

835 Barnet, Richard J. *Intervention and Revolution: America's Confrontation with Insurgent Movements around the World.* New York: World, 1968.

836 Bator, Victor. *Vietnam: A Diplomatic Tragedy.* New York: Oceana Publications, 1965.

837 Brandon, Henry. *Anatomy of Error: The Inside Story of the Asian War on the Potomac, 1954-1969.* Boston: Gambit, 1969.

838 Bromely, D.D. *Washington and Vietnam: An Examination of the Moral and Political Issues.* New York: Oceana Publications, 1966.

839 Buttinger, Joseph. *The Smaller Dragon: A Political History of Vietnam.* New York: Praeger, 1958.

840 ——. *Vietnam: A Dragon Embattled.* 2 Vols. New York: Praeger, 1967.

841 ——. *Vietnam: A Political History.* New York: Praeger, 1968.

842 Chomsky, Noam. *American Power and the New Mandarins.* New York: Pantheon, 1969.

843 Committee of Concerned Asian Scholars. *The Indochina Story.* New York: Bantam Books, 1970.

844 ——. *Indochina Story: A Critical Appraisal of American Involvement in Southeast Asia.* New York: Pantheon Books, 1971.

845 Cooper, Chester L. *The Lost Crusade: America in Vietnam.* New York: Dodd, Mead, 1970.

846 Critchfield, Richard. *The Long Charade: Political Subversion in the Vietnam War.* New York: Harcourt, Brace and World, 1968.

847 Davis, Vincent. "American Military Policy: Decision-making in the Executive Branch [1969]." *Naval War College Review* 22:9 (1970), pp. 4-23.

848 Devillers, P., and J. Lacouture. *Viet Nam: de la guerre française à la guerre américaine.* Paris: Éditions du Seuil, 1969.

849 Draper, Theodore. *Abuse of Power.* New York: Viking Press, 1966.

850 Effros, William O. *Quotations—Vietnam: 1945-1970.* New York: Random House, 1970.

851 Fall, Bernard B. *Last Reflections on a War.* New York: Doubleday, 1967.

852 ——. *The Two Vietnams: A Political and Military Analysis.* 2d ed. New York: Praeger, 1967.

853 ——. *Viet-Nam Witness, 1953-66.* New York: Praeger, 1966.

854 Fishel, Wesley R. *Vietnam: Is Victory Possible?* (Headline Series). New York: Foreign Policy Association, Feb. 1964.

855 ——. *The U.S. and Vietnam.* New York: Public Affairs Commission, 1966. Pamphlet # 391.

856 Goodwin, Richard. *Triumph or Tragedy: Reflections on Vietnam.* New York: Random House, 1966.

857 Halberstam, David. *The Making of a Quagmire.* New York: Random House, 1964.

858 ——. *The Best and the Brightest.* New York: Random House, 1972.

859 Herman, E.S., and R.B. DuBoff. *America's Vietnam Policy: The Strategy of Deception.* Washington, D.C.: Public Affairs Press, 1966.

860 Honey, P.J. *Genesis of a Tragedy: The Historical Background to the Vietnam War.* London: Benn, 1968.

861 Kahin, George McT., and John W. Lewis. *The United States in Vietnam.* New York: Dial Press, 1966.

862 Kattenburg, Paul M. "Viet Nam and U.S. Diplomacy, 1940-1970." *Orbis* 15:3 (Fall 1971), pp. 818-841.

863 Lacouture, Jean. *Vietnam Between Two Truces.* New York: Random House, 1966.

864 Lindholm, R.W., ed. *Vietnam: The First Five Years, An International Symposium.* East Lansing: Michigan State University Press, 1959.

865 Liska, George. *War and Order: Reflections on Vietnam and History.* Baltimore: Johns Hopkins Press, 1968.

866 McCarthy, Joseph E. *Illusion of Power: American Policy Toward Viet-Nam, 1954-1966.* New York: Carlton Press, 1967.

867 Mohn, A.H. *Vietnam.* Oslo: Gyldendal Norsk Forlat, 1965.

868 Morgenthau, H.J. *Vietnam and the United States.* Washington, D.C.: Public Affairs Press, 1965.

869 Melano, H.J.M. *The Viet-Nam Story.* Willingboro, New Jersey: Alexia Press, 1969.

870 Podwal, Mark H. *The Decline and Fall of the American Empire.* New York: Darien House, 1971.

871 Scheer, Robert. *How the United States Got Involved in Viet Nam.* Santa Barbara, California: Center for the Study of Democratic Institutions, 1965.

872 Schlesinger, Arthur M., Jr. *The Bitter Heritage: Vietnam and American Democracy, 1941-1966.* Boston: Houghton, Mifflin, 1966.

873 Schoenbrun, David. *Vietnam: How We Got In, How to Get Out.* New York: Atheneum, 1968.

874 Scott, Peter D. *The War Conspiracy: The Secret Road to the Second Indochina War.* New York: Bobbs-Merrill, 1972.

875 Shaplen, Robert. *Lost Revolution: The U.S. in Vietnam.* New York: Harper & Row, 1965.

876 ——. *Lost Revolution: U.S. in Vietnam, 1946-1966.* rev. ed. New York: Harper & Row, 1966.

877 ——. *The Road from War: Vietnam 1965-1970.* New York: Harper & Row, 1970.

878 ——. *The Road from War: Vietnam, 1965-1971.* New York: Harper & Row, 1971.

879 Stavins, R., R. Burnel, and M. Raskin. *Washington Plans An Aggressive War.* New York: Random House, 1971.

880 Stone, Isidor F. *Polemics and Prophecies, 1967-1970.* New York: Random House, 1970.

881 Sullivan, C.D., et al. *The Vietnam War; Its Conduct and Higher Direction.* Center for Strategic Studies, Georgetown University, Nov. 1968.

882 Thompson, Sir Robert. *No Exit from Vietnam.* New York: McKay, 1969.

883 Trager, Frank N. *Why Vietnam?* New York: Praeger, 1966.

884 White, Ralph K. *Nobody Wanted War: Misperception in Vietnam and Other Wars.* rev. ed. New York: Doubleday, 1970.

A.3 / Edited Collections

885 Boettiger, J.R., ed. *Vietnam and American Foreign Policy.* Boston: D.C. Heath, 1968.

886 Brown, Robert M., et al., eds. *Vietnam, Crisis of Conscience.* New York: Association Press, 1967.

887 Brown, S., and L. Ackland, eds. *Why Are We Still in Vietnam?* Westminster, Maryland: Random House, 1970.

888 Critchley, Julian, comp. *The Domino Theory: Laos and Cambodia.* London: Atlantic Information Centre for Teachers, 1970.

889 Fishel, W.E., ed. *Vietnam: Anatomy of a Conflict.* Itasca, Illinois: Peacock, 1968.

890 Gettleman, Marvin, et al., eds. *Conflict in Indochina.* New York: Vintage, 1970.

891 Gettleman, Marvin E., ed. *Vietnam: History, Documents and Opinions on a Major World Crisis.* 2d ed. New York: Fawcett, 1970.

892 Hamilton, M.P., ed. *The Vietnam War: Christian Perspectives.* Grand Rapids, Michigan: W.B. Eerdmans, 1967.

893 Isard, Walter, ed. *Vietnam: Some Basic Issues and Alternatives.* Cambridge, Massachusetts: Schenkman, 1969.

894 Kim, Jung-gun, ed. *Essays on the Vietnam War.* Granville: East Carolina University Press, 1970.

895 Kravor, Patricia A., ed. *Anatomy of an Undeclared War.* Boston: Beacon, 1972.

896 Ly Qui Chung, ed. *Between Two Fires: The Unheard Voices of Vietnam.* New York: Praeger, 1970.

897 Manning, Robert, and Michael Janeway, eds. *Who We Are: An Atlantic Chronicle of the United States and Vietnam.* Boston: Little, Brown, 1969.

898 Murray, Rubin, ed. *Vietnam.* London: Eyre & Spottiswoode, 1965.

899 Pfeffer, Richard M., ed. *No More Vietnams? The War and the Future of American Foreign Policy.* New York: Harper & Row, 1968.

900 Raskin, Marcus, and Bernard B. Fall, eds. *The Vietnam Reader: Articles and Documents on American Foreign Policy and the Vietnam Crisis.* New York: Vintage Books, 1965.

901 Ray, S., ed. *Vietnam Seen from East and West.* New York: Praeger, 1966.

902 Rezazadeh, Reza, ed. *VietNam: The Alternatives for American Policy.* Platteville: Wisconsin State University Press, 1965.

903 Sobel, Lester A., ed. *South Vietnam: Communist-U.S. Confrontation in Southeast Asia.* Vol. 1: *1961-1965.* Interim History Series. New York: Facts on File, 1969.

904 ——, ed. *South Vietnam: Communist-U.S. Confrontation in Southeast Asia.* Vol. 2: *1966-67.* Interim History Series. New York: Facts on File, 1969.

905 Sweezy, Paul M., ed. *Vietnam: The Endless War; from Monthly Review, 1954-1970.* New York: Monthly Review Press, 1970.

906 Wells, J.M., and M. Wilhelm, eds. *The People vs. Presidential War.* New York: Dunellen, 1970.

B / Politics & Vietnam

907 *Anatomy of an Undeclared War: Congressmen and Other Authorities Respond to the Pentagon Papers.* New York: International Universities Press, 1972.

908 Anders, Gunther. *Eskalation des Verbrechens; aus einem ABC der amerikanischen Aggression gegen Vietnam.* Berlin: Unron Verlag, 1971.

909 Aptheker, Herbert. *Mission to Hanoi.* New York: International Publishers, 1966.

910 Beal, C.W. *The Realities of Vietnam: A Ripon Society Appraisal.* Washington, D.C.: Public Affairs Press, 1968.

911 Berrier, Hilaire du. *Background to Betrayal: Tragedy of Vietnam.* Belmont, Massachusetts: Western Islands, 1965.

912 Bommarito, J.E. *The Truth About Viet Nam.* St. Louis, Missouri: Operation Alert Publications, 1966.

913 Broekmeijer, M.W.M.M. *South Vietnam, Victim of Misunderstanding.* Bilthoven: H. Nelissen, 1967.

914 Burchett, Wilfred G. *Vietnam Will Win!* New York: Guardian Books, 1968.

915 Cameron, James. *Here Is Your Enemy: Complete Report from North Vietnam.* New York: Holt, Rinehart and Winston, 1966.

916 Chaumont, Charles Marie. *Analyse critique de l'intervention américaine au Vietnam.* Bruxelles: Commission permanente d'enquête pour le Vietnam, 1968.

917 Coe, Charles. *Young Man in Vietnam.* New York: Four Winds Press, 1968.

918 Corson, William R. *The Betrayal.* New York: W.W. Norton, 1968.

919 Diamond, Dick. *The Walls Are Down.* Hanoi: Foreign Languages Publishing House, 1958.

920 Donlon, R.H.C. *Outpost of Freedom.* New York: McGraw-Hill, 1965.

921 Dooley, T.A. *Dr. Tom Dooley's Three Great Books: Deliver Us From Evil, Edge of Tomorrow, and The Night They Burned the Mountain.* New York: Farrar, Straus & Cudahy, 1960.

922 Eby, Omar. *A House in Hue.* Scottdale, Pennsylvania: Herald Press, 1969.

923 Ellsberg, D. *Escalating in a Quagmire.* Center of International Studies, M.I.T., Sept. 1970.

924 ——. *Kahn on Winning in Vietnam: A Review.* Santa Monica, California: Rand, P-3965, Nov. 1968.

925 ——. *Papers on the War.* New York: Simon & Schuster, 1972.

926 Ennis, Thomas Edson. *Vietnam: Land without Laughter.* Morgantown, West Virginia: Cooperative Extension Service, West Virginia University, 1966.

927 Feinberg, A.L. *Hanoi Diary.* Canada: Alger Press, 1968.

928 Field, Michael. *The Prevailing Wind: Witness in Indo-China.* London: Methuen, 1965.

929 Fitzgerald, Frances. *Fire in the Lake: The Vietnamese and the Americans in Vietnam.* New York: Atlantic Monthly Press (Little, Brown), 1972.

930 Fox, Len. *Friendly Vietnam.* Hanoi: Foreign Languages Publishing House, 1958.

931 Garrett, Banning, and Katherine Barkley. *Two, Three–Many Vietnams.* San Francisco: Canfield Press, 1971.

932 Greene, Felix. *Vietnam! Vietnam!* Palo Alto, California: Fulton Publishing Co., 1966.

933 Hassler, R. Alfred. *Saigon, USA.* New York: R.W. Baron, 1970.

934 Higgins, Marguerite. *Our Vietnam Nightmare.* New York: Harper & Row, 1965.

935 Hope, Bob. *Five Women I Love: Bob Hope's Vietnam Story.* New York: Doubleday, 1966.

936 Kalb, Marvin, and Elie Abel. *Roots of Involvement.* New York: W.W. Norton, 1971.

937 Kanh, Huynh K. "The War in Viet Nam: The U.S. Official Line–A Review Article." *Pacific Affairs* 42:1 (1969), pp. 58-67.

938 Kang, Pilwon. *The Road to Victory in Vietnam.* New York: Exposition Press, 1970.

939 Labin, Suzanne. *Sellout in Vietnam?* Springfield, Virginia: Crestwood Books, 1966.

940 ——. *Vietnam: An Eye-Witness Account.* Springfield, Virginia: Crestwood Books, 1964.

941 Lane, Thomas. *America on Trial: The War for Vietnam.* New Rochelle, New York: Arlington House, 1971.

942 Lederer, William J. *Our Own Worst Enemy.* New York: W.W. Norton, 1968.

943 Levchenko, Irina Nikolaevna. *Land Aflame.* Moscow: Progress Publishers, 1969.

944 Lowenfels, Walter. *Where Is Vietnam?* New York: Doubleday, 1967.

945 Luce, Don and John Sommer. *Viet Nam: The Unheard Voices.* Ithaca: Cornell University Press, 1969.

946 Lynd, Staughton, and Thomas Hayden. *The Other Side.* New York: New American Library, 1967.

947 Lyons, Daniel S. *Vietnam Crisis.* New York: Twin Circle Publishing, 1967.

948 MacDonald, C.B. "Official History and the War in Vietnam." *Military Affairs* 32 (Spring 1968), pp. 2-11.

949 Mailer, Norman. *Armies of the Night.* Cleveland, Ohio: World, 1968.

950 ——. *Why Are We in Vietnam?* New York: Berkley Publishing Corp., 1968.

951 McCarthy, Mary. *Reports from Vietnam.* New York: Harcourt, Brace and World, 1967.

952 McGrady, M. *Dove in Vietnam.* New York: Funk & Wagnalls, 1968.

953 Mulligan, H.A. *No Place to Die: The Agony of Viet Nam.* New York: Morrow, 1967.

954 Nutt, A.L. *On the Question of Communist Reprisals in Vietnam.* Santa Monica, California: Rand, P-4416, Aug. 1970.

955 Perlo, Victor. *The Vietnam Profiteers.* New York: New Outlook Publishers, 1966.

956 *The Politics of Escalation: A Study of United States Responses to Pressures for a Political Settlement of the Vietnam War, November 1963-January 1966.* Prepared by a working group organized by scholars at the University of California, at Berkeley, and Washington University, in St. Louis. Berkeley: 1966.

957 Ray, Michèle. *The Two Shores of Hell.* New York: McKay, 1968.

958 Rozier, William B. *To Battle a Dragon.* New York: Vintage, 1971.

959 Sager, Peter. *Report from Vietnam.* Bern: Swiss Eastern Institute, 1968.

960 Salisbury, Harrison E. *Behind the Lines—Hanoi: December 23, 1966-January 7, 1967.* New York: Harper & Row, 1967.

961 Salmon, Malcolm. *Focus on Indo-China.* Hanoi: Foreign Languages Publishing House, 1961.

962 Schurmann, Franz, et al. *The Politics of Escalation in Vietnam: A Citizens White Paper.* Boston: Beacon, 1966.

963 Sontag, Susan. *Trip to Hanoi.* New York: Farrar, Straus and Giroux, 1969.

964 Spruille, Jane Polk. *The Line is Drawn: Extracts from the Letters of Captain J.P. Spruill,* U.S. Army. Washington, D.C.: U.S. Government Printing Office, 1964.

965 Standard, William L. *Aggression: Our Asian Disaster.* New York: Random House, 1971.

966 Sully, Françoise. *We The Vietnamese: Voices from Vietnam.* New York: Praeger, 1971.

967 Thich Nhat Hanh. *Vietnam: Lotus in a Sea of Fire.* New York: Hill and Wang, 1967.

968 Thompson, James C., Jr. "How Could Vietnam Happen? An Autopsy." *Atlantic* 221:4 (Apr. 1968), pp. 47-53.

969 Vien, N.C. *Seeking the Truth.* New York: Vintage, 1967.

970 Weil, Charles A. *Curtains Over Vietnam.* Jericho, New York: Exposition Press, 1969.

971 Warbey, William. *Vietnam the Truth.* London: Merlin Press, 1965.

972 West, Richard. *Sketches from Vietnam.* New York: International Publications Service, 1968.

973 Wicker, Tom. *JFK and LBJ: The Influence of Personality Upon Politics.* New York: William Morrow, 1968.

974 Wolf, C., Jr. *The Logic of Failure: A Vietnam "Lesson."* Santa Monica, California: Rand, P-4654, June 1971.

975 Zils, Maria Susanne. *Vietnam: Hand ohne Frieden.* Weilheim/Oberbayern: O.W. Barth-Verlag, 1965.

976 Zinn, H. *Vietnam: The Logic of Withdrawal.* Boston: Beacon, 1967.

B.1 / Eisenhower Years

B.1a / Personalities/Policies

977 Beal, John R. *John Foster Dulles: A Biography.* New York: Harper, 1957.

978 Childs, Marquis. *The Ragged Edge: The Diary of a Crisis.* New York: Doubleday, 1955.

979 Do Vang Ly. "The Emergency of Vietnam." *Foreign Affairs Reports* 7 (Jan. 1958), pp. 1-19.

980 Donovan, Robert J. *Eisenhower: The Inside Story.* New York: Harper, 1956.

981 Drummond, R., and C. Coblentz. *Duel at the Brink: John Foster Dulles' Command of American Power.* New York: Doubleday, 1960.

982 Dunn, William B. *American Policy and Vietnamese Nationalism, 1950-1954.* Chicago: University of Chicago Press, 1960.

983 Eisenhower, Dwight D. *The White House Years: Mandate for Change, 1953-1956.* New York: Doubleday, 1963.

984 ——. *Waging Peace: The White House Years, 1956-1961.* New York: Doubleday, 1965.

985 Gurtov, Melvin. *The First Vietnam Crisis, Chinese Strategy and United States Involvement, 1953-1954.* New York: Columbia University Press, 1967.

986 "Intervention in Indo-China: Radford Knows What He Wants, But Will His Policy Work?" *New Republic* (June 14, 1954), pp. 3-7.

987 "Interview with General Nathan F. Twining." *U.S. News & World Report.* (Dec. 25, 1953), pp. 40-45.

988 Kennedy, John F. "What Should the U.S. Do in Indo-China?" *Foreign Policy Bulletin* 33 (May 15, 1954), pp. 4, 6.

989 MacAllister, Robert J. "The Great Gamble: United States Policy Toward South Viet Nam from July, 1954, to July, 1956." Unpublished PhD thesis, University of Chicago, 1958.

990 Ridgway, Gen. Matthew B. "My Battles in War and Peace." *Saturday Evening Post* (Jan. 21, 1956), pp. 17-19, 46-48.

991 ——. *Soldier: The Memoirs of Matthew B. Ridgway.* New York: Harper, 1956.

992 Roberts, Chalmers H. "The Day We Didn't Go to War." *Reporter* 11 (Sept. 14, 1954), pp. 31-35.

993 Robertson, W.S. "Progress in Free Viet-Nam." Department of State *Bulletin* 34 (June 11, 1956), pp. 972-974.

994 Shepley, James. "How Dulles Averted War." *Life* (Jan. 16, 1956), pp. 70-80.

995 Taylor, Maxwell D. *The Uncertain Trumpet.* New York: Harper, 1959.

B.1b / Politics

996 Corley, Francis J. "Vietnam Since Geneva." *Fordham University Quarterly* 33 (Winter 1958-59), pp. 515-568.

997 Crozier, Brian. "Indo-China: The Unfinished Struggle." *World Today* 12 (Dec. 1956), pp. 17-26.

998 ——. "The International Situation in Indochina." *Pacific Affairs* 29 (Dec 1956), pp. 309-323.

999 Dunn, William B. "How the West Could Win Vietnam's Support." *Foreign Policy Bulletin* 33 (May 15, 1954), pp. 1-2.

1000 Ennis, T.E. "Vietnam: Our Outpost in Asia." *Current History* 31 (July 1956), pp. 33-38.

1001 Fishel, Wesley R. "The Role of the Michigan State University Group in Vietnam." *Viet My* (Nov. 1963), pp. 39-42.

1002 Jumper, Roy. "The Communist Challenge to South Vietnam." *Far Eastern Survey* 25 (Nov. 1956), pp. 161-168.

1003 Karpikhim, A. "The United States Takes Over in South Viet-Nam." *International Affairs* (Moscow) 5 (Apr. 1956), pp. 83-91.

1004 Mansfield, Mike. "Reprieve in Vietnam." *Harper's* 212 (Jan. 1956), pp. 46-51.

B.2 / John F. Kennedy Years

B.2a / Personalities/Policies

1005 Bowles, Chester. *Promises to Keep.* New York: Harper & Row, 1971.

1006 Deane, Hugh. *The War in Vietnam.* New York: Monthly Review Press, 1963.

1007 Democratic Republic of Vietnam. *La Politique d'intervention et d'aggression des États-Unis au Sud.* Hanoi: Ministry of Foreign Affairs, 1962.

1008 Edwards, Theodore. "Kennedy's War in Vietnam." *International Socialist Review* 24 (Summer 1963), pp. 84-87.

1009 Heavner, T.J.C. "The Viet-Nam Situation." *U.S. Department of State Bulletin* 49 (Sept. 9, 1963), pp. 393-398.

1010 Henry, J.B., II, and W. Espinosa. "The Tragedy of Dean Rusk." *Foreign Policy* 4 (Fall 1971), pp. 166-189.

1011 Hilsman, R. *To Move a Nation: The Politics of Foreign Policy in the Administration of John F. Kennedy.* New York: Doubleday, 1967.

1012 Hurley, R.M. *President John F. Kennedy and Vietnam, 1961-1963.* Unpublished PhD thesis, University of Hawaii, 1970.

1013 Jeffries, Jean. "Why Vietnam is Kennedy's War." *National Review* 20 (Apr. 23, 1968), pp. 396-397, 411.

1014 Kennedy, John F. "America's Stake in Vietnam." In *A Symposium on America's Stake in Vietnam.* New York: American Friends of Vietnam, Sept. 1956, pp. 8-14.

1015 ——. *The Strategy of Peace.* New York: Harper, 1960.

1016 Lansdale, E.G. *In the Midst of Wars.* New York: Harper & Row, 1972.

1017 Mecklin, John. *Mission in Torment: An Intimate Account of the U.S. Role in Vietnam.* New York: Doubleday, 1965.

1018 Rusk, Dean. "The Stake in Viet-Nam." *U.S. Department of State Bulletin* 48 (May 13, 1963), pp. 727-735.

1019 Schlesinger, Arthur, Jr. *A Thousand Days: John F. Kennedy in the White House.* Boston: Houghton, Mifflin, 1965.

1020 Sorensen, Theodore C. *Kennedy.* New York: Harper & Row, 1965.

1021 Walton, Richard J. *Cold War and Counter-Revolution: The Foreign Policy of John F. Kennedy.* New York: Viking, 1972.

B.2b / Politics

1022 Black, E.F. "The Master Plan for Conquest in Vietnam." *Military Review* 43:6 (1963), pp. 51-57.

1023 Buchan, A. "Questions About Vietnam." *Encounter* [Great Britain] 30:172 (1968), pp. 3-12.

1024 Child, Frank C. "Vietnam: The Eleventh Hour." *New Republic* (Dec. 4, 1961), pp. 14-16.

1025 Cook, H.C.B. "The Situation in Vietnam." *Royal United Services Institution Journal* 107 (Aug. 1962), pp. 220-229.

1026 Devillers, Philippe. "Struggle for Unification of Vietnam." *China Quarterly* 9 (Jan/Mar 1962), pp. 2-23.

1027 Elegant, R.S. "The Task in Vietnam." *New Leader* 46 (Nov. 25, 1963), pp. 5-7.

1028 Goshal, Kumar. "War in South Vietnam." *New World Review* 31 (Oct. 1963), pp. 8-14.

1029 Hendry, J.B. "Economic Development Under Conditions of Guerrilla Warfare: The Case of Viet Nam." *Asian Survey* 2 (June 1962), pp. 1-12.

1030 "Indo-China: America's Algeria." *Dissent* 10 (Summer 1963), pp. 204-214.

1031 Kearney, V.S., and F.J. Buckley. "Vietnam Dilemma." *America* 109 (Sept. 7, 1963), pp. 237-240.

1032 Kristol, Irving. "Facing the Facts in Vietnam." *New Leader* 46 (Sept. 30, 1963), pp. 7-8.

1033 Ngo Dinh Thuc. "What's Really Going on in Vietnam." *National Review* (Nov. 5, 1963), pp. 388-390.

1034 Nolting, F.E. "The Turning Point: The Origin and Development of U.S. Commitment in Viet-Nam." *Foreign Service Journal* 45 (July 1968), pp. 18-20.

1035 Rose, J.A. "Dead End in Vietnam: We Can't Win, but We Need Not Lose." *New Republic* (Oct. 12, 1963), pp. 15-18.

1036 Schecter, J.L. "Bitter Harvest in Vietnam." *Progressive* 27 (Oct. 1963), pp. 10-15.

1037 Scigliano, Robert. "Vietnam: A Country at War." *Asian Survey* 3 (Jan. 1963), pp. 48-54.

1038 Simpson, H.R. "A Dirty Dangerous Business." *Foreign Service Journal* 40:4 (1963), pp. 46-50.

1039 "U.S. Imperialism and Vietnam." *Political Affairs* 42 (Nov. 1963), pp. 1-7.

1040 Vernon, Hilda. "Vietnam: U.S. Guilt and Dilemma." *Labour Monthly* 45 (Nov. 1963), pp. 515-518.

1041 Worthington, Peter. "Vietnam: School for U.S. Guerrillas." *Nation* 196 (Mar. 2, 1963), pp. 179-180.

B.3 / Lyndon B. Johnson Years

B.3a / Personalities/Policies

1042 Ball, George W. "The Issue in Viet-Nam." *U.S. Department of State Bulletin* 54 (Feb. 14, 1966), pp. 239-246.

1043 ——. "Top Secret: The Prophecy the President Rejected [in 1964]." *Atlantic* 230:1 (July 1972), pp. 35-49.

1044 Bundy, W.P. "American Policy in South Vietnam and Southeast Asia." *U.S. Department of State Bulletin* 52 (Feb. 8, 1965), pp. 168-175.

1045 ——. "The Path to Vietnam: A Lesson in Involvement." *U.S. Department of State Bulletin* 57 (Sept. 4, 1967), pp. 275-287.

1046 ——. "The Path to Vietnam: Ten Decisions." *Orbis* 11 (Fall 1967), pp. 647-663.

1047 ——. "A Perspective on U.S. Policy in Vietnam." *U.S. Department of State Bulletin* 52 (June 21, 1965), pp. 1001-1005.

1048 ——. "Reality and Myth Concerning South Viet Nam." *U.S. Department of State Bulletin* 52 (June 7, 1965), pp. 890-896.

1049 Bunker, Ellsworth. "Report on Vietnam." *U.S. Department of State Bulletin* 57 (Dec. 11, 1967), pp. 781-784.

1050 Burnham, James. "McNamara's Non-War." *National Review* 19:37 (Sept. 19, 1967), pp. 1012-1014.

1051 Clifford, Clark M. "A Viet Nam Appraisal: The Personal History of One Man's View and How It Evolved." *Foreign Affairs* 47:4 (1969), pp. 601-622.

1052 Evans, Rowland, and Robert Novak. *Lyndon B. Johnson: The Exercise of Power.* New York: New American Library, 1966.

1053 Frankel, M. "The Importance of Being Bundy." *New York Times Magazine* (Mar. 28, 1965), pp. 32-33.

1054 ——. "The President's 'Just-a-Minute' Man." *New York Times Magazine* (Sept. 12, 1965), pp. 48-49.

1055 Geyelin, Philip. *Lyndon B. Johnson and the World.* New York: Praeger, 1966.

1056 Goldberg, Arthur J. "United States Peace Aims in Viet-Nam." *U.S. Department of State Bulletin* 56 (Feb. 27, 1967), pp. 310-16.

1057 Goldman, Eric F. *The Tragedy of Lyndon Johnson.* New York: Knopf, 1969.

1058 Graff, H.F. "Teach-In on Vietnam by . . . the President, the Secretary of State, the Secretary of Defense and the Under-Secretary of State." *New York Times Magazine* (Mar. 20, 1966), p. 25.

1059 ——. *The Tuesday Cabinet: Deliberation and Decision on Peace and War under Lyndon B. Johnson.* Englewood Cliffs, New Jersey: Prentice-Hall, 1970.

1060 Head, Simon. "LBJ's Vietnam Options." *Far Eastern Economic Review* 58 (Oct. 26, 1967), pp. 182-188.

1061 Heren, Louis. *No Hail, No Farewell.* New York: Harper & Row, 1970.

1062 Hoopes, Townsend. *The Limits of Intervention.* New York: McKay, 1970.

1063 Humphrey, Hubert. "United States Tasks and Responsibilities in Asia." *U.S. Department of State Bulletin* 55 (Apr. 4, 1966), pp. 523-528.

1064 Johnson, Gen. H.K. "The Defense of Freedom in Viet-Nam." *U.S. Department of State Bulletin* 52 (Feb. 8, 1965), pp. 176-180.

1065 Johnson, Lyndon B. "Answering Aggression in Viet-Nam." *U.S. Department of State Bulletin* 57 (Oct. 23, 1967), pp. 519-522.

1066 ——. "The Defense of Viet-Nam: Key to the Future of Free Asia." *U.S. Department of State Bulletin* 56 (Apr. 3, 1967), pp. 534-539.

1067 ——. "Our Objective in Vietnam." *U.S. Department of State Bulletin* 55 (Sept. 12, 1966), pp. 368-371.

1068 ——. "Pattern for Peace on Southeast Asia." *U.S. Department of State Bulletin* 52 (Apr. 26, 1965), pp. 606-610.

1069 ——. "The U.S. Commitment to Peace—A Shield for Threatened Nations." *U.S. Department of State Bulletin* 57 (Dec. 25, 1967), pp. 851-854.

1070 ——. *The Vantage Point: Perspectives of the Presidency, 1963-1969.* New York: Holt, Rinehart & Winston, 1971.

1071 ——. "Viet-Nam: The Struggle to be Free." *U.S. Department of State Bulletin* 54 (Mar. 14, 1966), pp. 390-396.

1072 ——. "Viet-Nam: The Third Face of War." *U.S. Department of State Bulletin* 52 (May 31, 1965), pp. 838-841.

1073 ——. "We Will Stand in Viet-Nam." *U.S. Department of State Bulletin* 53 (Aug. 16, 1965), pp. 262-265.

1074 Katzenbach, Nicholas. "The Complex and Difficult Problems in Viet-Nam." *U.S. Department of State Bulletin* 57 (Nov. 6, 1967), pp. 602-604.

1075 Lansdale, E.G. "Viet Nam: Do We Understand Revolution?" *Foreign Affairs* 43 (Oct. 1964), pp. 75-86.

1076 Lodge, Henry Cabot. "Ambassador Lodge Discusses Viet-Nam in *New York Times* Interview." *U.S. Department of State Bulletin* 56 (May 22, 1967), pp. 795-800.

1077 ——. "How the World's Hottest Spot Looks to Me." *Life* 56:16 (Apr. 17, 1964), pp. 38D-38F.

1078 MacArthur, Douglas, II. "The Free World Stake in Viet-Nam." *U.S. Department of State Bulletin* 55 (Nov. 14, 1966), pp. 745-750.

1079 McNamara, R.S. "Secretary McNamara Discusses Buildup of Forces in Vietnam." *U.S. Department of State Bulletin* 53 (July 5, 1965), pp. 12-19.

1080 ——. "South Vietnam: The United States Policy." *Vital Speeches* 30 (Apr. 15, 1964), pp. 394-399.

1081 Morgenthau, Hans J. "Bundy's Doctrine of War Without End." *New Republic* 159 (Nov. 2, 1968), pp. 18-20.

1082 Moyers, Bill D. "One Thing We Learned in Vietnam." *Foreign Affairs* 46:4 (1968), pp. 657-664.

1083 Roberts, Charles. *LBJ's Inner Circle.* New York: Delacorte Press, 1965.

1084 Rostow, E.V. "A Certain Restlessness About Viet-Nam." *U.S. Department of State Bulletin* 58 (Mar. 25, 1968), pp. 405-416.

1085 Rovere, Richard. *Waist Deep in the Big Muddy: Personal Reflections on 1968.* Boston: Little, Brown, 1968.

1086 Rusk, Dean. "Communist Aggression: Vietnam." *Vital Speeches* 35 (Oct. 15, 1968), pp. 2-6.

1087 ——. "Firmness and Restraint in Viet-Nam." *U.S. Department of State Bulletin* 57 (Nov. 27, 1967), pp. 703-705.

1088 ——. *The Heart of the Problem: Secretary Rusk and General Taylor Review Viet-Nam Policy in Senate Hearings.* Washington, D.C.: U.S. Government Printing Office, 1966.

1089 ——. "Keeping Our Commitment to Peace." *U.S. Department of State Bulletin* 54 (April 4, 1966), pp. 514-521.

1090 ——. "Secretary Rusk Discusses Viet-Nam Situation on 'Face the Nation' Program." *U.S. Department of State Bulletin* 52 (Mar. 29, 1965), pp. 442-448.

1091 ——. "Secretary Rusk Reviews Efforts to Reach Peaceful Settlement in Southeast Asia." *U.S. Department of State Bulletin* 53 (July 5, 1965), pp. 5-12.

1092 ——. "The U.S. Commitment in Viet-Nam: Fundamental Issues." *U.S. Department of State Bulletin* 54 (Mar. 7, 1966), pp. 346-356.

1093 ——. "Viet-Nam: Four Steps to Peace." *U.S. Department of State Bulletin* 53 (July 12, 1965), pp. 50-55.

1094 ——, et al. "Viet-Nam: Winning the Peace." *U.S. Department of State Bulletin* 53 (Sept. 13, 1965), pp. 431-444.

1095 ——, and R.S. McNamara. "Political and Military Aspects of U.S. Policy in Vietnam." *U.S. Department of State Bulletin* 53 (Aug. 30, 1965), pp. 342-356.

1096 Sherril, Robert. *The Accidental President.* New York: Grossman, 1967.

1097 Soloveytchik, G. "Loss and Gain [Problems of LBJ]." *Contemporary Review* (Great Britain) 213:1228 (1968), pp. 230-237.

1098 ——. "President Johnson's Problems." *Contemporary Review* (Great Britain) 209:1208 (1966), pp. 120-126.

1099 Steinburg, Alfred. *Sam Johnson's Boy: A Close-up of the President from Texas.* New York: Macmillan, 1968.

1100 Taylor, Maxwell D. *Responsibility and Response.* New York: Harper & Row, 1967.

1101 ——. "Why Vietnam?" *World Affairs* 128 (Jan/Mar 1966), pp. 218-223.

1102 Thompson, Robert. "Squaring the Error." *Foreign Affairs* 46:3 (1968), pp. 442-453.

1103 Thompson, W.F.K. "Vietnam Task." *Royal United Service Institute Journal* 113:652 (Nov. 1968), pp. 344-345.

1104 Warner, Denis. "Vietnam: General Taylor Faces an All-Out War." *Reporter* 31 (Aug. 13, 1964), pp. 50-53.

B.3b / Politics

1105 Armstrong, H.F. "Power in a Sieve." *Foreign Affairs* 46:3 (1968), pp. 467-475.

1106 Baldwin, H.W. "The Case for Escalation." *New York Times Magazine* (Feb. 27, 1966), pp. 22, 79-82.

1107 Basich, Thomas. "Vietnam: The Confusion and the Commitment." *Dialog* 6 (Winter 1967), pp. 34-43.

1108 Brogan, W. "Naiveté versus Reality in Vietnam." *Atlantic* 220:1 (1967), pp. 48-55.

1109 Clifford, J.W. "Some Fallacies about the Vietnam War." *Catholic World* 203 (Sept. 1966), pp. 361-364.

1110 Critchfield, Richard. "Lessons of Vietnam." *Annals of American Academy of Politics and Social Sciences* 380 (1968), pp. 125-134.

1111 Draper, Theodore. "The American Crisis: Vietnam, Cuba and the Dominican Republic." *Commentary* 43:1 (1967), pp. 27-48.

1112 Elegant, R.S. "Vietnam: An American Tragedy." *New Leader* 47:20 (1964), pp. 5-7.

1113 Elston, G.A. "Vietnam: Some Basic Considerations." *Catholic World* 205 (May 1967), pp. 78-82.

1114 Fairbanks, H.G. "Facing Hard Facts in Vietnam." *Catholic World* 199 (May 1964), pp. 891-895.

1115 Fall, B.B. "Our Options in Vietnam." *Reporter* 30 (Mar. 12, 1964), pp. 17-22.

1116 ——. "Vietnam: The New Korea." *Current History* 50 (Feb. 1966), pp. 85-90, 117.

1117 ——. "The Year of the Hawks." *New York Times Magazine* (Dec. 12, 1965), p. 46.

1118 Fishel, W.R. "The Eleventh Hour in Vietnam." *Asian Survey* 5 (Feb. 1965), pp. 98-107.

1119 Fleming, D.F. "Vietnam: The Crashing Dominoes." *New World Review* 36 (1968), pp. 8-16.

1120 Ford, D.F. "Misadventure in Vietnam: 'The Only War We've Got.' " *Nation* 199 (Aug. 24, 1964), pp. 66-68.

1121 ——. "With the 'Redskins' in Vietnam." *Nation* 199 (July 27, 1964), pp. 29-31.

1122 Gange, John. "Misadventure in Vietnam: The Mix of Fact and Truth." *Nation* 199 (Aug. 24, 1964), pp. 63-66.

1123 Gavin, James M. "We Can Get Out of Vietnam." *Saturday Evening Post* 241 (Feb. 24, 1968), pp. 23-25.

1124 Gilpatric, R.L. "Will Vietnam Lead to World War III?" *New York Times Magazine* (May 30, 1965), p. 11.

1125 Girling, J.L.S. "Vietnam and the Domino Theory." *Australian Outlook* 21 (Apr. 1967), pp. 61-70.

1126 Graham, Dominick. "Vietnam and the Crisis in War." *Yale Review* 55 (June 1966), pp. 391-402.

1127 Grant, Donald. "Vietnam: Alternative to Disaster." *Nation* 198 (May 25, 1964), pp. 521-523.

1128 Halberstam, David. "The Ugliest American in Vietnam." *Esquire* 62:5 (1964), pp. 114-117, 137-140.

1129 Harries, Owen. "Should the U.S. Withdraw from Asia?" *Foreign Affairs* 47:1 (1968), pp. 15-25.

1130 Harrigan, Anthony. "We Can Win in Southeast Asia." *National Review* 17 (Mar. 9, 1965), pp. 187-188.

1131 Hartley, A. "Turning Points [Pres. Election, 1968]." *Encounter* (Great Britain) 31:182 (1968), pp. 56-60.

1132 Heckscher, August. "Democracy and Foreign Policy: The Case of Vietnam." *American Scholar* 35 (Autumn 1966), pp. 613-620.

1133 Higgins, Marguerite. "Saigon Summary." *America* 110 (Jan. 4, 1964), pp. 18-21.

1134 Hilsman, Roger. "The Policy Proposals: 'Strength and Conciliation.' " *Bulletin of the Atomic Scientists* (June 1965), pp. 41-42.

1135 Howe, Irving. "Vietnam: The Costs and Lessons of Defeat." *Dissent* 12 (Spring 1965), pp. 151-156.

1136 Huntington, S.P. "The Basis of Accommodation." *Foreign Affairs* 46:4 (1968), pp. 642-656.

1137 Kahin, G. McT., and J.W. Lewis. "Escalation and East Asia." *Bulletin of the Atomic Scientists* 23:1 (1967), pp. 20-24.

1138 Kamath, M.V. "Vietnam: Victim of Power Politics." *United Asia* (India) 17:3 (1965), pp. 193-198.

1139 Kennan, G.F. "Kennan on Vietnam." *New Republic* 154 (Feb. 26, 1966), pp. 19-30.

1140 Koch, Chris. "The View from North Vietnam." *War/Peace* 5 (Nov. 1965), pp. 4-7.

1141 "Kosygin's Visit to Hanoi: American Bombings." *Current Digest of the Soviet Press* 17:6 (1965), pp. 3-12.

1142 Lansdale, E.G. "Viet Nam: Still the Search for Goals." *Foreign Affairs* 47:1 (1968), pp. 92-98.

1143 Lefever, E.W. "Vietnam: Joining the Issues." *Catholic World* 205 (May 1967), pp. 72-77.

1144 Lens, Sidney. "The Myth of Chinese Aggression." *Liberation* 11:3 (1966), pp. 35-37.

1145 Lowenthal, Richard. "The Vietnamese Agony." *Encounter* [Great Britain] 26 (Jan. 1966), pp. 54-59.

1146 McDermott, John. "Portent for the Future: Welfare Imperialism in Vietnam." *Nation* 203 (July 25, 1966), pp. 76-88.

1147 McWilliams, W.C., and Dennis Hale. "Spain and Vietnam: Comparing Two Civil Wars." *Commonweal* 48 (Sept. 16, 1966), pp. 575-577.

1148 Morgenthau, H.J. "We Are Deluding Ourselves in Vietnam." *New York Times Magazine* (Apr. 18, 1965), p. 25.

1149 ——. "Who Makes Those Commitments?" *New Republic* (June 14, 1969), pp. 16-18.

1150 Moriarty, J.K. "Politics of Delusion." *Commonweal* 86 (Sept. 22, 1967), pp. 574-580.

1151 Murakami, Hideo. " 'Vietnam' and the Question of Chinese Aggression." *Journal of South Asia History* 7:2 (1966), pp. 11-26.

1152 Murphy, C.J.V. "Vietnam Hangs on U.S. Determination." *Fortune* 69:5 (1964), pp. 159-162, 227-232.

1153 Pfaff, William. "No Victory in Vietnam." *Commonweal* 82 (Apr. 23, 1965), pp. 135-137.

1154 Raskin, Marcus. "America's Night of the Generals." *Ramparts* 6 (July 1967), pp. 15-19.

1155 Scalapino, Robert A. "We Cannot Accept a Communist Seizure of Vietnam." *New York Times Magazine* (Dec. 11, 1966), pp. 47, 133-140.

1156 Scheer, Robert, and Warren Hinckle. "The 'Vietnam Lobby.' " *Ramparts* 4 (July 1965), pp. 16-25.

1157 Shaplen, Robert. "Viet Nam: Crisis of Indecision." *Foreign Affairs* 46:1 (1967), pp. 95-110.

1158 Skorov, A. "McNamara's Dirty War." *International Affairs* (Moscow) 10:8 (1964), pp. 61-64.

1159 Smith, R.S. "Viet-Nam: The War That Is Not a War." *Foreign Service Journal* 42:1 (1965), pp. 18-21.

1160 Sochwick, Howard. "Slow Train through Viet Nam's War." *National Geographic* 126 (Sept. 1964), pp. 412-444.

1161 Stucki, Lorenz. "From a Report on Indochina." *Swiss Review of World Affairs* 14 (June 1964), pp. 12-15.

1162 Van der Haag, Ernest. "Vietnam: After All Is Said and Done." *National Review* 18 (Nov. 29, 1966), pp. 1210-1212, 1237.

1163 Warner, Denis. "Vietnam: The Need for a Loyal Opposition." *Reporter* 37:10 (1967), pp. 23-25.

1164 ——. "Vietnam: The Politics of 'Peace.'" *Reporter* 32 (Apr. 8, 1965), pp. 40-42.

1165 Warner, Geoffrey. "Escalation in Vietnam: The Precedents of 1954." *International Affairs* 41 (Apr. 1965), pp. 267-277.

1166 Watt, Alan. "The Geneva Agreements 1954 in Relation to Vietnam." *Australian Quarterly* 39 (June 1967), pp. 7-23.

1167 Wegaman, Philip. "The Vietnam War and Paul Ramsey's Conscience." *Dialog* 6 (Autumn 1967), pp. 292-298.

1168 "What Johnson Faces in South Vietnam." *Look* 28:2 (1964), pp. 19-29.

1169 White, Ralph. "Misperception of Aggression in Vietnam." *Journal of International Affairs* 21 (1967), pp. 123-140.

1170 Witze, Claude. "Report from Vietnam." *Air Force and Space Digest* 47:8 (1964), pp. 12-16.

1171 Wolk, H.S. "Vietnam and the Warfare State Complex." *Air Force and Space Digest* 50 (Apr. 1967), pp. 39-43.

B.3c / Tonkin Gulf Resolution

1172 Austin, Anthony. *The President's War: The Story of the Tonkin Gulf Resolution and How the Nation Was Trapped in Vietnam.* Philadelphia: Lippincott, 1971.

1173 Finney, John. "Tonkin Gulf Attack." *New Republic* 158 (Jan. 27, 1968), pp. 19-22.

1174 ——. "The Tonkin Verdict." *New Republic* 158 (Mar. 9, 1968), pp. 17-19.

1175 Goulden, Joseph C. *Truth is the First Casualty: The Gulf of Tonkin Affair, Illusion and Reality.* Chicago: Rand McNally, 1969.

1176 Roberts, Adam. "The Fog of Crisis: The 1964 Tonkin Gulf Incidents." *World Today* (Great Britain) 26:5 (1970), pp. 209-217.

1177 Schmidt, John W. *The Gulf of Tonkin Debates, 1964 and 1967: A Study in Argument.* Unpublished PhD thesis, University of Minnesota, 1969.

1178 Stone, I.F. "The Tonkin Bay Mystery." *The New York Review of Books* 10 (Mar. 28, 1968), pp. 5-12.

1179 U.S. Senate. Committee on Foreign Relations. Hearings; *The Gulf of Tonkin: The 1964 Incidents. Pt. I.* (Feb. 20, 1968); *Pt. II* (Dec. 16, 1968). 90th Cong., 2d Sess., 1969.

1180 ——. *Termination of Southeast Asia Resolution.* Report No. 91-872 [by Fulbright]. (May 15, 1970). 91st Cong., 2d Sess., 1970.

1181 U.S. Senate. Committee on Foreign Relations and the Committee on Armed Services. Joint Hearing; *Southeast Asia Resolution.* (Aug. 6, 1964), 88th Cong., 2d Sess., 1964.

1182 Windchy, Eugene G. *Tonkin Gulf.* New York: Doubleday, 1971.

B.3d / Tet Offensive

1183 Gannett, Betty. "The NLF Offensive in Vietnam." *Political Affairs* 47 (Mar. 1968), pp. 1-9.

1184 Irving, F.F. "The Battle of Hue." *Military Review* 49:1 (1969), pp. 56-63.

1185 Leroy, Catherine. "A Tense Interlude with the Enemy in Hue." *Life* (Feb. 16, 1968), pp. 22-29.

1186 Livingston, Maj. George D., Jr. "Pershing II: Success Amid Chaos." *Military Review* 50:5 (1970), pp. 56-60.

1187 Markbreiter, T.N. "A Bitter Tet." *Far Eastern Economic Review* 59 (Feb. 22, 1968), pp. 331-333.

1188 Milstein, J.S. *The Vietnam War Since the 1968 Tet Offensive: A Quantitative Analysis.* New Haven: Department of Political Science, Yale University, 1967.

1189 Oberdorfer, Don. *Tet!* New York: Doubleday, 1971.

1190 Olson, John. "The Battle that Regained and Ruined Hue." *Life* 64 (Mar. 8, 1968), pp. 24-29.

1191 Pike, Douglas, "Giap's General Uprising." *Far Eastern Economic Review* 59 (Mar. 21, 1968), pp. 513-515.

1192 ——. "The Tet Offensive: A Setback for Giap; But Just How Big?" *Army* 18:4 (1968), pp. 57-61.

1193 Rolph, Hammond. "Viet Cong Seize War Initiative in Major Offensive." *Communist Affairs* 6 (Jan/Feb 1968), pp. 12-14.

1194 *South Viet Nam: A Month of Unprecedented Offensive and Uprising.* Hanoi: Giai Phong Publishing House, 1968.

1195 Williams, G. "America Seeks to Negotiate." *Contemporary Review* 213:1231 (1968), pp. 84-85, 89.

B.4 / Richard M. Nixon Years

B.4a / Personalities/Policies

1196 Gray, Francine du Plessix. "Kissinger: The Swinging Sphinx." *Ramparts* 11:6 (Dec. 1972), pp. 33-34, 58-62.

1197 Horowitz, David. "Nixon's Vietnam Strategy." *Ramparts* 11:2 (Aug. 1972), pp. 17-20.

1198 Jeffries, Jean. "McGovern on Vietnam: Slipping and Sliding." *New Guard* 12:9 (Nov. 1972), pp. 7-8.

1199 Kahin, George McT. "Nixon's Peace Plan: No Basis for Negotiation." *New Republic* (Feb. 12, 1972), pp. 12-14.

1200 Landau, David. *Kissinger: The Uses of Power.* Boston: Houghton, Mifflin, 1972.

1201 Loomis, W. "It's No Longer LBJ's War." *Data* 14:7 (July 1969), pp. 15-17.

1202 "McGovern's Peace Plan." *New Republic* (Oct. 21, 1972), p. 11.

1203 Nixon, Richard M. "The Pursuit of Peace in Viet-Nam." *U.S. Department of State Bulletin* 61 (Nov. 24, 1969), pp. 437-443.

1204 ——. "Strengthening the Total Fabric of Peace." *U.S. Department of State Bulletin* 59 (Oct. 6, 1969), pp. 297-302.

1205 ——. "A Vietnam Plan: The Silent Majority." *Vital Speeches* 36 (Nov. 15, 1969), pp. 66-70.

1206 Richardson, E.L. "The Foreign Policy of the Nixon Administration: Its Aims and Strategy." *U.S. Department of State Bulletin* 59 (Sept. 22, 1969), pp. 257-260.

1207 "Terms for Ending the War: What the Candidates Say." *U.S. News & World Report* 73 (Oct. 23, 1972), pp. 28-29.

B.4b / Politics

1208 Abel, Lionel. "The Position of Noam Chomsky." *Commentary* 47:5 (1969), pp. 35-41.

1209 ——. "Reply (to Noam Chomsky)." *Commentary* 48:4 (1969), pp. 26-43.

1210 Ashmore, H.S. "The Policy of Illusion; The Illusion of Policy." *Center Magazine* 3 (May-June 1970), pp. 2-10.

1211 "Back to Bombing." *New Republic* (Jan. 1 & 8, 1973), pp. 9-10.

1212 Ball, George W. "We Should De-escalate the Importance of Vietnam." *New York Times Magazine* (Dec. 21, 1969), pp. 6-7, 29-31, 34, 36.

1213 Buckley, T. "Is This Written in the Stars? See It through with Nguyen Van Thieu." *New York Times Magazine* (Sept. 26, 1971), p. 14.

1214 Bunker, Ellsworth. "A Close Look at Progress inside Vietnam." *U.S. News & World Report* 67 (Nov. 17, 1969), pp. 46-52.

1215 Chomsky, Noam. "Vietnam, the Cold War and Other Matters." *Commentary* 48:4 (1969), pp. 12-26.

1216 Clifford, Clark. "Set a Date in Vietnam. Stick to It. Get Out." *Life* 68:19 (May 22, 1970), pp. 34-38.

1217 Greene, Fred. "The Case for and against Military Withdrawal from Vietnam and Korea." *Annals of the American Academy of Political and Social Science* 390 (1970), pp. 1-17.

1218 Hilsman, Roger. "Must We Invade the North?" *Foreign Affairs* 46:3 (1968), pp. 425-441.

1219 Hoopes, Townsend. "Legacy of the Cold War in Indochina." *Foreign Affairs* 48:4 (1970), pp. 601-616.

1220 Huglin, Brig. Gen. H.C. "Our Gains from Success in Vietnam." *Air University Review* 20:2 (1969), pp. 71-78.

1221 Johnstone, W.C. "The Political-Strategic Significance of Vietnam." *Current History* 56:330 (1969), pp. 65-70.

1222 Klare, Michael. "The Great South Asian War." *Nation* (Mar. 9, 1970), pp. 265-273.

1223 Kramer, Helmut, and Helfried Bauer. "Imperialism, Intervention Capacity, and Foreign Policy Making: On the Political Economy of the U.S. Intervention in Indochina." *Journal of Peace Research* 4 (1972), pp. 285-302.

1224 Lawrence, D. "It's the Duty of the U.N. to Make Peace in Vietnam." *U.S. News & World Report* 72 (May 22, 1972), p. 104.

1225 Lilienthal, D.E. "Postwar Development in Viet Nam." *Foreign Affairs* 47:2 (1969), pp. 321-333.

1226 McCombs, P.A. "Letter from Saigon: How Can We Lose in Vietnam, Having Won?" *National Review* 22:51 (1970), pp. 1399-1402.

1227 Middleton, R. "The Hubris and Nemesis of Power [Vietnam vs. U.S. Revolution]." *Royal United Service Institution Journal* 114:654 (1969), pp. 70-72.

1228 Morgenthau, Hans J. "The New Escalation in Vietnam." *New Republic* (May 20, 1972), pp. 9-10.

1229 Nicholas, H.G. "Vietnam and the Traditions of American Foreign Policy." *International Affairs* 44:2 (1968), pp. 189-201.

1230 Rhyne, R.F. "[Military] Victory in Vietnam." *Military Review* 50:2 (1970), pp. 37-47.

1231 Smith, Gaines. "How Ho Started the War: A History Lesson for Richard Nixon." *New Guard* 12:4 (May 1972), pp. 10-12.

1232 Stone, I.F. "Will The War Go On until 1976?" *New York Review of Books* 29:4 (Sept. 21, 1972), pp. 14-16.

1233 Taylor, Maxwell D. "Lessons of Vietnam." *U.S. News & World Report* 73 (Nov. 27, 1972), pp. 22-26.

1234 "The Vietnam War–Prospect and Retrospect: An Interview with George McT. Kahin." *Center Magazine* 5:2 (1972), pp. 24-32.

1235 Waskow, Arthur I. "The Politics of the Pentagon Papers." *Peace and Change: A Journal of Peace Research* 1:1 (Fall 1972), pp. 1-10.

1236 Whitney, Craig R. "Giap Teaches Us a Lesson; But It's over Our Heads." *New York Times Magazine* (Sept. 24, 1972), pp. 16-17, 76-84.

1237 "Why Vietnam War Drags On." *U.S. News & World Report* (Jan. 1, 1973), pp. 9-12.

1238 "Will the Leaders now Lead?" *New Republic* (Dec. 30, 1972), pp. 7-8.

1239 Wolf, Charles, Jr. "The Logic of Failure: A Vietnam 'Lesson.' " *Journal of Conflict Resolution* 14:3 (Sept. 1972), pp. 397-401.

B.4c / Nixon Doctrine

1240 Barber, James A. "The Nixon Doctrine and the Navy." *Naval War College Review* (June 1971), pp. 5-15.

1241 Dower, John W. "Asia and the Nixon Doctrine: 10 Points of Note." *Bulletin of the Concerned Asian Scholars* 2 (Fall 1970), pp. 47-70.

1242 Girling, J.L.S. "The Guam Doctrine." *International Affairs* (Great Britain) 46:1 (1970), pp. 48-62.

1243 Gleason, R.L. "Quo Vadis? The Nixon Doctrine and Air Power." *Air University Review* 23:5 (1972), pp. 45-56.

1244 "President Nixon and President Thieu Confer at Midway Island." *U.S. Department of State Bulletin* 60 (June 30, 1969), pp. 549-554.

1245 "President Nixon's Round the World Trip." *U.S. Department of State Bulletin* 61 (Aug. 25, 1969), pp. 147-176.

1246 Sidey, Hugh. "Question of Belief in Hanoi and at Home." *Life* 67:2 (Oct. 10, 1969), p. 4.

1247 U.S. Senate. Committee on Foreign Relations. Report; *Perspective on Asia: The New U.S. Doctrine and Southeast Asia.* 91st Cong., 1st Sess., 1969.

1248 Van Vien, Gen. Cao. "Vietnam: What Next? The Strategy of Isolation." *Military Review* (Apr. 1972), pp. 22-30.

C / Congressional Views on Vietnam

1249 American Enterprise Institute for Public Policy Research. *What Pace Withdrawal?* [The McGovern-Hatfield Amendment] Washington, D.C.: 1970.

1250 Benton, M.J.G. *Wayne Morse and Vietnam: A Study of the Role of Dissenter.* Unpublished PhD thesis, University of Denver, 1968.

1251 Brooke, Edward W. "The United States and Vietnam." *World Affairs* 130 (Apr/June 1967), pp. 5-12.

1252 Church, Frank. "Interview (on Vietnam)." *Ramparts* 3:5 (1965), pp. 17-22.

1253 ——. "Vietnam: Disengagement Now." *Vital Speeches* 36 (Nov. 1, 1969), pp. 34-39.

1254 Docking, Robert. "Viet Nam: An Observer's Report." *Washburn Law Journal* 7 (1968), pp. 187-193.

1255 Fairlie, H. "The Senator [Fulbright] and World Power: Letter from America." *Encounter* (Great Britain) 30:176 (1968), pp. 57-66.

1256 Findley, Cong. Paul. "End the Vietnam War through the Rule of Law." *Social Science* 43:3 (1968), pp. 133-138.

1257 Fullbright, J. William. *The Arrogance of Power.* New York: Random House, 1967.

1258 ——. "We Must Negotiate Peace in Vietnam." *Saturday Evening Post* 239 (Apr. 9, 1966), pp. 10-14.

1259 ——, ed. *The Vietnam Hearings.* New York: Vintage, 1966.

1260 Goodell, Sen. Charles E. "Setting a Deadline for Withdrawal." *Current* 115 (1970), pp. 30-32.

1261 Gruening, E., and H.B. Beaser. *Vietnam Folly.* Washington, D.C.: National Press, 1967.

1262 Hartke, Sen. Vance. *The American Crisis in Vietnam.* New York: Bobbs-Merrill, 1968.

1263 Kennedy, Edward M. "A Fresh Look at Vietnam." *Look* 30 (Feb. 8, 1966), pp. 21-23.

1264 ——. "The 'Other War' in Vietnam." *New Leader* 50 (Nov. 20, 1967), pp. 6-9.

1265 Kennedy, Robert F. "Comment [on P. Findley's 'End the Vietnam War through the Rule of Law']." *Social Science* 43:3 (1968), pp. 138-139.

1266 ——. "Senator Robert Kennedy Explains His Position." *U.S. News & World Report* 60 (Mar. 14, 1966), pp. 68-70.

1267 ——. *To Seek a Newer World.* New York: Doubleday, 1967.

1268 Krause, Patricia A., ed. *Anatomy of an Undeclared War: Congressional Conference on the Pentagon Papers.* New York: International Universities Press, 1972.

1269 McCarthy, Eugene J. *The Limits of Power: America's Role in the World.* New York: Holt, Rinehart & Winston, 1967.

1270 McGee, Gale W. *The Responsibilities of World Power.* Washington, D.C.: National Press, 1968.

1271 ——. "Vietnam: A Living Example for Implementing the American Spirit." *Vital Speeches* 26 (May 1, 1960), pp. 440-443.

1272 McGovern, George S. "Affirmative Alternative in Vietnam." *Progressive* 29 (Mar. 1965), pp. 12-14.

1273 ——. "A Proposal for Vietnam." *New York Review of Books,* 6 (July 7, 1966), pp. 5-6.

1274 ——. "Vietnam: The Time Is Now." *Progressive* 33 (Sept. 1969), pp. 13-16.

1275 ——. "We Can Solve the Vietnam Dilemma." *Saturday Review* 48 (Oct. 16, 1965), pp. 37-38.

1276 Morse, Wayne. "Humpty Dumpty in Vietnam." *Progressive* 28:8 (1964), pp. 13-16.

1277 ——. "Protests Against Vietnam Policy." *Vital Speeches* 32:2 (Nov. 15, 1965), pp. 74-78.

1278 ——. *The Truth About Vietnam: Report on the U.S. Senate Hearings.* Analysis by W. Morse, edited by F.M. Robinson and E. Kemp. San Diego, California: Greenleaf Classics, 1966.

1279 U.S. Congress. Committee for a Vote on the War. *The Amendment to Fund the War: Report of the Steering Committee of the Congressional Committee for a Vote on the War.* Washington, D.C.: 1970.

1280 U.S. House of Representatives. Committee on Foreign Affairs. Hearings; *Termination of Hostilities in Indochina.* [May 16, 18, 23 and June 1, 1972] 92d Cong., 2d Sess., 1972.

1281 ——. *Report of the Special Study Mission to Asia.* [by L.L. Wolff and J.H. Burke, April 22, 1970] 91st Cong., 2d Sess., 1970.

1282 ——. *Report of the Special Study Mission to East and Southeast Asia.* [by E.R. Roybal, Dec., 1968] 90th Cong., 2d Sess., 1968.

1283 ——. *Report of the Special Study Mission to East and Southeast Asia.* [by E.R. Roybal, Feb. 18, 1969] 91st Cong., 1st Sess., 1969.

1284 ——. *Report on Vietnam.* [by Clement J. Zablocki] 89th Cong., 2d Sess., 1966.

1285 U.S. House of Representatives. Committee on Foreign Relations. *Report of the Special Study Mission to South and Southeast Asia.* [by R. Taft, Jr., May 5, 1969] 91st Cong., 1st Sess., 1969.

1286 U.S. Senate. Committee on Foreign Relations. Report; *China and the Vietnam War—Will History Repeat?* [by Senator Joseph S. Clark, Mar. 19, 1968] 90th Cong., 2d Sess., 1968.

1287 ——. *Report on Indochina.* [by Senator Mike Mansfield] 83d Cong., 2d Sess., 1954.

1288 ——. Report; *Stalemate in Vietnam.* [by Joseph S. Clark] 90th Cong., 2d Sess., 1968.

1289 ——. Report; *Viet Nam and Southeast Asia.* [by Senator Mike Mansfield *et al.*] 88th Cong., 1st Sess., 1963.

1290 ——. Report; *The Vietnam Conflict: The Substance and the Shadow.* [by Mansfield and others, Jan. 6, 1966] 89th Cong., 2d Sess., 1966.

1291 U.S. Senate Republican Policy Committee. *The War in Vietnam.* Washington, D.C.: Public Affairs Press, 1967.

1292 "Vietnam Debate: Dirksen vs. Fulbright." *New Leader* 50 (Oct. 23, 1967), pp. 9-19.

1293 Zablocki, C.J. "Recent Events in South Vietnam: Who Is Responsible?" *Vital Speeches* 30 (Dec. 15, 1963), pp. 133-134.

D / Policies, Politics, & Critics

D.1 / U.S. Involvement Legal?

1294 Alford, N.H., Jr. "The Legality of American Military Involvement in Vietnam: A Broader Perspective." *Yale Law Journal* 75 (1966), pp. 1109-1121.

1295 Andonian, J.K. "Law and Vietnam." *American Bar Association Journal* 54 (May 1968), pp. 457-459.

1296 Blaustein, A.P. "Current Legal Bibliography: Viet Nam." *Law Library Journal* 61 (1968), pp. 20-22.

1297 Deutsch, Eberhard. "Legality of the War in Vietnam." *Washburn Law Journal* 7 (1968), pp. 153-186.

1298 Falk, Richard A. "International Law and the United States Role in the Viet Nam War." *Yale Law Journal* 75 (1966), pp. 1122-1160.

1299 ——. *The Six Legal Dimensions of the Vietnam War.* Research Monograph No. 34. Princeton: Center of International Studies, Princeton University, 1968.

1300 ——. "U.S. in Vietnam: Rationale and Law." *Dissent* 13 (May/June 1966), pp. 275-284.

1301 ——, ed. *The Vietnam War and International Law.* 3 Vols. Princeton: Princeton University Press, 1968-1972.

1302 Friedmann, Wolfgang. "Law and Politics in the Vietnamese War: Commentary." *American Journal of International Law* 61 (1967), pp. 776-784.

1303 Hull, Roger, and J. Novogrod. *Law and Vietnam.* Dobbs Ferry, New York: Oceana Publications, 1968.

1304 Lawyer's Committee on American Policy Towards Vietnam. *Vietnam and International Law: An Analysis of the Legality of U.S. Military Involvement.* Flanders, New Jersey: O'Hare Books, 1967.

1305 Liska, G. *War and Order, Reflections on Vietnam and History.* Baltimore: Johns Hopkins Press, 1968.

1306 Lobel, W.N. "Legality of the United States' Involvement in Vietnam: a Pragmatic Approach." *University of Miami Law Review* 23 (Summer 1969), pp. 792-814.

1307 Meeker, Leonard C. "The Legality of United States Participation in the Defense of Viet Nam." *U.S. Department of State Bulletin* 54 (Mar. 28, 1966), pp. 474-489.

1308 ——. "Viet-Nam and the International Law of Self-Defense." *U.S. Department of State Bulletin* 56 (Jan. 9, 1967), pp. 54-63.

1309 Messing, J.H. "American Actions in Vietnam: Justifiable in International Law?" *Stanford Law Review* 19 (June 1967), pp. 1307-1336.

1310 Moore, John Norton. *Law and the Indo-China War.* Princeton: Princeton University Press, 1972.

1311 ——. "Law and Politics in the Vietnamese War: A Response to Professor Friedman." *American Journal of International Law* 61 (Oct. 1967), pp. 1039-1053.

1312 ——. "The Lawfulness of Military Assistance to the Republic of Vietnam." *American Journal of International Law* 61:1 (1967), pp. 1-34.

1313 Murphy, C.F., Jr. "Indochina: Lingering Issues of Law and Policy." *Duquesne Law Review* 10 (Winter 1971), p. 155ff.

1314 ——, and M.Q. Sibley. "War In Vietnam: A Discussion." *Natural Law Forum* 12 (1967), pp. 196-209.

1315 Partan, D.G. "Legal Aspects of the Vietnam Conflict." *Boston University Law Review* 46 (1966), pp. 281-316.

1316 Possony, S.T. *Aggression and Self-Defense: The Legality of U.S. Action in South Vietnam.* FPRI Monograph Series No. 6. Philadelphia: Foreign Policy Research Institute, University of Pennsylvania, 1966.

1317 Robertson, D.W. "Debate Among American International Lawyers About the Vietnam War." *Texas Law Review* 46 (July 1968), pp. 898-913.

1318 Wright, Quincy. "Legal Aspects of the Viet-Nam Situation." *American Journal of International Law* 60 (1966), pp. 750-769.

D.2 / Presidential Powers Exceeded?

1319 Bader, W.B. "Congress and National Strategy." *Naval War College Review* 22:6 (1970), pp. 9-18.

1320 Baldwin, D.A. "Congressional Initiative in Foreign Policy." *Journal of Politics* 28:4 (1966), pp. 754-773.

1321 Buckwalter, Doyle W. "The Congressional Concurrent Resolution: A Search for Foreign Policy Influences." *Midwest Journal of Political Science* 14:3 (1970), pp. 434-458.

1322 "Congress, the President, and the Power to Commit Forces to Combat." *Harvard Law Review* 81 (June 1968), pp. 1771-1805.

1323 Dvorin, Eugene P., ed. *The Senate's War Powers: Debate on Cambodia from the Congressional Record.* Chicago: Markham, 1971.

1324 Javits, Sen. Jacob K. "The Congressional Presence in Foreign Relations." *Foreign Affairs* 48:2 (1970), pp. 221-234.

1325 Moore, J.N. "The National Executive and the Use of the Armed Forces Abroad." *Naval War College Review* 28 (Jan. 1969), pp. 28-38.

1326 Reveley, W. Taylor, III. "Presidential War-Making: Constitutional Prerogative or Usurpation?" *Virginia Law Review* (Nov. 1969), pp. 1243-1305.

1327 U.S. Senate. Committee on Foreign Relations. *Documents Relating to the War Powers of Congress, the President's Authority as Commander-in-Chief and the War in Indochina.* [July 1970] 91st Cong., 2d Sess., 1970.

1328 Velvel, L.R. "The War in Viet Nam: Unconstitutional, Justifiable, and Jurisdictionally Attackable." *Kansas Law Review* 16 (1968), pp. 449-503.

1329 Wells, John M., comp. *The People vs. Presidential War.* New York: Dunellen, 1970.

1330 Windchy, E.G. "The Right to Make War." *New Republic* (Jan. 29, 1972), pp. 19-23.

1331 Wormuth, F.D. "The Vietnam War, The President versus the Constitution." *A Center Occasional Paper* 1:3. Santa Barbara, California: Center for the Study of Democratic Institutions, 1968.

E / U.N. & Vietnam

1332 Bargman, Abraham. "Can the U.N. Act on Vietnam?" *War/Peace Report* 7 (Oct. 1967), pp. 12-13.

1333 Bloomfield, L.P. *The U.N. and Vietnam.* New York: Carnegie Endowment for International Peace, 1968.

1334 Goldberg, Arthur J. "Ambassador Goldberg Submits Viet-Nam Question to U.N. Security Council." *U.S. Department of State Bulletin* 54 (Feb. 14, 1966), pp. 229-239.

1335 ——. "The Responsibility of the United Nations in the Search for Peace in Viet-Nam." *U.S. Department of State Bulletin* 57 (Nov. 20, 1967), pp. 667-672.

1336 Mezerik, A.G., comp. *Viet Nam and the U.N., 1967: National and International Policy.* New York: International Review Service, 1967.

1337 Pilkington, Betty. "Vietnam: The U.N. Peeks In." *Nation* 197 (Nov. 2, 1963), pp. 273-275.

1338 Reuss, H.S. "Let the U.N. Handle It: Peacekeeping in Vietnam." *Commonweal* 82 (July 23, 1965), pp. 523-526.

1339 Schacter, Oscar. "Intervention and the United Nations." *Stanford Journal of International Studies* 3 (1968), pp. 5-12.

1340 United Nations. Report; *The Violation of Human Rights in South Viet Nam.* U.N. Document A/5630, 1963.

1341 U.S. Senate. Committee on Foreign Relations. Hearings; *Submission of the Vietnam Conflict to the United Nations.* [Oct. 26, 27 and Nov. 2, 1967] 90th Cong., 1st Sess., 1967.

1342 "Vietnam: Statements by Secretary-General on Recent Developments." *U.N. Monthly Chronicle* 2 (May 1965), pp. 21-24.

F / Negotiations

F.1 / General

1343 "After the [Bombing] Pause: Motion or Progress?" *Newsweek* 67 (Feb. 14, 1966), pp. 17-23.

1344 American Friends Service Committee. *Peace in Vietnam: A New Approach in South East Asia.* New York: Hill and Wang, 1966.

1345 Ashmore, Harry, and William Boggs. *Mission to Hanoi.* New York: Putnam's, 1968.

1346 Baldwin, H.J. "We Must Choose: (1) 'Bug Out,' (2) Negotiate, (3) Fight." *New York Times Magazine* (Feb. 21, 1965), pp. 8-9, 62-63.

1347 Browne, M.W. "Are Negotiations Possible? No." *War/Peace Report* 7 (Jan. 1967), pp. 6-7.

1348 Burchett, Wilfred. "How Hanoi and the N.L.F. See Chances for Peace." *War/Peace Report* 7 (Nov. 1967), pp. 3-6.

1349 ——. "Negotiations on Vietnam? How it Looks from the 'Other Side.'" *War/Peace* 6 (Nov. 1966), pp. 3-5.

1350 ——. "Why North Vietnam Rejects 'Unconditional Negotiations.'" *War/Peace* 5 (Dec. 1965), pp. 7-9.

1351 Buttinger, Joseph. "Can the Negotiations Bring Peace to Vietnam?" *Dissent* 15:4 (1968), pp. 296-300.

1352 "Can Vietnam be Neutralized?" *War/Peace Report* 4:4 (1964), pp. 3-7.

1353 Cooper, C.L. "The Complexities of Negotiation." *Foreign Affairs* 46:3 (1968), pp. 454-466.

1354 Cousins, Norman. "How the U.S. Spurned Three Chances for Peace in Vietnam." *Look* 33 (July 29, 1969), pp. 45-48.

1355 Critchley, Julian, and Betty Hunt. *The Vietnam War Negotiations.* London: World and School Crisis Papers, 1968.

1356 Cutrone, J.F.H. "Peace in Vietnam: An Acceptable Solution." *Military Review* 46 (Nov. 1966), pp. 60-68.

1357 Devillers, Philippe. "Preventing the Peace: Report from an Intermediary." *Nation* 203 (Dec. 5, 1966), pp. 597-603.

1358 Donhoff, Marion. "In the Shadow of Vietnam: The Great Powers more Rigid, Asia more Flexible." *International Affairs* (London), 42:4 (1966), pp. 609-618.

1359 Downs, Hunton. "Diplomacy: Saigon in Retrospect." *Ramparts* 6 (Dec. 1967), pp. 12-19, 22.

1360 Draper, Theodore. "How Not to Negotiate." *New York Review of Books* 8 (May 4, 1967).

1361 Duff, P. *The Credibility Gap: A Chronological Record of Attempts to Achieve a Political Solution Leading to Peace in Vietnam.* London: International Confederation for Disarmament and Peace, 1967.

1362 Durbrow, Elbridge. "Negotiating with the Communists: Firmness is the Key." *Air Force and Space Digest* 51:9 (1968), pp. 48-52.

1363 Eden, Anthony. *Toward Peace in Indochina.* London: Oxford University Press, 1966.

1364 Falk, Richard A. *A Vietnam Settlement: The View from Hanoi.* Princeton: Center of International Studies, Princeton University, 1968.

1365 Fallers, L.A., et al. "The Policy Proposals: 'A Negotiated Stalemate.'" *Bulletin of the Atomic Scientists* (June 1965), pp. 42-44.

1366 Gordon, B.K. *Toward Disengagement in Asia.* London: Prentice-Hall, 1969.

1367 Grant, Zalin. "The Bombing Halt." *New Republic* 159 (Nov. 9, 1968), pp. 13-15.

1368 ——. "Why Saigon Wants No Early Cease-Fire." *New Republic* 159 (Dec. 21, 1968), pp. 15-17.

1369 Gr. Br. Foreign Office. *Recent Exchange Concerning Attempts to Promote a Negotiated Settlement of the Conflict in Viet-Nam.* London: H.M.S.O., 1965.

1370 Halberstam, David. "Bargaining With Hanoi." *New Republic* (May 11, 1968), pp. 14-16.

1371 Hickey, Gerald C. *Accommodation and Coalition in South Vietnam.* Santa Monica, California: Rand, P-4213, Jan. 1970.

1372 Honey, P.J. "North Vietnam and Peace Negotiations." *China New Analysis* 726 (Sept. 20, 1968), pp. 1-7.

1373 Hudson, Richard. "The Nearest to Negotiations Yet." *War/Peace Report* 7 (Mar. 1967), pp. 3-4.

1374 Jenkins, B. *Why the North Vietnamese Keep Fighting.* Santa Monica, California: Rand, P-4395, Aug. 1970.

1375 Johnson, Lyndon B. "United States Halts the Bombing of North Vietnam." *U.S. Department of State Bulletin* 59 (Nov. 18, 1968), pp. 517-519.

1376 Kahn, Herman. "If Negotiations Fail." *Foreign Affairs* 46:4 (1968), pp. 627-641.

1377 Kissinger, Henry A. "The Viet Nam Negotiations." *Foreign Affairs* 47:2 (1968), pp. 211-234.

1378 Kolko, Gabriel. "Vietnam: la guerre et la diplomatie américaine depuis janvier 1968." *Partisans* 48 (June/Aug 1969), pp. 81-106.

1379 ——. "Vietnam War and Diplomacy." *London Bulletin* 11 (Aug. 1969).

1380 Kraft, Joseph. "In Search of Kissinger." *Harper's* (Jan. 1971), pp. 54-61.

1381 Kraslow, David, and Stuart H. Loory. *The Secret Search for Peace in Vietnam.* New York: Vintage, 1969.

1382 Kung, Hsien-wu. "Why Does the United States Make Concessions in the War in Vietnam?" *Asian Outlook* 4 (June 1969), pp. 40-44.

1383 Lacouture, Jean. "How to Talk to Mr. Ho." *Ramparts* 5 (Oct. 1966), pp. 42-46.

1384 Lens, Sidney. "What Hanoi Wants." *Progressive* 31 (Sept. 1967), pp. 18-20.

1385 McCullouch, Frank. "Peace Feelers: This Frail Dance of the Seven Veils." *Life* 64 (Mar. 22, 1968), pp. 32-38.

1386 Moskin, J. Robert. "The Hard-Line Demand: Victory—Exclusive Report from Hanoi." *Look* 34:26 (Dec. 29, 1970), pp. 20-25.

1387 Nguyen Van Ba. "Bases for a Valid Settlement." *Vietnamese Studies* 18/19 (Sept. 1968), pp. 303-335.

1388 Nicolson, Nigel. "Diplomatic Initiative on Vietnam." *Listener* 74 (July 22, 1965), pp. 111-112, 142.

1389 Palmer, Joe M. "Political Negotiations in Vietnam." *Military Review* 46:9 (1966), pp. 62-69.

1390 Phan Guang Dan. "We Must Contact Our Opponents." *War/Peace Report* 8 (Aug/Sept 1968), pp. 12-16.

1391 "President Johnson's Proposal for Negotiation on Viet-Nam Rejected by Ho Chi Minh." *U.S. Department of State Bulletin* 56 (Apr. 10, 1967), pp. 595-597.

1392 Reicher, Reuben. *Une Paix immédiate au Viet-Nam est-elle possible?* Paris: S.G.R.A.D.I., 1966.

1393 Roberts, Adam. "Hanoi's Offer to Talk." *World Affairs* 24 (May 1968), pp. 176-178.

1394 Swomly, J.M., Jr. "Peace Negotiations and President Johnson." *Minority of One* 10:9 (1968), pp. 10-12.

1395 ——, and R.W. Selton. "Rational Victory." *U.S. Naval Institute Proceedings* 94:2 (1968), pp. 26-32.

1396 Thee, M., ed. *Vietnam Peace Proposals, Documents 1954-1968.* Oslo: International Peace Research Institute, Mar. 1969.

1397 Trager, F.N. "Back to Geneva '54? An Act of Political Folly!" *Vietnam Perspectives* 1:1 (1965), pp. 1-7.

1398 Tran Van Dinh. "Are Negotiations Possible? Yes." *War/Peace Report* 7 (Jan. 1967), pp. 7-10.

1399 ——. "Reunification: Key to Peace in Vietnam." *War/Peace Reports* 6 (Dec. 1966), pp. 3-4.

1400 Woito, R. *Vietnam Peace Proposals.* Berkeley, California: World Without War Council, 1967.

1401 Wolf, Charles, Jr. "Vietnam Prospects and Precepts." *Asian Survey* 9:3 (1968), pp. 157-162.

1402 Van Thai, V. *Fighting and Negotiating on Vietnam: A Strategy.* Santa Monica, California: Rand, RM-5997-ARPA, July 1969.

F.2 / Paris Talks

1403 Burchett, Wilfred. "The Paris Talks and the War." *Liberation* 13:5 (1968), pp. 29-31.

1404 ——. "Vietnam: One Year of the Peace Talks." *New World Review* 37:2 (1969), pp. 2-9.

1405 Buttinger, Joseph. "Toward Peace at Paris?" *Dissent* 16 (Mar/Apr 1969), pp. 108-112.

1406 Davis, Derek. "What Price Peace at Paris?" *Far Eastern Economic Review* 60 (May 30, 1968), pp. 473-476.

1407 Devillers, Philippe. "The Paris Negotiations on Vietnam." *World Today* (Great Britain), 25:8 (1969), pp. 339-350.

1408 Hayden, Tom. "The Impasse in Paris." *Ramparts* 3 (Aug. 24, 1968), pp. 18-21.

1409 Kahin, George McT. "Impasse at Paris." *New Republic* 159 (Oct. 12, 1968), pp. 23-26.

1410 Mustafa, Zubeida. "The Paris Peace Talks." *Pakistan Horizon* 22:1 (1969), pp. 29-38.

1411 Shaplen, Robert. "Seats at the Table." *New Yorker* 44 (Nov. 16, 1968), pp. 193-206.

1412 ——. "Until the Chairs Rot." *New Yorker* 45 (July 5, 1969), pp. 36-57.

1413 Smith, H. "The Paris Talks Started 471 Days Ago . . . Harriman Suggests a Way Out of Vietnam." *New York Times Magazine* (Aug. 24, 1969), p. 24.

1414 Stone, I.F. "The Paris Peace Talks." *New York Review of Books* 13 (June 19, 1969), pp. 1 ff.

1415 Terrill, Ross. "Making Peace at Paris: A Special Report on the Negotiations." *Atlantic Monthly* 222 (Dec. 1968), pp. 4-33.

1416 Tran Van Dinh. "The Other Side of the Table." *Washington Monthly* 1:1 (Jan. 1970), pp. 74-80.

1417 Wainwright, W.H. "The Paris Peace Talks: Diplomacy and Stagecraft." *Antioch Review* 29:4 (1969), pp. 505-514.

F.3 / Paris Talks: Final Phase (1972-73)

1418 "Can the U.S. Make the Truce Stick?" *U.S. News & World Report* (Feb. 12, 1973), pp. 17-20.

1419 Clubb, O. Edmund. "The Cease-Fire." *Nation* 216:7 (Feb. 12, 1973), pp. 198-201.

1420 "The Elusive Peace Deal." *Newsweek* (Nov. 13, 1972), pp. 42, 47, 50.

1421 "For Indo-China, the War is Far from Over." *U.S. News & World Report* (Feb. 5, 1973), pp. 20-22.

1422 "Getting Ready for Truce: A Rush of Arms to Vietnam." *U.S. News & World Report* (Nov. 27, 1972), pp. 18-19.

1423 Hubbard, H. "Clouds Over Paris." *Newsweek* 80 (Dec. 4, 1972), pp. 26-27.

1424 Karnow, Stanley. "Truce or Peace? The Vietnam Accord." *New Republic* (Jan. 27, 1973), pp. 19-20.

1425 "Kissinger: An Interview with Oriana Fallaci." *New Republic* (Dec. 16, 1972), pp. 17-22.

1426 [Kissinger, Henry A.] "Dr. Kissinger Discusses Status of Negotiations Toward Viet-Nam Peace—A Transcript of October 30 News Conference." *U.S. Department of State Bulletin* 67 (Nov. 13, 1972), pp. 549-558.

1427 Nixon, Richard M. "Significant Breakthrough in the Viet-Nam Negotiations—Remarks on October 26." *U.S. Department of State Bulletin* 67 (Nov. 13, 1972), pp. 558-560.

1428 "Official Text of the Cease-Fire Agreement." *U.S. News & World Report* (Feb. 5, 1973), pp. 66-71.

1429 "Thieu at the Bridge: Kissinger-Tho Discussions." *National Review* 24 (Nov. 24, 1972), p. 1288.

1430 U.S. Department of State. Bureau of Public Affairs. *Documentation on Viet-Nam [Cease-fire] Agreement.* (News Release) Washington, D.C., Jan. 24, 1973.

1431 "The Vietnam Peace." *U.S. News & World Report* (Feb. 5, 1973), pp. 16-19.

G / Other Nations & U.S. Involvement

1432 Alexeyev, E., and V. Zhurkin. "U.S.A.: Wanton Escalation." *International Affairs* (Moscow) 14:8 (1965), 59-63.

1433 "The *ASAHI* Poll on Vietnam." *Japan Quarterly* 12 (Oct/Dec 1965), pp. 463-466.

1434 Australia. Department of External Affairs. *Viet-Nam, Australia and Asia: Attitudes of Asian Countries to Viet-Nam and Australia's Role There.* Canberra: 1967.

1435 ——. *"Viet Nam Since the 1954 Geneva Agreements.* Canberra: 1964.

1436 ——. "Vietnam: Documents on Communist Aggression." *Current Notes on International Affairs* 33:1 (1962), pp. 27-40.

1437 "Bases of Canada's Policy on Vietnam." *External Affairs* (Ottawa) 19 (Apr. 1967), pp. 131-135.

1438 Brown, R.L. "The Japanese and Vietnam." *Contemporary Review* 208 (May 1966), pp. 234-236.

1439 Cooksey, Robert. "Australian Public Opinion and Vietnam Policy." *Dissent* (Melbourne) 22 (1968), pp. 5-11.

1440 Fall, B.B. "Vietnam: European View Points." *New Republic* 153 (Aug. 21, 1965), pp. 13-15.

1441 Findley, P.T. *Protest Politics and Psychological Warfare: The Communist Role in the Anti-Vietnam War and Anti-Conscription Movement in Australia.* Melbourne: Hawthorn Press, 1968.

1442 Fletcher, James. "British Support on Vietnam?" *National Review* 18 (Apr. 19, 1966), pp. 167-168.

1443 ——. "The English and the Vietnam War." *National Review* 19:25 (1967), pp. 684-687, 706.

1444 Huizinga, J.H. "A European's View of the Vietnam War." *Reporter* 36:5 (1967), pp. 30-36.

1445 Link, Ruth. "Ambassador Holland and the Swedes." *Crisis* 78:2 (1971), pp. 43-48.

1446 Rawson, D.W. "The Vietnam War and the Australian Party System." *Australian Outlook* 23 (Apr. 1969), pp. 58-67.

1447 Reese, Gunter. "Between Verdicts: German Students' View of the War." *Motive* 27:8 (1967), pp. 48-52.

1448 Rigin, Y. "Canada and the War in Viet-Nam." *International Affairs* (Moscow) 5 (May 1968), pp. 57-62.

1449 Sar Desai, D.R. "South Asia and the Vietnam War." *United Asia* 20 (July/Aug 1968), pp. 210-217.

1450 Singh, L.P. "Canada, the United States and Vietnam." *Journal of Commonwealth Political Studies* 6 (July 1968), pp. 125-148.

1451 Steel, Ronald. "De Gaulle on Vietnam." *Commonweal* 80 (Apr. 24, 1964), pp. 141-143.

1452 Story, Richard. "Repercussions in Japan." *Studies on the Soviet Union* 6:2 (1966), pp. 74-82.

1453 University Study Group on Vietnam. *Vietnam and Australia—Documents—Interpretations.* Sydney: Bridge Printery, 1966.

1454 Warner, Denis. "Australia Votes to Stay in Vietnam." *Reporter* 35:11 (1966), pp. 29-31.

1455 Watt, Alan. *Vietnam: An Australian Analysis.* Melbourne: F.W. Cheshire (for the Australian Institute of International Affairs), 1968.

V / MILITARY OPERATIONS

A / Strategy & Tactics

A.1 / General

1456 "Aggression from the North." *Army* 15 (Apr. 1965), pp. 66-79.

1457 Baldwin, H.A. "Vietnam Balance Sheet." *Reporter* 37:6 (Oct. 1967), pp. 14-18.

1458 Beaufré, A. "Aspects stratégiques du problème Vietnamien." *Internationale Spectator* (The Hague) 20 (Feb. 22, 1966), pp. 260-267.

1459 Bell, J.C. "Dien Bien Phu: Giap's Last Win?" *Military Review* 48 (Feb. 1968), pp. 84-91.

1460 Bradford, Lt. Col. Z.B., Jr. "U.S. Tactics in Vietnam." *Military Review* (April 1972), pp. 63-76.

1461 Braestrup, Peter. "The Abrams Strategy in Vietnam." *New Leader* 52 (June 9, 1969), pp. 3-5.

1462 Brownlow, C. "Bomb Pause Causes Major Tactics Shift." *Aviation Week and Space Technology* 84:7 (Feb. 14, 1966), pp. 27-29.

1463 Butz, J.S., Jr. "Do They Want Us There? Are We Fighting Honorably? Can We Win?" *Air Force and Space Digest* 49:9 (1966), pp. 62-68.

1464 Cleland, John R.D. "Principle of the Objective and Vietnam." *Military Review* 46:7 (1966), pp. 82-86.

1465 Conley, M.C. "Communist Thought and Viet Cong Tactics." *Asian Studies* 8 (1968), pp. 206-222.

1466 Denno, B.F. "Military Prospects in Vietnam." *Orbis* 9 (Summer 1965), pp. 411-417.

1467 Dudman, Richard. "Military Policy in Vietnam." *Current History* 50 (Feb. 1966), pp. 81-97, 115.

1468 Durst, Col. Jay B. "Limited Conventional War; Can It Be Successful?" *Military Review* 50:1 (1970), pp. 56-63.

1469 Galula, David. "Military Considerations in Vietnam." *Studies on the Soviet Union* 6:2 (1966), pp. 29-42.

1470 Hartle, A.E. "Momentum in Attack." *Army* 17:5 (May 1967), pp. 35-38.

1471 Hayden, Tom. "The Prospects of the North Vietnam Offensive." *Ramparts* 11:2 (Aug. 1972), pp. 21-25, 51-56.

1472 Heilbrun, Otto. "How Many Men to Vietnam?" *Military Review* 45:12 (1965), pp. 27-33.

1473 ——. "Strategy in Vietnam." *Royal United Service Institution Journal* 112 (Aug. 1967), pp. 257-260.

1474 Kinnard, H.W.O. "Vietnam Has Lessons for Tomorrow's Army." *Army* 18 (Nov. 1968), pp. 77-80.

1475 Lofgren, Charles A. "How New Is Limited War?" *Military Review* 47:7 (1967), pp. 16-23.

1476 Marshall, S.L.A. "Fighting a Sticky War: A Strategy for Vietnam." *New Leader* 47:16 (1964), pp. 12-15.

1477 ——. "The Military Mess." *New Leader* 48:5 (1965), pp. 3-6.

1478 McConnell, J.P. "The Role of Airpower in Vietnam: Strategic Persuasion." *Vital Speeches* 32:1 (Oct. 15, 1965), pp. 12-15.

1479 Moore, W.C. "History, Vietnam, and the Concept of Deterrence." *Air University Review* 20:6 (1969), pp. 58-63.

1480 Norman, Lloyd. "No More Koreas." *Army* 15 (May 1965), pp. 22-29.

1481 Palmer, D.R. "Ho's Mistake." *Military Review* 47 (Apr. 1967), pp. 35-39.

1482 Pfaff, William. "Checkmate in Vietnam." *Commonweal* 85 (Feb. 24, 1967), pp. 585-586.

1483 Plattner, C.M. "Limited-War Concepts Weighed in Battle." *Aviation Week and Space Technology* 84:5 (Jan. 31, 1966), pp. 42-46.

1484 Porter, D.G. "Is This a Limited War?" *Commonweal* 85 (Mar. 24, 1967), pp. 9-11.

1485 Rolph, Hammond. *Vietnamese Communism and the Protracted War.* Chicago: American Bar Association Standing Committee on Education About Communism and Its Contract with Liberty under Law, 1971.

1486 Sams, Kenneth. "Air Power: The Decisive Weapon." *Air Force and Space Digest* 49 (Mar. 1966), pp. 69-83.

1487 Sights, Col. A.P., Jr. "Graduated Pressure in Theory and Practice." *U.S. Naval Institute Proceedings* 96:7 (1970), pp. 40-45.

1488 Stillman, Edmund. "Smart Bombs and Dumb Strategy." *Saturday Review of the Society* 55:31 (July 29, 1972), pp. 27-32.

1489 Stilwell, R.G. "Evolution in Tactics–The Vietnam Experience." *Army* 20:2 (Feb. 1970), pp. 14-21.

1490 Swenson, M.F. "The Vietnamese War: A Case of Misjudged Staying Power." *Air Force and Space Digest* 50 (Dec. 1967), pp. 42-44.

1491 Taylor, Gen. M.D. "Post-Vietnam Role of the Military in Foreign Policy." *Air University Review* 19:5 (1968), pp. 50-58.

1492 Thompson, Robert. " 'What Went Wrong?' The Failure of American Strategy in Vietnam." *Interplay* 2:9 (1969), pp. 13-16.

1493 Trager, F.N. "Vietnam: The Military Requirements for Victory." *Orbis* 8 (Fall 1964), pp. 563-583.

1494 U.S. House of Representatives. Committee on Armed Services. Hearings; *Military Posture.* [Mar-Aug 1969] 91st Cong., 1st Sess., 1969.

1495 U.S. Senate. Committee on Armed Services. Hearings; *Investigation of the Preparedness Program on the Situation in South Vietnam as it Relates to:* I. *The Enemy Threat;* II. *Free World Forces (other than U.S.);* III. *Revolutionary Development Program;* IV. *The Economy of South Vietnam.* 90th Cong., 1st Sess., 1967.

1496 U.S. Senate. Committee on Foreign Relations. Hearings; *Moral and Military Aspects of the War in South East Asia.* [May 7, 12, 1970] 91st Cong., 2d Sess., 1970.

1497 "Viet Nam: From Tactical Victories to Strategic Defeat?" *Orbis* 11 (Spring 1967), pp. 14-18.

1498 *Visions of Victory: Selected Vietnamese Communist Military Writings.* Ed. by P.J. McGarvey. (Hoover Institution Publication No. 81). Stanford: Hoover Institution, 1969.

1499 Weller, J. *Fire and Movement: Bargain Basement Warfare in the Far East.* New York: Crowell, 1967.

1500 West, Francis J., Jr. "Stingray '70." *U.S. Naval Institute Proceedings* 95:11 (1969), pp. 26-37.

1501 Witze, C. "How Not to Win." *Air Force Magazine* 53:12 (Dec. 1970), pp. 10-12.

A.2 / The Generals

1502 Clark, Blair. "Westmoreland Appraised: Questions and Answers." *Harper's* (Nov. 1970), pp. 96-101.

1503 Devillers, Philippe. "Vietnam: The Generals Sing an Old Song." *Nation* 205 (Sept. 18, 1967), pp. 233-238.

1504 Furgurson, E.B. *Westmoreland: The Inevitable General.* Boston: Little, Brown, 1968.

1505 Leinster, Colin. "The Two Wars of General Lew Walt." *Life* 62 (May 26, 1967), pp. 77-84.

1506 "Viet Nam: The Generals Speak." *Survival* 9 (Feb. 1967), pp. 52-62.

1507 Weller, Jac. "Wellington against Abrams: Were the Old Ways Better?" *Army Quarterly and Defense Journal* (Great Britain) 100:1 (1970), pp. 60-70.

1508 Westmoreland, William C. "General Westmoreland Reports on Vietnam War: Interview with the U.S. Commander." *U.S. News & World Report* 61 (Nov. 28, 1966), pp. 44-49.

1509 ——. "Progress Report on the War in Viet-Nam." *U.S. Department of State Bulletin* 57 (Dec. 11, 1967), pp. 785-788.

1510 ——. "A Report to the Congress by the Commander of U.S. Military Forces in Vietnam." *U.S. Department of State Bulletin* 56 (May 15, 1967), pp. 738-741.

1511 ——. "Year-End Report: No Mission Impossible." *Army* 18:11 (Nov. 1968), pp. 27-30, 45.

1512 Wheeler, Earle G. "The Challenge Came in Vietnam." *Vital Speeches* 33 (Dec. 16, 1966), pp. 130-133.

1513 ——. "The U.S. Achievements in Viet-Nam." *U.S. Department of State Bulletin* 56 (Feb. 6, 1967), pp. 186-192.

A.3 / Guerrilla Warfare

1514 Browne, Malcolm W. *The New Face of War.* New York: Bobbs-Merrill, 1965.

1515 Buchanan, W.J., and R.A. Hyatt. "Capitalizing on Guerrilla Vulnerabilities." *Military Review* 48:8 (1968), pp. 3-40.

1516 Burchett, Wilfred G. *Vietnam: Inside Story of the Guerrilla War.* New York: International Publishers, 1965.

1517 Calvert, J.M. "The Pattern of Guerrilla Warfare." *Military Review* 46:7 (1966), pp. 13-18.

1518 Cooper, Bert, et al. *Case Studies in Insurgency and Revolutionary Warfare: Vietnam, 1941-1954.* Washington, D.C.: Special Operations Research Office, American University, 1964.

1519 Cross, James Eliot. *Conflict in the Shadows: The Nature and Politics of Guerrilla War.* New York: Doubleday, 1963.

1520 Deutch, M.J. "The Economics of Insurgency." *Vietnam Perspectives* 2:4 (1967), pp. 3-10.

1521 Furlong, W.B. "Training for the Front-All-Around-You War." *New York Times Magazine* (Oct. 24, 1965), p. 184.

1522 Gastil, R.D. *Four Papers on the Vietnamese Insurgency.* New York: Hudson Institute, 1967.

1523 Greene, Lt. Col. T.N., ed. *The Guerrilla—and How to Fight Him.* New York: Praeger, 1962.

1524 Guevara, Ernesto Che. *Guerrilla Warfare.* New York: Monthly Review, 1961.

1525 Harrigan, Anthony. *A Guide to the War in Viet Nam.* Boulder, Colorado: Panther Publications, 1966.

1526 Hilsman, Roger. "American Response to the Guerrilla." *Chicago Today* 4:2 (1967), pp. 34-39.

1527 Mao Tse-tung. *Basic Tactics.* Trans. and intro. by S.R. Schram. New York: Praeger, 1966.

1528 Paige, J.M. "Inequality and Insurgency in Vietnam: A Re-Analysis." *World Politics* 23:1 (1970), pp. 24-37.

1529 Paret, Peter, and John W. Shy. *Guerrillas in the 1960s.* rev. ed. New York: Praeger, 1962.

1530 Prosser, Major L.F. "The Bloody Lessons of Indochina." *The Army Combat Forces Journal* 5 (June 1955), pp. 23-30.

1531 Reinhardt, G.C. *Guerrilla-Combat Strategy and Deterrence in Southeast Asia.* Santa Monica, California: Rand, P-2706, Jan. 1964.

1532 Russell, C.A., and R.E. Hildner. "The Role of Communist Ideology in Insurgency." *Air University Review* (Jan-Feb 1971), pp. 42-48.

1533 Sansom, Robert L. *The Economics of Insurgency in the Mekong Delta of Vietnam.* Cambridge, Massachusetts: M.I.T. Press, 1970.

1534 Simpson, H.R. "Offshore Guerrilla War." *Naval War College Review* 22:2 (1969), pp. 17-20.

1535 Sparks, Will. "Guerrillas in Vietnam." *Commonweal* 76 (June 29, 1962), pp. 343-346.

1536 Taber, Robert. *The War of the Flea: A Study of Guerrilla Warfare Theory and Practice.* New York: Lyle Stuart, 1965.

A.4 / Counterinsurgency

1537 Clutterbuck, Richard L. *The Long, Long War: Counterinsurgency in Malaya and Vietnam.* New York: Praeger, 1966.

1538 Duncan, Donald. *The New Legions* [Green Berets]. New York: Random House, 1967.

1539 Farmer, J. *Counterinsurgency: Principles and Practices in Viet-Nam.* Santa Monica, California: Rand, P-3039, Dec. 1964.

1540 ——. *Counterinsurgency: Vietnam 1962-1963.* Santa Monica, California: Rand, P-2778, Aug. 1963.

1541 "The Green Berets, Special Report." *The Sunday Times Magazine* (London), (Nov. 9, 1969).

1542 Joiner, C.A. "The Ubiquity of the Administrative Role in Counterinsurgency." *Asian Studies* 7 (Aug. 1967), pp. 540-554.

1543 McMahon, Richard A. "The Indirect Approach." *Army* (Aug. 1969), pp. 56-63.

1544 Pohle, V., and C. Menges. *Time and Limited Success as Enemies of the Viet Cong.* Santa Monica, California: Rand, P-3491, Oct. 1967.

1545 Pustay, John S. *Counterinsurgency Warfare.* New York: Free Press, 1965.

1546 Rolland, Pierre. *Countre-Guerrilla.* Paris: Louvois, 1956.

1547 Smythe, Donald. "Pershing and Counterinsurgency." *Military Review* 46:9 (1966), pp. 85-92.

1548 Sochurek, H. "American Special Forces in Action in Vietnam." *National Geographic* 127:1 (Jan. 1965), pp. 38-64.

1549 Tanham, G.K., and D.J. Duncanson. "Some Dilemmas of Counterinsurgency." *Foreign Affairs* 48 (Oct. 1969), pp. 113-122.

1550 Thompson, Robert. *Defeating Communist Insurgency: The Lessons of Malaya and Vietnam.* New York: Praeger, 1966.

1551 Tringuier, Roger. *Modern Warfare: A French View of Counterinsurgency.* New York: Praeger, 1964.

1552 Weed, A.C., II. "Army Special Forces and Vietnam." *Military Review* 49:8 (1969), pp. 63-68.

1553 Wood, John S., Jr. "Counterinsurgency Coordination at the National and Regional Level." *Military Review* 46:3 (1966), pp. 80-85.

1554 Wren, Christopher. "The Facts Behind the Green Beret Myth." *Look* 30 (Nov. 1, 1966), pp. 28-36.

A.5 / Search & Destroy

1555 Baxter, Gordon. *13/13, Vietnam: Search and Destroy.* Cleveland, Ohio: World, 1967.

1556 Beshore, B.T. "The Name of the Game is 'Search and Destroy.'" *Army* 17:2 (Feb. 1967), pp. 56-59.

1557 Blacker, Irwin R. *Search and Destroy.* New York: Random House, 1966.

1558 McEnery, J.W. "'Mainstreet': A Successful Cordon and Search." *Armor* 78 (Jan/Feb 1969), pp. 36-39.

1559 Roberts, G. "Search and Destroy Follows New Tactics." *New York Times* (Sept. 10, 1968), pp. 1-2.

A.6 / Pacification & Strategic Hamlets

1560 Allen L.A. "The U.S. and Southeast Asia: Pacification in Quang Tri." *New Leader* 47:12 (1964), pp. 9-12.

1561 Buttinger, Joseph. "How to 'Pacify' Vietnam." *War/Peace Report* 7 (June/July 1967), pp. 8-9.

1562 Corson, W.R. "Pacification Program." In *The Vietnam War: Its Conduct and Higher Management.* Washington, D.C.: Center for Strategic Studies, Georgetown University, 1968.

1563 Cushman, J.H. "Pacification: Concepts Developed in the Field by the RVN 21st Infantry Division." *Army* 16 (Mar. 1966), pp. 21-29.

1564 Donnell, John C. "Pacification Reassessed." *Asian Survey* 7 (Aug. 1967), pp. 567-576.

1565 Duncanson, D.J. "Pacification and Democracy in South Vietnam." *World Today* 23 (Oct. 1967), pp. 410-418.

1566 Dunn, J.F. "A New Look at Pacification." *Military Review* 50:1 (1970), pp. 84-87.

1567 Elliott, D.W.P., and W.A. Stewart. *Pacification and the Viet Cong System in Dinh Tuong: 1966-1967.* Santa Monica, California: Rand, RM-5788-ISA/ARPA, Jan. 1969.

1568 Ellsberg, D. *The Day Loc Tien Was Pacified.* Santa Monica, California: Rand, P-3793, Feb. 1968.

1569 Glick, E.B. "Military Civic Action: Thorny Art of the Peace Keepers." *Army* 17:9 (Sept. 1967), pp. 67-70.

1570 Goodman, A.E. *Government and the Countryside: Political Accommodation and South Vietnam's Communal Groups.* Santa Monica, California: Rand, P-3924, Sept. 1968.

1571 Higgins, J.W. *Temporary Villages for Refugees: Costs, Problems, and Opportunities.* Santa Monica, California: Rand, RM-5444-ISA/ARPA, Aug. 1968.

1572 Komer, R.W. "Clear, Hold and Rebuild." *Army* 20:5 (May 1970), pp. 16-24.

1573 ——. *Impact of Pacification on Insurgency in South Vietnam.* Santa Monica, California: Rand, P-4443, Aug. 1970.

1574 ——. "Impact of Pacification on Insurgency in South Vietnam." *Journal of International Affairs* 25:1 (1971), pp. 48-69.

1575 Martin, J.A. "Operation Helping Hand." *U.S. Naval Institute Proceedings* 96:10 (Oct. 1970), pp. 99-100.

1576 Meyerson, Harvey. *Vinh Long.* Boston: Houghton, Mifflin, 1970.

1577 Mitchell, E.J. *Land Tenure and Rebellion: A Statistical Analysis of Factors Affecting Government Control in South Vietnam.* Santa Monica, California: Rand, RM-5181-ARPA (Abridged), June 1967.

1578 Nguyen Zuan Lai. "The Failure of 'Pacification.'" *Vietnamese Studies* 20 (Dec. 1968), pp. 191-253.

1579 Nighswanger, W.A. *Rural Pacification in Vietnam.* New York: Praeger, 1967.

1580 O'Donnell, J.B. "The Strategic Hamlet Program in Kien Hoa Province, South Vietnam: A Case Study of Counterinsurgency." In Peter Kunstadter, ed., *Southeast Asian Tribes, Minorities and Nations.* Princeton: Princeton University Press, 1967, pp. 703-744.

1581 Olsen, A.N. "Teaming Up to Build a Nation." *U.S. Naval Institute Proceedings* 95:10 (1969), pp. 34-43.

1582 Osborne, M.E. *Strategic Hamlets in South Vietnam: A Survey and a Comparison.* Data Paper number 55, Southeast Asia Program, Cornell University, Apr. 1965.

1583 Pool, Ithiel de Sola. "Further Thoughts on Rural Pacification and Insurgency." *Peace Research Society (International) Papers* 10 (1968), pp. 23-35.

1584 Posterman, R.L. "Land Reform in South Vietnam: A Proposal for Turning the Tables on the Viet Cong." *Cornell Law Review* 53 (Nov. 1967), pp. 26-44.

1585 "Rebuilding a Nation in the Midst of War." *Army* 20:10 (Oct. 1970), pp. 111-116.

1586 Reston, J. "We May Win the War but Lose the People." *New York Times Magazine* (Sept. 12, 1965), pp. 42-43.

1587 Rowe, T.E. "More Precious Than Bullets." *Army* 21:3 (Mar. 1971), pp. 38-44.

1588 Schell, Jonathan. *The Village of Ben Suc.* New York: Knopf, 1967.

1589 Shaplen, Robert. "A Reporter in Vietnam: The Delta, the Plateau, and the Mountains." *The New Yorker* (Aug. 11, 1962), pp. 48-77ff.

1590 Smith, W.A. "Strategic Hamlets in Vietnam." *Military Review* 44:5 (1964), pp. 17-23.

1591 Starner, Frances, and Ben Tre. "Pacification in South Vietnam: Any Umbrellas?" *Far Eastern Economic Review* 69:28 (1970), pp. 19-20, 69-71.

1592 Tormey, J.H. "Arteries of Pacification." *Army* 17:8 (Aug. 1967), pp. 59-60.

1593 U.S. House of Representatives. Committee on Armed Services. Report; *Progress of the Pacification Program.* [Feb. 9, 1970] 91st Cong., 2d Sess., 1970.

1594 U.S. House of Representatives. Committee on Foreign Affairs. Hearings; *Rural Development in Asia.* 2 parts. [Feb-May 1967] 90th Cong., 1st Sess., 1967.

1595 ——. Report; *Measuring Hamlet Security in Vietnam.* Report No. 91-25. [by J.V. Tunney, Feb. 25, 1969] 91st Cong., 1st Sess., 1969.

1596 U.S. Marine Corps. *U.S. Marine Corps Civic Action Efforts in Vietnam, March 1965-March 1966.* [by Capt. R.H. Stolfi] Washington, D.C.: Historical Branch, U.S. Marine Corps, 1968.

1597 U.S. Senate. Committee on Foreign Relations. Hearings; *Vietnam: Policy and Prospects, 1970.* [on Civil Operations and Rural Development Support Programs] 91st Cong., 2d Sess., 1970.

1598 Warner, Denis. "Vietnam: The Ordeal of Pacification." *Reporter* 35:9 (1966), pp. 25-28.

1599 Welsh, David. "Pacification in Vietnam." *Ramparts* 6:3 (1967), pp. 36-41.

1600 West, F.J., Jr. "The Fast Rifles: A Strategy for Grassroots Pacification in Vietnam." *Public and International Affairs* 5:1 (1967), pp. 99-109.

1601 Weyand, F.C. "Winning the People in Hau Nghia Province." *Army* 17 (Jan. 1967), pp. 52-55.

1602 Zasloff, Joseph. "Rural Resettlement in South Vietnam: The Agroville Program." *Pacific Affairs* 35 (Winter 1962-63), pp. 327-340.

1603 ——. *Rural Resettlement in Vietnam: An Agroville in Development.* Saigon: Michigan State University Vietnam Advisory Group, 1961.

A.7 / Military Intelligence

1604 Bennett, D.G. "Intelligence, Vietnam." *Military Review* 46 (Aug. 1966), pp. 72-77.

1605 Girouard, R.J. "District Intelligence in Vietnam." *Armor* 75 (Nov/Dec 1966), pp. 10-14.

1606 Heilbrun, Otto. "Tactical Intelligence in Vietnam." *Military Review* 48 (Oct. 1968), pp. 85-87.

1607 Martinsen, Peter. "Interrogating Prisoners." *Liberation* 12:9 (1967/68), pp. 14-31.

1608 Sahlins, Marshall. "The Best Torture: 'Once You've Broken Him Down. . . .' " *Nation* 201 (Oct. 25, 1965), pp. 266-269.

1609 Seagraves, R.W.A. "NILO–The Naval Intelligence Liaison Officer in Vietnam." *U.S. Naval Institute Proceedings*, 94:12 (Dec. 1968), pp. 145-146.

A.8 / Military Logistics

1610 Arnold, E.R. "Signal Communications in Vietnam." *Military Review* 47 (Mar. 1967). pp. 92-96.

1611 Brownlow, C. "Aircraft Variety Marks Airlift to Vietnam." *Aviation Week and Space Technology* 86:20 (May 15, 1967), pp. 76-79.

1612 ——. "Tactical Air Lift Vital to Forces in Field." *Aviation Week and Space Technology* 82:22 (May 31, 1965), pp. 78-82.

1613 Burke, R.L. "Corps Logistic Planning in Vietnam." *Military Review* 49 (Aug. 1969), pp. 3-11.

1614 Hanks, J. "Engineers in Vietnam: Builders and Fighters." *Army* 23:10 (Oct. 1968), pp. 57-62.

1615 Hickman, W. "Vietnam Communications Network Growing Into Southeast Asia's Best." *Electronics* 39:20 (Oct. 3, 1966), pp. 167-170.

1616 Hoefling, J.A. "Outflanking the Terminal Complex; The Way to Total Mobility." *Army* 17:4 (Apr. 1967), pp. 34-41.

1617 Hooper, E.B. "The Service Force, Pacific Fleet, in Action." *Naval Review* (1968), pp. 116-127.

1618 Huff, K.P. "Building the Advanced Base at Da Nang." *Naval Review* (1968), pp. 89-113.

1619 Kendall, L.C. "U.S. Merchant Shipping and Vietnam." *Naval Review* (1968), pp. 129-147.

1620 King, H.T. "Naval Logistic Support, Qui Nhon to Phu Quoc." *Naval Review* (1969), pp. 86-111.

1621 McKinney, J.B. "Signal Planning Needs Innovators." *Army* 18:3 (Mar. 1968), pp. 36-42.

1622 Merdinger, C.J. "Civil Engineers, Seabees, and Bases in Vietnam." *U.S. Naval Institute Proceedings* 96:5 (May 1970), pp. 256-275.

1623 Newport, H.S. "Inventory Control in the Combat Zone." *Army* 17:8 (Aug. 1967), pp. 61-64.

1624 Oliver, E.F. "A Chain of Ships." *U.S. Naval Institute Proceedings* 95:11 (1969), pp. 92-107.

1625 Resor, S.R. "Number One Objective Is Support of Vietnam Forces." *Armed Forces Management* 12:2 (Nov. 1965), pp. 40-41.

1626 Scholin, A.R. "Logistics: Lifeline to Southeast Asia." *Air Force and Space Digest* 48:2 (1965), pp. 42-44, 47-48.

1627 Soper, J.B. "A View from FMF Pac of Logistics in the Western Pacific." *U.S. Naval Institute Proceedings* 98:5 (May 1972), pp. 224-239.

1628 Swindler, M.G. "Base Depot Upgrade." *Ordnance* 56:308 (Sept-Oct 1971), pp. 143-146.

1629 U.S. House of Representatives. Committee on Armed Services. Report; *Military Construction Requirements in Southeast Asia.* [Mar. 11, 1970] 91st Cong., 2d Sess., 1970.

1630 U.S. House of Representatives. Committee on Government Operations. Hearings; *Military Supply Systems, 1969.* 91st Cong., 1st Sess., 1969.

1631 Williams, R.C. "How to Succeed in the Construction Business by Really Trying." *U.S. Naval Institute Proceedings* 95:9 (1969), pp. 70-80.

B / Combat Operations

B.1 / General

1632 *American Failure and Dry Season Offensives.* (Vietnamese Studies, No. 20). San Francisco: China Books and Periodicals, 1971.

1633 Amos, H.O. "Artillery Support of Vietnamese." *Military Review* 46:8 (1966), pp. 30-41.

1634 Burrows, Larry. "New U.S. Front in a Widening War: The Delta, Steamy, Teeming Heartland of the Vietcong." *Life* 62 (Jan. 13, 1967), pp. 22-31.

1635 Coleman, J.D. "Saturation Patrolling." *Army* 17:12 (Dec. 1967), pp. 54-57.

1636 Dalby, M.C. "Operations in Vietnam." *Royal United Service Institution Journal* 111:641 (Feb. 1966), pp. 4-13.

1637 Dickerson, Sherwood. "A Taste of What's to Come in the Ugly Delta War." *Reporter* 36:4 (1967), pp. 37-39.

1638 Donovan, Hedley. "Vietnam: Slow, Tough, but Coming Along." *Life* 62 (June 2, 1967), pp. 68-77.

1639 Fitzgerald, F. "Life and Death of a Vietnamese Village." *New York Times Magazine* (Sept. 4, 1966), p. 4.

1640 Flint, R.K. "Campaigning with the Infantry in Vietnam." *Air Force Magazine* 53:8 (Aug. 1970), pp. 47-51.

1641 Fourniau, C. *Le Vietnam: face à la guerre.* Paris: 1966.

1642 Gunderman, G.L. "Ambush." *Armor* 76:3 (1967), pp. 15-19.

1643 Gusmith, H.R. "Messages Sent in Symbols Will Link Multilingual Troops." *Electronics* 39:15 (July 25, 1966), pp. 108-112.

1644 Hackworth, D.H. "Battle Analysis: The Truth of Battle Can Be Learned only from the Soldiers Who Fight It." *Army* 17:7 (July 1967), pp. 33-35.

1645 Harris, M.M. "First Team Moves South." *Army* 19:5 (May 1969), pp. 43-48.

1646 Harrigan, Anthony. "Ground Warfare in Vietnam." *Military Review* 47 (Apr. 1967), pp. 60-67.

1647 Hughes, D.R. "Clean Sweep on Election Day." *Army* 18:5 (May 1968), pp. 40-46.

1648 Humphrey, Capt. V.W. "The Dragoon Concept." *Military Review* (Jan. 1972), pp. 17-25.

1649 Marshall, S.L.A. "Men Facing Death: The Destruction of an American Platoon." *Harper's Magazine* (Sept. 1966), pp. 47-57.

1650 McCaffrey, W.J. "Vietnam in 1970: Year of Transition." *Army* 20:10 (Oct. 1970), pp. 95-109.

1651 Mildren, F.T. "From Mekong to DMZ: A Fighting Year for the U.S. Army's Best." *Army* 18:11 (Nov. 1968), pp. 83-95.

1652 Moser, Don, and C. Rentmeester. "Battle Jump: U.S. Paratroopers in a Stepped-up War." *Life* 62 (Mar. 10, 1967), pp. 72-77.

1653 "Mounted Combat in Vietnam." *Armor* 77:4 (1968), pp. 9-17, 57-62.

1654 Nguyen Van Hieu. "Eye-witness Report from War Zone C." *Minority of One* 9 (July/Aug 1967), pp. 22-24.

1655 Pisor, R.L. "Saigon's Fighting MP's." *Army* 18:4 (Apr. 1968), pp. 37-41.

1656 Pruden, W., Jr. *Vietnam: The War.* New York: Dow Jones, 1965.

1657 Pscherer, S.W. "Learning from Charlie." *Army* 18:7 (July 1968), pp. 53-57.

1658 Raine, David. "Vietnam: A Night Ambush." *Contemporary Review* 208 (May 1966), pp. 237-239.

1659 Raymond, J. "When G.I. Joe Meets Ol' Charlie." *New York Times Magazine* (July 25, 1965), pp. 4-5.

1660 Rigg, Robert B. *How to Stay Alive in Vietnam.* Harrisburg, Pennsylvania: Stackpole, 1966.

1661 Rose, J.A. "I'm Hit! I'm Hit!" *Saturday Evening Post* 236:11 (Mar. 23, 1963), pp. 34-47.

1662 Sack, J.M. "An Account of One Company of American Soldiers." *Esquire* (Oct. 1966), pp. 79-86, 140-164.

1663 Schell, Jonathan. *The Military Half: An Account of Destruction in Quang Ngai and Quang Tin.* New York: Vintage, 1968.

1664 Smith, R.W., and N.L. Tiller, Sr. "Hole-Hunting for Dragon's Teeth." *Army* 19:8 (Aug. 1969), pp. 50-53.

1665 Tully, W.B., Jr. "Company B." *Armor* 76:5 (1967), pp. 12-19.

1666 U.S. Department of Army. *Guide to Selected Viet Cong Equipment and Explosive Devices.* (No. 381-11). Washington, D.C.: U.S. Government Printing Office, 1966.

1667 U.S. Pacific Command. *Report on the War in Vietnam (as of June 30, 1968).* Section I: (Admiral U.S.G. Sharp, Commander in Chief, Pacific) *Report on Air and Naval Campaigns Against North Vietnam and Pacific Command-wide Support of the War, June 1964-July 1968;* Section II: (General W.C. Westmoreland, Commander, U.S. Military Assistance Command, Vietnam) *Report on Operations in South Vietnam, January 1964-June 1968.* Washington, D.C.: U.S. Government Printing Office, 1968.

B.2 / Battles

1668 Albright, John, et al. *Seven Firefights in Vietnam.* Washington, D.C.: U.S. Government Printing Office, 1970.

1669 Chamberlain, E.W., Jr. "The Assault at Ap Bac." *Army* 18:9 (1968), pp. 50-57.

1670 Cushman, J.H. "How We Did It in Thua Thien." *Army* 20:5 (1970), pp. 48-54.

1671 Donlon, Roger, and Warren Rogers. "The Battle for Nam Dong." *Saturday Evening Post* 238:21 (1965), pp. 38-42, 46-53.

1672 Garretson, R.B., Jr. "The Battle of Binh An." *Armor* 78 (July/Aug 1969), pp. 25-28.

1673 Grogan, T.L. "The Battle of An Bao II." *Armor* 78 (July/Aug 1969), pp. 29-31.

1674 Heiberg, E.R. "Closing the Plei Trap Road." *Military Review* 49:7 (1969), pp. 83-88.

1675 Hofmann, R.A. "The Affray at Slope 30." *Armor* 77:1 (1968), pp. 13-18.

1676 Kinnard, H.W.O. "A Victory in the La Drang: The Triumph of a Concept." *Army* 17:9 (Sept. 1967), pp. 71-91.

1677 Marshall, S.L.A. *Ambush; The Battle of Dau Tieng; Also Called the Battle of Dong Minh Chau, War Zone C, Operation Attleboro, and Other Deadfalls in South Vietnam.* New York: Cowles, 1969.

1678 ——. *Battles in the Monsoon: Campaigning in the Central Highland, South Vietnam, Summer 1966.* New York: Morrow, 1966.

1679 ——. *Bird: The Christmastide Battle.* New York: Cowles, 1968.

1680 ——. *West to Cambodia.* New York: Cowles, 1968.

1681 Mataxis, T.C. "War in the Highlands." *Army* 15:15 (1965), pp. 49-55.

1682 Meissner, J.P. "The Battle of Duc Lap." *Army* 19:5 (1969), pp. 50-56.

1683 Mirsky, Jonathan. "The Tombs of Ben Suc: 'Too Blind Stupid to See.' " *Nation* 205 (Oct. 23, 1967), pp. 397-400.

1684 Peatross, O.F. "Application of Doctrine: Victory at Van Tuong Village." *Naval Review* (1967), pp. 2-13.

1685 Schlitz, W.P. "The Siege of Ben Het." *Air Force and Space Digest* 52 (Aug. 1969), pp. 48-49.

1686 Shepherd, Jack. "American Militarism: Incident at Van Duong." *Look* 33 (Aug. 12, 1969), pp. 26-31.

B.3 / Battle for Khe Sanh

1687 Duncan, David Douglas. "Khe Sanh." *Life* 64 (Feb. 23, 1968), pp. 20-31.

1688 Galvin, J.R. "The Relief of Khe Sanh." *Military Review* 50:1 (1970), pp. 88-94.

1689 Herr, Michael. "Conclusion at Khesanh." *Esquire* 72 (Oct. 1969), pp. 118-123, 202.

1690 ——. "Khesanh." *Esquire* 72 (Sept. 1969), pp. 118-123, 150.

1691 McLaughlin, B.W. "Khe Sanh: Keeping an Outpost Alive: An Appraisal." *Air University Review* 20:1 (1968), pp. 57-77.

1692 Sayle, M. "The Relief of Khe Sanh: How 80,000 Tons of Bombs Saved the Marines." *London Sunday Times* (Apr. 14, 1967), pp. 6-7.

1693 Shore, M.S. *The Battle for Khe Sanh.* Washington, D.C.: Historical Branch, G-3 Division, Headquarters, U.S. Marine Corps, 1969.

B.4 / Helicopter Tactics

1694 Brownlow, C. "Helicopter Tactics Shaped by Experience." *Aviation Week and Space Technology* 86:22 (May 31, 1965), pp. 67-76.

1695 Famiglietti, G. "The Chopper War in Vietnam." *Aerospace International* 3 (July-Aug 1967), pp. 20-28.

1696 Haid, Maj. D.J. "How to Shoot a Duck [armed helicopters]." *Military Review* 45:9 (1965), pp. 3-12.

1697 Hammer, A. "Better Guns for Choppers." *Ordnance* 56:308 (Sept-Oct 1971), pp. 138-142.

1698 Hampe, D.E. "Tactics and the Helicopter." *Military Review* 46:3 (1966), pp. 60-63.

1699 Jackson, Sen. Henry. "A Key to Victory in Vietnam [helicopters]." *Army* (Mar. 1963), pp. 22 ff.

1700 Mertel, K.D. "The Agility of Air Mobility." *Army* 17:5 (1967), pp. 26-30.

1701 Meyerson, Harvey. "Choppers and the New Kind of War." *Look* 32 (Apr. 30, 1968), pp. 92-100.

1702 Trueman, H.P. "The Helicopter and Land Warfare; Applying the Vietnam Experience." *Brassey's Annual 1971* (1971), pp. 190-204.

1703 Westmoreland, W.C. "A New Concept of Warfare." *Aerospace International* 3 (July-Aug 1967), p. 8.

1704 Witze, C. "The U.S. Army Flies to Fight and Win." *Aerospace International* 3 (July-Aug 1967), pp. 13-17.

B.5 / Riverine Forces

1705 Baker, J.W., and L.C. Dickson. "Army Forces in Riverine Operations." *Military Review* 47:8 (1967), pp. 64-74.

1706 Bates, C.C., G. Tselepis, and D. Von Nieda. "Needed: Shallow Thinking." *U.S. Naval Institute Proceedings* 94:11 (Nov. 1968), pp. 44-51.

1707 Chapelle, C. "Water War in Viet Nam." *National Geographic* (Feb. 1966), pp. 271-296.

1708 Conn, V. "The Brown Water Navy: A Story About U.S. Navymen Who Go Down the Rivers in Small Boats in Viet Nam." *Navy Magazine* 12:3 (Mar. 1969), pp. 18-22.

1709 Emery, T.R.M. "River Power." *U.S. Naval Institute Proceedings* 96:8 (Aug. 1970), pp. 117-121.

1710 Malone, P.B., III. "JTEBGIG: Delta Dance of Death." *Army* 19:7 (July 1969), pp. 48-52.

1711 Meyer, R.M. "The Ground-Sea Team in River Warfare." *Military Review* 46:9 (1966), pp. 54-61.

1712 Mumford, R.E. "Jackstay: New Dimensions in Amphibious Warfare." *Naval Review* (1968), pp. 69-87.

1713 "River Gunfire Support Ship." *U.S. Naval Institute Proceedings.* 94:2 (Feb. 1968), pp. 100-101.

1714 Smith, A.C., Jr. "Rung Sat Special Zone, Vietnam's Mekong Delta." *U.S. Naval Institute Proceedings* 94:4 (Apr. 1968), pp. 116-121.

1715 Spore, J.B. "Floating Assault Force: Scourge." *Army* 18:2 (Feb. 1968), pp. 28-32.

1716 Swarztrauber, S.A. "River Patrol Relearned." *U.S. Naval Institute Proceedings* 96:5 (May 1970), pp. 122-157.

1717 "U.S. Brown Water Navy Disbanded, Heads Home." *Navy Magazine* 12:10 (Oct. 1969), pp. 26-27.

1718 Well, W.C. "The Riverine Force in Action, 1966-1967." *Naval Review* (1969), pp. 48-83.

B.6 / Personal Accounts

1719 Biberman, Edward. "Vietnam: An Artist's View of War." *Mankind* 2:3 (1969), pp. 24-34.

1720 Briscoe, E.G. *Diary of a Short-timer in Vietnam.* New York: Vantage, 1970.

1721 Broughton, Col. Jack *Thud Ridge.* Philadelphia: Lippincott, 1969.

1722 Dudman, Richard. *Forty Days with the Enemy.* New York: Liveright, 1971.

1723 Duncan, D. "Memoirs of a Special Forces Hero: The Whole Thing Was a Lie." *Ramparts* (Feb. 1966), pp. 13-24.

1724 Duncan, David Douglas. *This Is War.* New York: Bantam, 1967.

1725 Glasser, Ronald J. *365 Days.* New York: Braziller, 1971.

1726 Herbert, Lt. Col. Anthony B. *Soldier.* New York: Holt, Rinehart & Winston, 1972.

1727 ——. "Soldier—A Memoir." *Ramparts* 11:7 (Jan. 1973), pp. 27-32, 50-52.

1728 Herr, M. "Hell Sucks: Impressions from the Only War We've Got." *Esquire* (Aug. 1968), pp. 66-69, 109-110.

1729 Hughes, Larry. *You Can See a Lot Standing under a Flare in the Republic of Vietnam: My Year at War.* New York: Morrow, 1969.

1730 Johnson, R.W. *Postmark: The Mekong Delta.* Westwood, New Jersey: Revell, 1968.

1731 Marks, R.E. *The Letters of Pfc. Richard E. Marks, USMC.* Philadelphia: Lippincott, 1967.

1732 O'Connor, John J. *A Chaplain Looks at Vietnam.* New York: World, 1968.

1733 Parks, David. *G.I. Diary.* New York: Harper and Row, 1968.

1734 Pickerell, James. *Vietnam in the Mud.* Indianapolis: Bobbs-Merrill, 1966.

1735 Reed, David. *Up Front in Vietnam.* New York: Funk and Wagnalls, 1967.

1736 Rosenberger, J.W. "How the Soldiers View Vietnam." *Progressive* 32 (Mar. 1968), pp. 22-24.

1737 Sadler, Barry. *I'm a Lucky One.* New York: Macmillan, 1967.

1738 Tucker, J.G. *Arkansas Men at War.* Little Rock, Arkansas: Pioneer Press, 1968.

C / Combat Forces

C.1 / U.S. Air Force

1739 "Air War in Vietnam: The Statistical Side." *Air Force and Space Digest* 50 (Mar. 1967), pp. 78-85.

1740 Anthis, R.H. "Airpower: The Paradox in Vietnam." *Air Force and Space Digest* 50 (Apr. 1967), pp. 34-38.

1741 Brownlow, C. "Pause Cuts Soaring Loss Rates." *Aviation Week and Space Technology* 89:3 (July 15, 1968), pp. 14-16.

1742 ——. "USAF Boosts North Viet ECM Jamming." *Aviation Week and Space Technology* (Feb. 6, 1967), pp. 22-24.

1743 ——. "U.S. to Boost Vietnam Air Commitment." *Aviation Week and Space Technology* 84:6 (Feb. 7, 1966), pp. 22, 24.

1744 Butz, J.S., Jr. "Those Bombings in North Vietnam." *Air Force and Space Digest* 49 (Apr. 1966), pp. 42-54.

1745 ——. "Hit 'em Where They Is!" *Air Force Magazine* 52:3 (Mar. 1969), pp. 64-68.

1746 Casey, W.R. "AC-119's Flying Battleship." *Air Force and Space Digest* 53:2 (Feb. 1970), pp. 48-50.

1747 Clelland, Don. "Air Interdiction: Its Changing Conditions." *Air Force and Space Digest* 52 (June 1969), pp. 52-56.

1748 Drendel, Lou. *The Air War in Vietnam.* New York: Arco, 1968.

1749 Greene, Jerry. "Airpower's Buildup in Vietnam." *Air Force and Space Digest* 48 (June 1965), pp. 33-43.

1750 Hai Thu. *North Vietnam Against U.S. Air Force.* Hanoi: 1967.

1751 Harvey, F. "Air War in Vietnam; Special Feature." *Flying* 79 (Nov. 1966), pp. 38-95.

1752 ——. *Air War: Vietnam.* New York: Bantam Books, 1967.

1753 Helmore, P.W. "Air Operations in Vietnam; I and II." *Royal United Service Institution Journal* 112:2 (Feb. 1967), pp. 16-31.

1754 Hense, Frank F.E., Jr. "Aircraft Maintenance Training for Southeast Asia." *Air University Review* 19:6 (1968), pp. 37-41.

1755 Kipp, R.M. "Counterinsurgency from 30,000 Feet: The B-52 in Vietnam." *Air University Review* 29:2 (1968).

1756 McGlasson, W.D. "Those Gung Ho Guardsmen in Vietnam." *Air Force and Space Digest* 51:11 (1968), pp. 191-196.

1757 Meyers, G.L. "Why Not More Targets in the North?" *Air Force and Space Digest* 50 (May 1967), pp. 74, 77-78.

1758 Plattner, C.M. "Force Buildup Keyed to Wider Escalation." *Aviation Week and Space Technology* 84:1 (Jan. 3, 1966), pp. 16-20.

1759 ——. "North Sortie Rate Pressed as Political Purpose Fails." *Aviation Week and Space Technology* 84:8 (Feb. 21, 1966), pp. 76-85.

1760 ——. "SAMs Spur Changes in Combat Tactics, New Equipment." *Aviation Week and Space Technology* 84:4 (Jan. 24, 1966), pp. 26-31.

1761 Sams, Kenneth. "The Air War in Vietnam: Countering Escalation." *Air Force and Space Digest* 48:12 (1965), pp. 72-73, 76, 79-80, 83.

1762 ——. "Tactical Air Support: Balancing the Scales." *Air Force and Space Digest* 48:8 (1965), pp. 37-40.

1763 Scholin, A.R. "Mission: Recce North." *Air Force and Space Digest* 51 (May 1968), pp. 42-46.

1764 ——. "U.S. Tactical Aircraft in Southeast Asia: A Gallery of Air Weapons in Vietnam." *Air Force Magazine* 50:3 (Mar. 1967), pp. 118-133.

1765 ——. "When the Iron Is Hot (Tac Air)." *Air Force and Space Digest* 50:12 (1967), pp. 64-68.

1766 Sights, A.P., Jr. "Tactical Bombing: The Unproved Element." *Air Force and Space Digest* 52 (July 1969), pp. 39-44.

1767 Simler, G.B. "North Vietnam's Air Defense System." *Air Force and Space Digest* 50 (May 1967), pp. 81-82.

1768 Sullivan, C.D. "Air War Against the North." In *The Vietnam War: Its Conduct and Higher Direction.* Washington, D.C.: Center for Strategic Studies, Georgetown University, 1968.

1769 Teplinsky, B. "The Air War Over Indochina." *International Affairs* (Moscow) 2 (Feb. 1967), pp. 40-47.

1770 "USAF, Navy Bombard MiG Installations at Hoa Lac, Key Bases in North Vietnam." *Aviation Week and Space Technology* 86:19 (May 8, 1967), pp. 18-23.

1771 U.S. House of Representatives. Committee on Armed Services. Hearings; *Close Air Support.* (Sept-Oct 1965) 89th Cong., 1st Sess., 1965.

1772 U.S. Senate. Committee on Armed Services. Hearings; *Air War Against North Vietnam.* (Aug. 16-29, 1967) 5 Parts. 90th Cong., 1st Sess., 1967.

1773 ——. Hearings; *U.S. Tactical Air Power Program.* (May-June 1968) 90th Cong., 2d Sess., 1968.

1774 Verrier, Anthony. "Strategic Bombing: The Lessons of World War II and the American Experience in Vietnam." *Royal United Service Institution Journal* 112 (May 1967), pp. 157-161.

1775 Weiss, G. "Tac Air: Present and Future Lessons, Problems, and Needs." *Armed Forces Journal* 109 (Sept. 1971), pp. 30-36.

1776 Witze, Claude. "What Kind of Air War in Vietnam?" *Air Force and Space Digest* 50 (Oct. 1967), pp. 42-46.

C.2 / U.S. Army

1777 Ashworth, S.T., III. "Armor Can Operate in the Delta." *Armor* 76:2 (1967), pp. 4-10.

1778 "Aviation: New Dimension for the U.S. Army in Vietnam." *Aerospace International* 3 (July-Aug 1967), pp. 7-8.

1779 Binder, L.J. "The Hundred Mile an Hour War." *Army* 19:3 (Mar. 1969), pp. 16-32.

1780 Engler, J.E. "U.S. Army Vietnam in 1966." *Army* 16 (Oct. 1966), pp. 105-110.

1781 Gibson, James M. "The Separate Brigade." *Military Review* 50:5 (1970), pp. 82-86.

1782 Harvey, T.H., Jr. "Air Cavalry in Battle: A New Concept in Action." *Armor* 77:3 (1968), pp. 5-10.

1783 Mertel, K.D. *Year of the Horse: Vietnam—1st Air Cavalry in the Highlands.* New York: Exposition Press, 1968.

1784 Quinn, Woodrow L. "Dogs in Counter-mine Warfare." *Infantry* (July-Aug 1971), pp. 16-18.

C.3 / U.S. Marine Corps

1785 Leftwich, W.G., Jr. ". . . and few Marines." *U.S. Naval Institute Proceedings* 94 (Aug. 1968), pp. 34-45.

1786 McCutcheon, K.B. "Marine Aviation in Vietnam, 1962-1970." *U.S. Naval Institute Proceedings* 97 (May 1971), pp. 123-155.

1787 Simmons, E.H. "Marine Corps Operations in Vietnam, 1965-1966." *Naval Review* (1968), pp. 2-35.

1788 ——. "Marine Corps Operations in Vietnam, 1967." *Naval Review* (1969), pp. 112-141.

1789 ——. "Marine Corps Operations in Vietnam, 1968." *U.S. Naval Institute Proceedings* 96:5 (1970), pp. 290-320.

C.4 / U.S. Navy

1790 Cagle, M.W. "Task Force 77 in Action off Vietnam." *U.S. Naval Institute Proceedings* 98:5 (May 1972), pp. 68-109.

1791 Carrison, D.J. "Influence of the Viet-Nam War." In *U.S. Navy.* New York: Praeger, 1968.

1792 Clapp, A.J. "Shu-fly Diary." *U.S. Naval Institute Proceedings* 89:10 (1963), pp. 42-53.

1793 Collins, F.C., Jr. "Maritime Support of the Campaign in I Corps." *U.S. Naval Institute Proceedings* 97:5 (May 1971), pp. 158-179.

1794 Gayle, G.D. "Naval Operations Supporting the Commitment." In *The Vietnam War; Its Conduct and Higher Management.* Washington, D.C.: Georgetown University, 1968.

1795 Hodgman, J.A. "Market Time in the Gulf of Thailand." *Naval Review* (1968), pp. 38-67.

1796 Middleton, W.D. "Seabees in Vietnam." *U.S. Naval Institute Proceedings* 93 (Aug. 1967), pp. 54-64.

1797 Miller, R.T. "Fighting Boats of the United States." *Naval Review* (1968), pp. 297-329.

1798 Moeser, Robert D. *U.S. Navy: Vietnam.* Annapolis, Maryland: U.S. Naval Institute, 1969.

1799 "Naval Gunfire Support." *U.S. Naval Institute Proceedings* 94:7 (July 1968), pp. 95-96.

1800 "Navy's Skywarrior Has New Role: Aerial Tanker over Tonkin Gulf." *Navy Magazine* 10:6 (June 1967), p. 37.

1801 "1967 Seventh Fleet Summary." *Naval Review* (1969), pp. 366-371.

1802 Padgett, H.E., and J.A. Garrow. "Saigon-The Navy Reported Today . . . ." *U.S. Naval Institute Proceedings* 95:4 (Apr. 1969), pp. 132-137.

1803 Plattner, C.M. "Combat Dictates Shift in Navy Tactics." *Aviation Week and Space Technology* 84:6 (Feb. 7, 1966), pp. 65-72.

1804 Powers, R.C. "Beans and Bullets for Sea Lords." *U.S. Naval Institute Proceedings* 96:12 (Dec. 1970), pp. 95-97.

1805 Rodgers, R.H. "America's Best Weapon." *U.S. Naval Institute Proceedings* 91:9 (Sept. 1968), pp. 106-108.

1806 Schreadley, R.L. "The Naval War in Vietnam 1950-1970." *U.S. Naval Institute Proceedings* 97:5 (May 1971), pp. 182-209.

1807 ——. "Sea Lords." *U.S. Naval Institute Proceedings* 96:8 (Aug. 1970), pp. 22-31.

1808 "Sea Power, 1966-1967." *Naval Review* (1968), pp. 291-292.

1809 Searle, W.F., Jr. "The Case for Inshore Warfare." *Naval Review* (1966), pp. 1-23.

1810 "Seventh Fleet's Sea Dragons Scorch North Viet Nam with Their Fire." *Navy Magazine* 10:6 (June 1967), pp. 38-39.

1811 Stephan, C.R. "Trawler!" *U.S. Naval Institute Proceedings* 94:9 (Sept. 1968), pp. 61-71.

1812 Torrance, H.S. "Naval and Maritime Events, 1 July 1967-30 June, 1968." *Naval Review* (1969), pp. 280-338.

1813 "U.S. Naval Operations Against North Vietnam, August 1964-November 1968." *Naval Review* (1969), pp. 360-362.

1814 U.S. Senate. Committee on Armed Services. Hearings; *Investigation of the Preparedness Program: U.S. Navy and U.S. Marine Corps in Southeast Asia.* 90th Cong., 1st Sess., 1967.

1815 Vito, A.H., Jr. "Carrier Air and Vietnam: An Assessment." *U.S. Naval Institute Proceedings* 93 (Oct. 1967), pp. 66-75.

1816 West, F.J. "Stingray '70." *U.S. Naval Institute Proceedings* 95:801 (Nov. 1969), pp. 27-28.

1817 Whitney, C.R. "Naval Gunfire in Vietnam." *Ordnance* 53:294 (May/June 1969), pp. 602-606.

1818 Winter, R.M. "Armor Afloat in Vietnam." *U.S. Naval Institute Proceedings* 94:11 (Nov. 1968), pp. 132-134.

1819 Yohanan, R.R. "Joint Training for Inshore Naval Operations." *U.S. Naval Institute Proceedings* 94:3 (Mar. 1968), pp. 130-132.

C.5 / Foreign Military Units

1820 "Allies Join the Parade Home." *U.S. News and World Report* 71 (July 19, 1971), p. 21.

1821 Burge, M.E.P. "Australian Gunners in South Vietnam." *Journal of the Royal Artillery* 95:2 (Sept. 1968), pp. 84-92.

1822 Kemp, Ian. *British G.I. in Vietnam.* London: Robert Hale, 1969.

1823 MacKay, Ian. *Australians in Vietnam.* Adelaide: Rigby, 1968.

1824 Marks, Thomas A. "Professionalism in the Royal Thai Army." *U.S. Naval Institute Proceedings* 99:1 (Jan. 1973), pp. 46-53.

1825 McNamara, E.G. "Australian Military Operations in Vietnam." *Royal United Services Institute Journal* 113:652 (Nov. 1968), pp. 310-316.

1826 Millar, T.B. "Australia and the War in Vietnam." *Brassey's Annual 1969* (1969), pp. 226-233.

1827 "Money for Men [Korean Troops]." *New Republic* 165 (Oct. 9, 1971), p. 1ff.

1828 Newman, K.E., ed. *The Anzac Battalion; A Record of the Tour of 2nd Battalion, The Royal Australian Regiment; 1st Battalion, the Royal New Zealand Infantry Regiment in South Vietnam, 1967-68.* 2 Vols. Brookvale, New South Wales: Printcraft Press, 1968.

1829 O'Neill, R.J. *Vietnam Task: The 5th Battalion; the Royal Australian Regiment, 1966/67.* Melbourne: Cassell, 1968.

1830 Rasmussen, R.R. "ROK Operations in Central Vietnam." *Military Review* 48 (Jan. 1968), pp. 51-55.

1831 Starner, F.L. "The White Horses [Korean Troops in Vietnam]." *Far Eastern Economic Review* 57 (Sept. 21, 1967), pp. 567-572.

1832 U.S. Senate. Committee on Armed Services. Hearings; *Investigation of the Preparedness Program; On the Situation in South Vietnam as It Relates to:* Part II: *Free World Forces (Other than U.S.).* 90th Cong., 1st Sess., 1967.

1833 "Vietnam Troop Contributors Hold Conference at Washington: Communiqué April 23, 1971." *U.S. Department of State Bulletin* 64 (May 17, 1971), pp. 635-638.

D / Weapons Policies & Practices

D.1 / General

1834 Coughlin, W.J., and M. Getler. "Report from Vietnam." *Missiles and Rockets* 18:13 (Mar. 28, 1966), pp. 44-70.

1835 Cushmac, G.E. "Enemy Napalm in Vietnam." *Army* 18:8 (1968), pp. 58-59.

1836 "DDR&E Looks for Solutions to Next Vietnam." *Space/Aeronautics* 46:5 (Oct. 1966), pp. 25, 30, 34.

1837 Fall, B.B. "Vietnam Blitz: A Report on the Impersonal War." *New Republic* 153 (Oct. 9, 1965), pp. 17-21.

1838 Famigletti, G. "Hardware Being Battle Tested in Vietnam." *Data* 12:5 (May 1967), pp. 18-21.

1839 "Fighting Guerrillas from the Lab." *Time* 69 (Oct. 7, 1966), pp. 69-70.

1840 Hackworth, D.H. "Target Acquisition: Vietnam Style." *Military Review* 48 (Apr. 1968), pp. 73-79.

1841 Hamlin, R.E. "Side-Firing Weapon Systems: A New Application of an Old Concept." *Air University Review* 21:2 (Jan-Feb 1970), pp. 77-88.

1842 Hymoff, E. "Stalemate in Indo-China: Technology vs. Guerrillas." *Bulletin of the Atomic Scientists* 27:9 (Nov. 1971), pp. 27-30.

1843 Jaubert, A. "Zapping the Viet Cong by Computer." *New Scientist* 53:789 (Mar. 30, 1972), pp. 685-688.

1844 Kalisch, R.B., and T.P. Baker, Jr. "DOD Basic Research and Limited Conflict." *Office of Aerospace Research Reviews* 7:7 (July 1968), pp. 10-11.

1845 Kanegis, A., et al. *Weapons for Counterinsurgency: Chemical/Biological, Antipersonnel, Incendiary.* Philadelphia: American Friends Service Committee, 1970.

1846 Kirchner, D.P. "Antiguerilla Armament." *Ordnance* 56:308 (Sept-Oct 1971), pp. 127-130.

1847 Leitenberg, Milton. "America in Vietnam: Statistics of a War." *Survival* 14:6 (1972), pp. 268-274.

1848 Ludwigsen, E.C. "The Technology Explosion and the Coming Generation of Army Weapons and Equipment." *Army* (Oct. 1969), pp. 147-158.

1849 Mason, J.F. "Jungle Fighters on Chesapeake Bay." *Electronics* 40:2 (Jan. 23, 1967), pp. 153-154, 158-159.

1850 ——. "The War that Needs Electronics." *Electronics* 39:10 (May 16, 1966), pp. 96-118.

1851 "New Weapons for Vietnam War." *U.S. News & World Report* 65 (Aug. 19, 1968), p. 75.

1852 "Pentagon Stresses Tactical Gear to Meet Needs of Vietnam Conflict." *Electronics* 40 (Jan. 9, 1967), pp. 135-138.

1853 Smith, D.A. "Educated Missiles." *Ordnance* 56:311 (Mar-Apr 1972), pp. 384-385.

1854 Takman, John. *Napalm: Streitschrift und Dokumentation.* Berlin: Union Verlag, 1968.

1855 "U.S. Army Weapons in Vietnam." *Interavia/International Defense Review* 3 (1967), pp. 256-261.

1856 Weiss, G. "AC-130 Gunships Destroy Trucks and Cargo." *Armed Forces Journal* 109:1 (Sept. 1971), pp. 18-19.

1857 Weller, J. "Good and Bad Weapons for Vietnam." *Military Review* 48:10 (Oct. 1968), pp. 57-64.

D.2 / Bombing

1858 Behar, Abraham. "I Bombardamenti di Obiettivi Civili nel Vietnam del Nord (The Bombing of Civilian Objectives in North Vietnam)." *Il Porte* (Italy) 23:7/8 (1967), pp. 897-913.

1859 Butz, J.S., Jr. "Airpower in Vietnam: The High Price of Restraint." *Air Force and Space Digest* 49:11 (1966), pp. 40-44.

1860 Chaliand, Gerard. "Bombing of Dai Lai." *Liberation* 12:9 (1967/68), pp. 67-69.

1861 Crichton, Robert. "Our Air War." *New York Review of Books* (Jan. 4, 1968), pp. 3-5.

1862 Drummond, S. "Korea and Vietnam: Some Speculations about the Possible Influences of the Korean War on American Policy in Vietnam." *Army Quarterly and Defense Journal* 97:1 (1968), pp. 65-71.

1863 Greene, Jerry. "U.S. Airpower in Vietnam: Scalpel Rather than Broadsword." *Air Force and Space Digest* 48 (May 1965), pp. 33-36.

1864 Hoeffding, O. *Bombing North Vietnam: An Appraisal of Economic and Political Effects.* Santa Monica, California: Rand, RM-5213-1-ISA, Dec. 1966.

1865 Lacoste, Yves. "Bombing the Dikes." *Nation* 215:10 (Oct. 9, 1972), pp. 298-301.

1866 Landau, David. "The Diplomacy of Terror: Behind the Decision to Bomb the Dikes." *Ramparts* 11:4 (Oct. 1972), pp. 21-25, 52-56.

1867 Littauer, Raphael, and Norman Uphoff, eds. *The Air War in Indochina.* Boston: Beacon, 1972.

1868 Osborne, John. "Bombs Away." *New Republic* (Jan. 6 & 13, 1973), pp. 14-15.

1869 Pfeiffer, E.W. "Land War, I: Craters." *Environment* 13:9 (Nov. 1971), pp. 1-5.

1870 Porter, D. Gareth. "Bombing the Dikes." *New Republic* (June 3, 1972), pp. 19-20.

1871 Russett, Bruce M. "Vietnam and Restraints on Aerial Warfare." *Ventures* 9:1 (1969), pp. 55-61.

1872 Saundby, Air Marshal Sir Robert. "The Ethics of Bombing." *Air Force and Space Digest* 50:6 (June 1967), pp. 48-50, 53.

1873 Slater, Philip. "Kill Anything that Moves [a reaction to Harvey's Air War–Vietnam]." In *The Pursuit of Loneliness: American Culture at the Breaking Point.* Boston: Beacon, 1970, pp. 29-52.

1874 "United States Bombing of Hanoi and Haiphong." *Current Notes on International Affairs* (Australia) 37:6 (1966), pp. 397-398.

1875 U.S. Senate. Committee on Foreign Relations. Staff Study No. 5: *Bombing as a Policy Tool in Vietnam: Effectiveness.* (Based on the Pentagon Papers, Oct. 12, 1972) 92d Cong., 2d Sess., 1972.

1876 Van Tien Dung. "People's War Against Air War of Destruction." *Vietnamese Studies* 20 (Dec. 1968), pp. 63-86.

1877 Vander Els, Theodore. "The Irresistible Weapon." *Military Review* 51:8 (1971), pp. 80-90.

1878 Ver Wey, W.D. "Bombing of the North after Tonkin and Pleiku: Reprisals?" *Revue Belge de Droit International* 5 (1969), pp. 460-479.

1879 Wald, George. "Our Bombs Fall on People." *Washington Monthly* (May 1972), pp. 8-10.

1880 Westing, A.H., and E.W. Pfeiffer. "The Cratering of Indochina." *Scientific American* 226:5 (May 1972), pp. 20-29.

D.3 / Electronic Battlefield

1881 Allman, T.D. "The Blind Bombers." *Far Eastern Economic Review* 75:5 (Jan. 29, 1972), pp. 18-20.

1882 "The Components and Manufacture of the Electronic Battlefield." *National Action/Research on the Military-Industrial Complex.* Philadelphia: American Friends Service Committee, 1971.

1883 "Congress Briefed on Electronic Battlefield." *Armed Forces Journal* 108:8 (Dec. 21, 1970), pp. 10-11.

1884 Dickson, P., and J. Rothchild. "The Electronic Battlefield: Wiring Down the War." *Washington Monthly* (May 1971), pp. 6-14.

1885 Frisbee, J.L. "Igloo White." *Air Force Magazine* 54:6 (June 1971), pp. 48-53.

1886 Haseltine, W. "The Automated Air War." *New Republic* (Oct. 16, 1971), pp. 15-17.

1887 Heiman, G. "Beep to Bang." *Armed Forces Management* (July 1970), pp. 36-39.

1888 Malloy, M. "The Death Harvesters." *Far Eastern Economic Review* 75:5 (Jan. 29, 1972), pp. 16-18.

1889 McClintic, R.G. "Rolling Back the Night." *Army* 19:8 (Aug. 1969), pp. 28-35.

1890 Norman, L. "McNamara's Fence: Our Eyes and Ears Along the DMZ." *Army* 18:8 (Aug. 1968), pp. 28-32.

1891 Proxmire, Sen. William. "Pentagon Conceals Facts on 3 Billion Dollar Electronic Battlefields." *Congressional Record* (Mar. 23, 1971), S 3618-22.

1892 Reid, M. "Turning Night into Day." *Electronics* 39:18 (Sept. 5, 1966), pp. 139-141.

1893 Seigel, L. "Vietnam's Electronic Battlefield." *Pacific Research and World Empire Telegram* 2 (Sept-Oct 1971), pp. 1-8.

1894 "Southeast Asia Sensor Fields: More Eyes and Ears." *Armed Forces Journal* (Mar. 1, 1971), pp. 38-39.

1895 U.S. Senate. Committee on Armed Services. Hearings; *Investigation into Electronic Battlefield Program.* 91st Cong., 2d Sess., 1970.

1896 Weiss, G.L. "Battle for Control of Ho Chi Minh Trail." *Armed Forces Journal* 108:12 (Feb. 15, 1971), pp. 18-22.

D.4 / Fire Storms

1897 "B-52's Drop Fire Bombs on Red Sanctuary Near Cambodia." *St. Louis Post Dispatch,* Jan. 28, 1967.

1898 "Blow to a Stronghold: Forest Fires Razing Red Haven." *St. Louis Post Dispatch,* Apr. 12, 1968.

1899 "Cong Flee Blazing Jungle Stronghold." *Sunday Times* (London), Apr. 14, 1968.

1900 Shapley, D. "Technology in Vietnam: Fire Storm Project Fizzled Out." *Science* 177 (July 21, 1972), pp. 239-241.

D.5 / Rome Plows

1901 Baldwin, H.W. "Rome Plow Helps Allies Clear Vietnam Jungles." *New York Times,* Jan. 12, 1968.

1902 Kiernan, J.M. "Combat Engineers in the Iron Triangle." *Army* 17:6 (June 1967), pp. 42-45.

1903 "Land Clearing Emerges as a Top Tactic of the War." *Engineering News Record* 184:3 (June 15, 1970), p. 27.

1904 Ploger, R.R. "Different War—Same Old Ingenuity." *Army* 18:9 (Sept. 1968), pp. 70-75.

1905 Westing, A.H. "Land War. II: Levelling the Jungle." *Environment* 13:9 (Nov. 1971), pp. 6-10.

1906 "When the Landscape is the Enemy." *Newsweek* (Aug. 7, 1972), p. 15.

D.6 / Weather Modification

1907 Kotsch, W.J. "Forecast: Change." *U.S. Naval Institute Proceedings* 94:1 (1968), pp. 69-77.

1908 Shapley, D. "Rainmaking: Rumored Use over Laos Alarms Arms Experts, Scientists." *Science* 176 (June 16, 1972), pp. 1216-1220.

1909 Sheehan, L.J. "Atmospheric Visibility in Southeast Asia." *Office of Aerospace Research Reviews* 8:3 (May-June 1969), pp. 12-13.

1910 Studer, T.A. "Weather Modification in Support of Military Operations." *Air University Review* 20:6 (1969), pp. 44-50.

D.7 / Chemical Warfare

1911 Beecher, W. "Chemicals vs. the Viet Cong: 'Right' or 'Wrong.' " *National Guardsman* 20:2 (1966), pp. 2-6.

1912 Briantais, J.M., et al. *Massacres: la guerre chimique en Asie du sud-est.* Paris: François Maspero, 1970.

1913 Do Xuan Sang. "U.S. Crimes of Chemical Warfare in South Vietnam." In *U.S. War Crimes in Vietnam.* Hanoi: Juridical Sciences Institute, State Commission of Social Sciences, 1968.

1914 Guignard, J.P. *Vietnam: documents sur la guerre chimique et bactériologique.* Genève: Comité National Suisse d'Aide au Vietnam, 1967.

1915 Harrigan, A. "The Case for Gas Warfare." *Armed Forces Chemical Journal* 17 (1963), pp. 12-13.

1916 Hersh, S.M. *Chemical and Biological Warfare: America's Hidden Arsenal.* New York: Bobbs-Merrill, 1968.

1917 Kahn, M.F. "CBW in Use: Vietnam." In *CBW: Chemical and Biological Warfare.* S. Rose, ed. London: Harrap, 1968.

1918 Langer, E. "Chemical and Biological Warfare: I. The Research Program. II. The Weapons and the Politics." *Science* 155 (1967), pp. 174-179, 299-303.

1919 Lederrey, E. "Guerrilla et guerre chimique." *Revue Militaire Suisse* 108 (1963), pp. 233-236.

1920 McCarthy, R.D. *The Ultimate Folly: War by Pestilence, Asphyxiation, Defoliation.* New York: Knopf, 1969.

1921 Neilands, J.B., et al. *Harvest of Death: Chemical Warfare in Cambodia and Indochina.* New York: Free Press, 1972.

1922 ——. "Vietnam: Progress of the Chemical War." *Asian Studies* 10:3 (1970), pp. 209-229.

1923 Pfeiffer, E.W. "Chemical Warfare in Vietnam and the American Scientific Community." *Scientific World* 12:6 (1968), pp. 16-19.

1924 Russell, Lord Bertrand. "Chemical Warfare in Vietnam." *New Republic* 149 (July 6, 1963), p. 30.

1925 "Spice Rack and Summit: A Season's Discontent over Classified Research." *Pennsylvania Gazette* 7 (1967), pp. 14ff.

1926 U.S. Departments of Army, Navy and Air Force. *Armed Forces Doctrine for Chemical and Biological Weapons Employment and Defense.* (FM 101-40; NWP 36(c); AFM 355-2; LFM 03). Washington, D.C.: U.S. Government Printing Office, Apr. 1964.

D.7a / Gas

1927 Blumenfeld, S., and M. Meselson. "The Military Value and Political Implications of the Use of Riot Control Agents in Warfare." In *The Control of Chemical and Biological Warfare.* New York: Carnegie Endowment for International Peace, 1971.

1928 "CB Defense." *Ordnance* 52 (1968), pp. 548, 550.

1929 "CB Defense: Fifty-year-old Edgewood Arsenal Develops New Equipment." *Ordnance* 53 (1968), pp. 30, 32.

1930 "Communists Use Nausea Gas in Cambodia." *Times* (London), Oct. 8, 1970, p. 8.

1931 Draw, J. "Lethal-gas Attack by Viet Cong." *Daily Telegraph,* Apr. 7, 1970.

1932 Goldblat, J. "Are Tear Gas and Herbicides Permitted Weapons?" *Science and Public Affairs* 26:4 (1970), pp. 13-16.

1933 "How Gas Is Being Used in Vietnam." *U.S. News and World Report* 60:1 (Jan. 31, 1966), pp. 8, 10.

1934 "Lethal Nerve Gas in Vietnam Charged." *New York Times,* May 8, 1970.

1935 "Red Troops in Cambodia Use Nausea Gas, Execute Civilians." *International Herald Tribune,* Oct. 8, 1970.

1936 "Silent Weapons: Role of Chemicals in Lower Case Warfare." *Army Digest* 23 (1968), pp. 6-11.

1937 Smith, J.A. "Gas in Vietnam: Opening Wedge for 'CB' Warfare." *National Guardian* 17 (Apr. 3, 1965), p. 3.

1938 U.S. Department of Army. *Employment of Riot Control Agents, Flame, Smoke, Antiplant Agents and Personnel Detectors in Counter-guerrilla Operations.* Training Circular 3-16. Washington, D.C.: Department of Army, Apr. 1969.

1939 "Vietcong Tear Gas Grenades Found." *Times* (London), Nov. 12, 1966.

D.7b / Herbicides

1940 Boffey, P.M. "Herbicides in Vietnam: AAAS Study Runs into a Military Roadblock." *Science* 170 (1970), pp. 42-45.

1941 Brightman, C. " 'Weed Killers' and the University at the Front." *Viet-Report* 2:4/5 (1966), pp. 9-14, 33-48.

1942 Brown, D.E. "The Use of Herbicides in War: A Political/Military Analysis." In *The Control of Chemical and Biological Weapons.* New York: Carnegie Endowment for International Peace, 1971, pp. 39-63.

1943 Constable, J., and M. Meselson. "Ecological Impact of Large Scale Defoliation in Vietnam." *Sierra Club Bulletin* 56:4 (1971), pp. 4-9.

1944 Cook, R.E., W. Haseltine, and A.W. Galston. "What Have We Done to Vietnam?" *New Republic* 162:2 (1970), pp. 18-21.

1945 "Defoliants, Deformities: What Risk?" *Medical World News* 11:9 (1970), pp. 15-17.

1946 Fair, S.D. "No Place to Hide: How Defoliants Expose the Viet Cong." *Army* 14:2 (1963), pp. 54-55.

1947 ——. "No Place to Hide: How Defoliants Expose the Viet Cong." *Armed Forces Chemical Journal* 18 (1964), pp. 5-6.

1948 Galston, A.W. "Herbicides in Vietnam." *New Republic* 157:22 (1967), pp. 19-21.

1949 ——. "Warfare with Herbicides in Vietnam." In J. Harte and R.H. Socolow, eds., *Patient Earth.* New York: Holt, Rinehart, and Winston, 1971, pp. 136-50.

1950 Gonzalez, A.F. "Defoliation–A Controversial U.S. Mission in Vietnam." *Data on Defense and Civil Systems* 13:10 (1968), pp. 12-15.

1951 "Government Begins Buildup of Defoliants to Meet Increasing Use in Vietnam." *Chemical and Engineering News* 46 (1968), pp. 26-27.

1952 Mayer, J. "Starvation as a Weapon: Herbicides in Vietnam." *Scientist and Citizen* 9 (1967), pp. 115-121.

1953 ——, and V.W. Sidel. "Crop Destruction in South Vietnam." *Christian Century* 83 (1966), pp. 829-832.

1954 McConnel, A.F., Jr. "Mission: Ranch Hand." *Air University Review* 21 (Jan-Feb 1970), pp. 89-94.

1955 Price, D.K., et al. "On the Use of Herbicides in Vietnam." *Science* 161 (1968), pp. 253-256.

1956 Tschirley, F.H. "Defoliation in Vietnam." *Science* 163 (Feb. 21, 1969), pp. 779-796.

1957 U.S. House of Representatives. Committee on Science and Astronautics. Report; *Technology Assessment of Vietnam Defoliant Matter: A Case History* [by F.P. Huddle] 91st Cong., 1st Sess., 1969.

1958 U.S. Senate. Committee on Commerce. Subcommittee on Energy, Natural Resources and the Environment. Hearings; *Effects of 2,4,5-T on Man and Environment.* [Apr. 1970] 91st Cong., 2d Sess., 1970.

1959 Westing, A.H. "Forestry and the War in South Vietnam." *Journal of Forestry* 69 (1971), pp. 777-783.

1960 Whiteside, Thomas. *Defoliation.* New York: Ballantine, 1970.

1961 ——. *The Withering Rain: America's Herbicidal Folly.* New York: Dutton, 1971.

D.8 / Psychological Warfare

1962 Bost, F.H. "Tool for Friendship." *Army* 18:7 (July 1968), pp. 34-36.

1963 Bullard, M.R. "Political Warfare in Vietnam." *Military Review* 49 (Oct. 1969), pp. 54-59.

1964 Cunningham, C. "A Carrot or a Stick for Charlie." *Army* 18:4 (Apr. 1968), pp. 68-69.

1965 Johnson, W.F. "Neglected Deterrent: Psychological Operations in 'Liberation Wars.' " *Military Review* 48 (May 1968), pp. 81-90.

1966 Jones, M.R. "The Polite Little Other War." *Army* 18:8 (Aug. 1968), pp. 43-44.

1967 Moulis, W.J. "Key to a Crisis." *Military Review* 46:2 (1966), pp. 9-14.

1968 Nathan, R.S. "Psychological Warfare: Key to Success in Viet Nam." *Orbis* 11:1 (Spring 1967), pp. 182-198.

1969 Reiling, V.G., Jr., and G.W. Scott. "Psychological Operations in Vietnam." *U.S. Naval Institute Proceedings* 94:7 (July 1968), pp. 122-125.

1970 "The Word Front." *Army* 18:11 (Nov. 1968), p. 96.

D.9 / Ecocide in Vietnam

1971 Johnstone, W.C. "Ecocide and the Geneva Protocol." *Foreign Affairs* 49 (1970/71), pp. 711-720.

1972 Orians, G.H., and E.W. Pfeiffer. "Ecological Effects of the War in Vietnam." *Science* 168 (1970), pp. 544-554.

1973 Schell, O., Jr. "Silent Vietnam: How We Invented Ecocide and Killed a Country." *Look* 35:7 (1971), pp. 55, 57-58.

1974 "Vietnam: Jungle Conflict Poses New R & D Problems." *Science* 152 (Apr. 8, 1966), pp. 187-190.

1975 Weisberg, B., ed. *Ecocide in Indochina: The Ecology of War.* San Francisco: Canfield Press, 1970.

1976 Westing, A.H. "Ecocide in Indochina." *Natural History* 80:3 (1971), pp. 56-61, 88.

E / Vietnamization

E.1 / General

1977 Arnett, Peter. "The ARVN: Prospects for the Army of South Vietnam." *Current History* 57:340 (1969), pp. 333-338.

1978 Beecher, W. "Vietnamization: A Few Loose Ends." *Army* 20:11 (Nov. 1970), pp. 12-17.

1979 Brownlow, C. "DOD Accelerates Viet Air Force Buildup." *Aviation Week and Space Technology* 91:3 (July 21, 1969), pp. 24-25.

1980 ——. "Viet Air Force Gains in Professionalism." *Aviation Week and Space Technology* 97:6 (Aug. 7, 1972), pp. 16-18.

1981 Buckley, T. "The ARVN Is Bigger and Better, But–." *New York Times Magazine* (Oct. 12, 1969).

1982 Croizat, Col. Victor J. "Vietnamese Naval Forces: Origins of the Species." *U.S. Naval Institute Proceedings* 99:2 (Feb. 1973), pp. 49-58.

1983 Glazer, Nathan. "Vietnam: The Case for Immediate Withdrawal." *Commentary* 51:5 (1971), pp. 33-37.

1984 Johnson, R.H. "Vietnamization: Can It Work?" *Foreign Affairs* 48:4 (1970), pp. 629-647.

1985 Kane, D.T. "Vietnamese Marines in Joint Operations." *Military Review* 48 (Nov. 1968), pp. 26-33.

1986 Lake, P.M. "About Vietnamization." *National Review* 23 (July 13, 1971), p. 761.

1987 Langguth, A.J. "The Vietnamization of General Di." *New York Times Magazine* (Sept. 6, 1970), p. 5.

1988 Madouse, R.A. "The Vietnamese Naval Academy." *U.S. Naval Institute Proceedings* 95 (Mar. 1969), pp. 48-57.

1989 McCarthy, F. "Winning the Ultimate Victory through Vietnamization." *Army* 21:1 (Jan. 1971), pp. 4-6.

1990 Murphy, R.P.W., and E.F. Black. "The South Vietnamese Navy." *U.S. Naval Institute Proceedings* 90:1 (1964), pp. 53-61.

1991 Oglesby, Carl. "Vietnamization Has Failed." *Commonweal* (Mar. 21, 1969), pp. 11-12.

1992 Race, Jeffrey. "Vietnamization: The Third Time Around." *Far Eastern Economic Review* 69:33 (1970), pp. 12-13.

1993 Sams, Kenneth. "How the Vietnamese Are Taking Over Their Own Air War." *Air Force* (Apr. 1971), p. 30.

1994 Stutzer, N.H. "Vietnamization Progress." *Ordnance* 56:309 (Nov-Dec 1971), pp. 226-229.

1995 Taylor, Col. Jim. "Helping to Build the UNAF." *Air Force and Space Digest* 53:12 (1970), pp. 47-49.

1996 Ton Vy. "Vietnamization." *Vietnamese Studies* 28 (1970), pp. 33-73.

1997 "Total of 648 River Patrol Boats to Be Given to Vietnam Navy." *U.S. Naval Institute Proceedings* 96:12 (Dec. 1970), p. 102.

1998 U.S. Department of State. Bureau of Public Affairs. *Indochina Progress Report: Assessment of Vietnamization, Address to Nation; by Richard Milhous Nixon, April 7, 1971.* Washington, D.C.: U.S. Government Printing Office, 1971.

1999 Vietnam Council on Foreign Relations. *The Armed Forces of the Republic of Viet Nam.* Saigon: 1969.

2000 "W. Averell Harriman Says: 'Vietnamization is Immoral.' " *Look* 34:23 (Nov. 17, 1970), pp. 38-40.

2001 Warner, Denis. "The South Vietnamese Army: Can It Replace Our GI's?" *Look* 32 (Dec. 10, 1968), pp. 77-86.

2002 "What It Means for Vietnamization." *Time* 97 (Apr. 5, 1971), pp. 25-26.

2003 White, J.M. "AcToV—The U.S. Navy's Accelerated Turnover Program." *U.S. Naval Institute Proceedings* 96:2 (Feb. 1970), pp. 112-113.

E.2 / Military Advisors

2004 Berle, P.A. "The Adviser's Role in South Vietnam." *Reporter* 58 (Feb. 8, 1968), pp. 24-26.

2005 Brown, R.F. "Role of the Junk Fleet Advisor in Base Defense." *U.S. Naval Institute Proceedings* 94:10 (Oct. 1968), pp. 128-130.

2006 "Naval Advisor Vietnam." *U.S. Naval Institute Proceedings* 95:9 (Sept. 1969), pp. 102-104.

2007 Ray, Capt. James F. "The District Advisor." *Military Review* 45:5 (1965), pp. 3-8.

2008 Slaff, A.P. "Naval Advisor Vietnam." *U.S. Naval Institute Proceedings* 95:4 (Apr. 1969), pp. 39-44.

2009 Tregaskis, R. *Vietnam Diary.* New York: Holt, Rinehart, and Winston, 1963.

F / War Crimes

F.1 / General

2010 "The Bloody Hands of the Viet Cong." *Army* 12:7 (1962), pp. 67-77.

2011 Carey, A.E. *Australian Atrocities in Vietnam.* Sydney: Gould, Convenor, Vietnam Action Campaign, 1968.

2012 Chomsky, Noam. "After Pinkville." *New York Review of Books* (Jan. 1, 1970), pp. 3-14.

2013 Davidson, A.L. "Vietnam: When Terror Is Not Statistics." *American Opinion* 11 (Feb. 1968), pp. 73-84.

2014 Dellinger, Dave. "Unmasking Genocide." *Liberation* 12:9 (1967/68), pp. 3-12.

2015 *The Dellums Committee: Hearings on War Crimes in Vietnam, An Inquiry into Command Responsibility in Southeast Asia.* Ed. with intro. by the Citizens Commission of Inquiry. New York: Vintage, 1972.

2016 [Duffy, Lt. James B.'s trial.] "Tan Am Base Vietnam: Feb. 12–1000 Hrs." *Scanlan's* (Apr. 1970), pp. 1-11.

2017 Eppridge, Bill, and Don Moser. "Vietcong Terror in a Village." *Life* 59:10 (1965), pp. 28-33, 68-70.

2018 Falk, Richard, et al., eds. *Crimes of War.* New York: Random House, 1971.

2019 Falk, Richard A. "War Crimes: The Circle of Responsibility." *Nation* (Jan. 26, 1970), pp. 77-82.

2020 Fallaci, Oriana. "An Interview with a Vietcong Terrorist." *Look* 32 (Apr. 16, 1968), pp. 36-42.

2021 Farer, T.J. "Laws of Wars 25 Years after Nuremberg." *International Conciliation* 583 (May 1971), pp. 5-54.

2022 Ferencz, B.B. "War Crimes Law and the Vietnam War." *American University Law Review* 17 (June 1968), pp. 403-420.

2023 "Geneva Convention of 1949: Application in the Vietnamese Conflict." *Virginia Journal of International Law* 5 (1965), pp. 243-265.

2024 Herman, E.S. *"Atrocities" in Vietnam: Myths and Realities.* Boston: Pilgrim Press, 1970.

2025 Hoopes, Townsend. "The Nuremberg Suggestion." *Washington Monthly* (Jan. 1970), pp. 18-21.

2026 International Commission of Jurists. "Human Rights in Armed Conflict: Vietnam." *Bulletin* 34 (June 1968), pp. 41-45.

2027 "International Law and Military Operations Against Insurgents in Neutral Territory." *Columbia Law Review* 68 (1968), pp. 1127-1148.

2028 Knoll, Erwin. "The Mysterious Project Phoenix." *Progressive* 34:2 (1970), pp. 19-21.

2029 ——, and Judith N. McFadden, eds. *War Crimes and the American Conscience.* New York: Holt, Rinehart and Winston, 1970.

2030 *Livre noir des crimes américains au Vietnam.* Paris: Payard, 1970.

2031 Mallin, J. *Terror in Vietnam.* Princeton: Van Nostrand, 1966.

2032 McWilliams, Wilson Carey. *Military Honor after MyLai.* (Special Studies No. 213) New York: Council on Religion and International Affairs, 1972.

2033 Melman, Seymour, et al. *In the Name of America: The Conduct of the War in Vietnam by the Armed Forces of the United States. . . .* New York: Clergy and Layman Concerned About Vietnam, 1968.

2034 Meyrowitz, Henir. "Le Droit de la guerre dans le conflict vietnamien." *Annuaire Français de Droit International* 13 (1967), pp. 143-201.

2035 Miller, R.H. "Convention on the Non-applicability of Statutory Limitations to War Crimes and Crimes against Humanity." *American Journal of International Law* 65 (July 1971), p. 476.

2036 *New Facts: Phu Loi Mass Murder in South Viet Nam.* Hanoi: Foreign Languages Publishing House, 1959.

2037 Norden, Eric. "American Atrocities in Vietnam." *Liberation* 10:11 (Feb. 1966), pp. 14-27.

2038 Pahm Cuong. "War Crimes and Genocide." *Vietnamese Studies* 18/19 (Sept. 1968), pp. 275-302.

2039 Pike, D. *The Viet Cong Strategy of Terror.* Saigon: U.S. Mission, 1970.

2040 Polner, Murray. "Vietnam War Stories." *Trans-action* 6:10 (1968), pp. 8-20.

2041 Reel, A. Frank. "Must We Hang Nixon Too?" *Progressive* (Mar. 1970), pp. 26-29.

2042 Reston, James, Jr. "Is Nuremberg Coming Back to Haunt Us?" *Saturday Review* (July 18, 1970), pp. 14-17, 61.

2043 Russell, B., and S. Russell. *War and Atrocity in Vietnam.* London: Bertrand Russell Peace Foundation, 1964.

2044 Sacharoff, M. "Bibliography of Recent and Forthcoming Books on U.S. War Crimes in Indochina." *New Republic* 164 (Jan. 2, 1971), pp. 29ff.

2045 Sahlins, Marshall. "The Destruction of Conscience in Vietnam." *Dissent* 13 (Jan-Feb 1966), pp. 36-62.

2046 Taylor, Telford. *Nuremberg and Vietnam: An American Tragedy.* Chicago: Quadrangle Books, 1970.

2047 *U.S. War Crimes in Viet Nam.* Hanoi: Juridical Science Institute, State Commission of Social Sciences, 1968.

2048 Wald, George. "Corporate Responsibility for War Crimes." *New York Review of Books* (July 2, 1970), pp. 4-6.

2049 Wilson, Andrew. "The War in Vietnam: How Relevant Are the Rules of War?" *Current* 114 (Jan. 1970), pp. 3-6.

F.2 / The Stockholm Conference

2050 Aptheker, Herbert. "The Stockholm Conference on Vietnam." *Political Affairs* 46 (Aug. 1967), pp 47-58.

2051 Coats, Kenneth, et al. *Prevent the Crime of Silence: Reports from the Sessions of the International War Crimes Tribunal Founded by Bertrand Russell.* Baltimore: Penguin, 1971.

2052 DeWeerd, H.A. *Lord Russell's War Crimes Tribunal.* Santa Monica, California: Rand, P-3561, Mar. 1967.

2053 The International War Crimes Tribunal. *Stockholm and Copenhagen, 1967: Against the Crime of Silence; Proceedings of the Russell International War Crimes Tribunal.* New York: Bertrand Russell Peace Foundation, 1968. Also published as: Duffet, J., ed. *Against the Crime of Silence. Proceedings of the Russell International War Crimes Tribunal.* Flanders, New Jersey: O'Hare Books, 1968.

2054 Jack, Homer A. "Confrontation in Stockholm." *War/Peace Report* 7 (Aug/Sept 1967), pp. 7-9.

2055 Lynd, Staughton. "The War Crimes Tribunal: A Dissent." *Liberation* 12:9 (1967/68), pp. 76-79.

2056 Russell, B. *War Crimes in Vietnam.* London: Allen & Unwin, 1967.

2057 Sartre, Jean Paul. *On Genocide; And a Summary of the Evidence and the Judgments of the International War Crimes Tribunal.* Boston: Beacon, 1968.

2058 Viet-Nam. Republique du Livre Blanc. Vol. 1: *Le Jugement de Stockholm;* Vol. 2: *Le Jugement final.* Tribunal Russell, Paris, N.R.F., 1968. Saigon: 1968.

F.3 / My Lai

2059 "An American Atrocity." *Esquire* 72 (Aug. 1969), pp. 59-63, 132.

2060 Barthelmes, Wes. "Mylai and the National Conscience—II: Cry, Our Beloved Country." *Commonweal* (Apr. 30, 1971), pp. 186-187.

2061 Everett, Arthur, et al. *Calley.* New York: Dell, 1971.

2062 Falk, Richard A. "Circle of Responsibility." *Nation* (Jan. 27, 1970), pp. 77-82.

2063 Grant, Z.B. "Mylai Was Not an 'Isolated Incident.'" *New Republic* 161 (Dec. 20, 1969), pp. 9-11.

2064 Gershen, Martin. *Destroy or Die: The True Story of Mylai.* New Rochelle, New York: Arlington House, 1971.

2065 Greenhaw, Wayne. *The Making of a Hero: The Story of Lt. William Calley, Jr.* Louisville, Kentucky: Touchstone Publishing Co., 1971.

2066 Hammer, Richard. *The Court-Martial of Lt. Calley.* New York: Coward, McCann & Geoghegan, 1971.

2067 ——. *One Morning in the War: The Tragedy at Son My.* London: Hart-Davis, 1970.

2068 Hersh, Seymour M. *My Lai 4.* New York: Random House, 1970.

2069 "Is There a Bit of Calley in Us?" *Look* (June 1, 1971), pp. 76-77.

2070 "The Massacre at Mylai." *Life* 67:23 (Dec. 5, 1969), pp. 36-44.

2071 McCarthy, Mary. *Medina.* New York: Harcourt, Brace & Jovanovich, 1972.

2072 Novak, Michael. "Mylai and the National Conscience—I: The Battle Hymn of Lt. Calley . . . and the Republic." *Commonweal* (Apr. 30, 1971), pp. 183-186.

2073 Opton, E.M., Jr., and R. Duckles. "Mental Gymnastics on Mylai." *New Republic* (Feb. 21, 1970), pp. 14-16.

2074 Paust, Capt. Jordan J. "MyLai and Vietnam: Norms, Myths and Leader Responsibility." *Military Law Review* 57 (Summer 1972), pp. 99-187.

2075 "Punishment for War Crimes: Duty or Discretion?" *Michigan Law Review* 69 (June 1971), pp. 1312-1346.

2076 Tiede, Tom. *Calley: Soldier or Killer?* New York: Pinnacle Books, 1971.

2077 U.S. House of Representatives. Committee on Armed Services. Hearings; *Investigation of the My Lai Incident.* [July 15, 1970] 91st Cong., 2nd Sess., 1970.

G / POW Issue

2078 "Ambassador Bruce Discusses Problem of U.S. Prisoners of War in Southeast Asia." *U.S. Department of State Bulletin* 63 (Dec. 21, 1970), pp. 737-747.

2079 "Back to the Hills (Raid on POW Camp at Son Tay)." *Economist* 237 (Nov. 28, 1970), pp. 14-16.

2080 Borman, Frank. "U.S. Prisoners of War in Southeast Asia." *U.S. Department of State Bulletin* 63 (Oct. 12, 1970), pp. 405-418.

2081 Branch, Taylor. "Prisoners of War, Prisoners of Peace." *Washington Monthly* (Aug. 1972), pp. 39-54.

2082 Chafee, J.H. "P.O.W. Treatment: Principles versus Propaganda." *U.S. Naval Institute Proceedings* 97:7 (1971), pp. 14-17.

2083 Denno, B.F. "The Fate of American POWs in Vietnam." *Air Force and Space Digest* 51 (Feb. 1968), pp. 40-45.

2084 Fall, B.B. " 'Unrepentant, Unyielding.' An Interview with Viet Cong Prisoners." *New Republic* 156 (Feb. 4, 1967), pp. 19-24.

2085 Fallaci, Oriana. "From North Vietnam: Two American POW's." *Look* 33 (July 15, 1969), pp. 30-35.

2086 "The Geneva Convention and the Treatment of Prisoners of War in Vietnam." *Harvard Law Review* 80 (Feb. 1967), pp. 851-868.

2087 "The Geneva Convention of 1949: Application in the Vietnamese Conflict." *Virginia Journal of International Law* 5 (1965).

2088 Hauser, R.E. "U.S. Brings Hanoi's Treatment of American Prisoners of War to Attention of U.N. Committee." *U.S. Department of State Bulletin* 61 (Dec. 1, 1969), pp. 471-476.

2089 Hemphill, J.A. "PW and Captured Document Doctrine." *Military Review* 49:11 (1969), pp. 65-71.

2090 Levie, H.S. "Maltreatment of Prisoners of War in Vietnam." *Boston University Law Review* 48 (1968), pp. 323-359.

2091 Lien, M.L. "The Plight of the Prisoners We Have Not Forgotten." *Air Force and Space Digest* 53:6 (1970), pp. 32-37.

2092 Neilands, J.B. "Due piloti americani ad Hanoi (Two American Pilots in Hanoi)." *Il Ponte* (Italy) 23:7/8 (1967), pp. 926-928.

2093 Ognibene, Peter J. "Politics and POWs." *New Republic* (June 3, 1972), pp. 17-19.

2094 Overly, N.M. "Held Captive in Hanoi: An Ex-POW Tells How It Was." *Air Force and Space Digest* 53:11 (1970), pp. 86-90.

2095 Pitzer, D.L., and W. Rogers. "The Animal Called POW: My Years in a Vietcong Prison." *Look* 33 (Feb. 18, 1969), pp. 46-51.

2096 Richardson, W.K. "Prisoners of War as Instruments of Foreign Policy." *Naval War College Review* 23:1 (1970), pp. 47-64.

2097 Rogers, Warren. "P.O.W. North Vietnam: Are U.S. Prisoners Mistreated?" *Look* 31 (July 25, 1967), pp. 53-55.

2098 Rowe, James N. *Five Years to Freedom.* Boston: Little, Brown, 1971.

2099 Stockstill, L.R. "The Forgotten Americans of the Vietnam War." *Air Force and Space Digest* 52 (Oct. 1969), pp. 38-49.

2100 U.S. House of Representatives. Committee on Armed Services. Hearings; *Problems of Prisoners of War and Their Families.* [Mar. 6, 1970] 91st Cong., 2d Sess., 1970.

2101 U.S. House of Representatives. Committee on Foreign Affairs. Hearings; *American Prisoners of War in Southeast Asia, 1970.* [Apr-May 1970] 91st Cong., 2d Sess., 1970.

2102 ——. Hearings; *American Prisoners of War in Southeast Asia, 1971.* 92d Cong., 1st Sess., 1971.

2103 ——. Hearings; *American Prisoners of War in Southeast Asia, 1972.* 92d Cong., 2d Sess., 1972.

2104 ——. Hearings; *American Prisoners of War in Vietnam.* [Nov. 13-14, 1969] 91st Cong., 1st Sess., 1969.

2105 "U.S. Prisoners in North Vietnam." *Life* 63 (Oct. 20, 1967), pp. 21-34.

2106 U.S. Senate. Committee on Foreign Relations. Hearings; *Bombing Operations and the Prisoners-of-War Rescue Mission in North Vietnam.* [Nov. 24, 1970] 91st Cong., 2d Sess., 1970.

2107 ——. Report; *American Prisoners of War in Southeast Asia.* [Calendar No. 698, Rpt. No. 91-705] [Feb. 16, 1970] 91st Cong., 2d Sess., 1970.

2108 Van Dyke, J.M. "Prisoners from Hanoi: Were They Tortured?" *Nation* 209 (Oct. 6, 1969), pp. 332, 334-335.

H / Casualties of War

2109 Alcock, N.Z., and K. Lowe. "The Vietnam War as a Richardson Process." *Journal of Peace Research* 6 (1969), pp. 105-112.

2110 Brass, Alister J.D. *Bleeding Earth: A Doctor Looks at Vietnam.* Sydney: Alpha Books, 1969.

2111 Briand, Rena. *No Tears to Flow: Woman at War.* Melbourne: Heineman, 1969.

2112 Conn, Harry. "Refugees: The World's Forgotten People." *American Federationist* 73:9 (Sept. 1966), pp. 17-20.

2113 Cutting, R.T., et al. *Congenital Malformations, Hydatidiform Moles and Stillbirths in the Republic of Vietnam, 1960-1969.* Washington, D.C.: Department of Defense, 1970.

2114 *Epidemiological Situation in Vietnam.* World Health Organization, EB 41/42, Jan. 1968.

2115 Evans, Barbara. *Caduceus in Saigon: A Medical Mission to South Vietnam.* London: Hutchinson, 1968.

2116 Fiedler, Leslie. "Who Really Died in Vietnam?" *Saturday Review of the Society* (Dec. 1972), pp. 40-43.

2117 Flood, Charles B. *The War of the Innocents.* New York: McGraw-Hill, 1970.

2118 Grant, Z.B. "Civilians Caught in the Vietnam Crossfire." *New Republic* 159 (Aug. 17, 1968), pp. 11-12.

2119 Hayes, Marcia. "Plague Goes to War." *Far Eastern Economic Review* 59 (Mar. 7, 1968), pp. 418-420.

2120 Kelman, R.B. "Vietnam: A Current Issue in Child Welfare." *Social Work* 13:4 (Oct. 1968), pp. 15-20.

2121 Lang, Daniel. *Casualties of War.* New York: McGraw-Hill, 1970.

2122 Luce, Don. "No Way Home: Vietnam's Refugees." *Christian Century* 84 (Oct. 11, 1967), pp. 1279-1281.

2123 Marks, E.B. "Saigon: The Impact of the Refugees." *Reporter* 36:1 (1967), pp. 33-36.

2124 Sack, John. *Body Count: Lt. Calley's Story.* London: Hutchinson, 1971.

2125 Schulze, Gene. *The Third Face of War (Medical and Sanitary Operations).* Austin, Texas: Pemberton, 1970.

2126 Sunderland, Sydney. *Australian Civilian Medical Aid to Viet-Nam: Report, March 1969.* Canberra: Department of External Affairs, 1969.

2127 Terry, Susan. *House of Love: Life in a Vietnamese Hospital.* London: Newnes, 1967.

2128 "To Make Children Whole Again." *Look* (July 23, 1968), pp. 30-34.

2129 Turpin, J.W. *Vietnam Doctor: The Story of Project Concern.* New York McGraw-Hill, 1966.

2130 U.S. Senate. Committee on Foreign Relations. Hearings; *Vietnam Children's Care Agency.* [Apr. 5, 1972] 92d Cong., 2d Sess., 1972.

2131 U.S. Senate. Committee on the Judiciary. Hearings; *Civilian Casualty, Social Welfare, and Refugee Problems in South Vietnam.* [May-Oct 1968] 90th Cong., 1st Sess., 1968.

2132 ——. Hearings; *Refugees and Civilian War Casualty Problems in Laos and Cambodia.* [May 7, 1970] 91st Cong., 2d Sess., 1970.

2133 ——. Hearings; *War-Related Civilian Problems in Indochina.* 92d Cong., 1st Sess., 1971.

2134 ——. Report; *Civilian Casualty and Refugee Problems in South Vietnam: Findings and Recommendations.* [May 9, 1968] 90th Cong., 2d Sess., 1968.

2135 ——. Report; *Refugee Problems in South Vietnam: Report Pursuant to S. Res. 49.* [Senate Rpt. No. 1058] 89th Cong., 2d Sess., 1966.

2136 "Viet Deformities: Will We Ever Know?" *Medical World News* 12:4 (1971), pp. 4-5.

I / Military Personnel

2137 Army Times. *American Heroes of the Asian Wars.* New York: Dodd, 1968.

2138 Beecher, W. "Crisis of Confidence." *Army* 17:1 (Jan. 1967), pp. 45-48.

2139 Bletz, Col. D.F. "After Vietnam: A Professional Challenge." *Military Review* 51:8 (1971), pp. 11-15.

2140 Bourne, Peter G. *Men, Stress and Vietnam.* Boston: Little, Brown, 1970.

2141 ——. *The Psychology and Physiology of Stress: With Special Reference to the Studies on the Viet Nam War.* New York: Academic Press, 1969.

2142 Boyle, Richard. *Flower of the Dragon: The Breakdown of the U.S. Army in Vietnam.* San Francisco: Ramparts Press, 1972.

2143 Cole, E.F. "Replacement Operations in Vietnam." *Military Review* 48 (Feb. 1968), pp. 3-8.

2144 Danto, B.L., and R.L. Sadoff. "Court-martial in Vietnam." *Corrective Psychiatry and Journal of Social Therapy* 15 (Fall 1969), pp. 65-72.

2145 "From Vietnam to a VA Hospital: Assignment to Neglect." *Life* 68:19 (May 22, 1970), pp. 25-31.

2146 Furlong, W.B. "The Re-Entry Problem of the Vietvets." *New York Times Magazine* (May 7, 1967), p. 23.

2147 Grant, Z.B. "American Defectors with the Viet Cong." *New Republic* 159 (Sept. 17, 1968), pp. 15-16.

2148 ——. "Whites against Blacks in Vietnam." *New Republic* 160 (Jan. 18, 1969), pp. 15-16.

2149 Greenberg, Abe, and C.H. McKeown. "Discrimination? A Minority Review [U.S. Navy]." *U.S. Naval Institute Proceedings* 92:2 (June 1971), pp. 104-106.

2150 Heaton, L.D. "Medical Support in Vietnam." *Army* 16 (Oct. 1966), pp. 125-128.

2151 Hersh, Seymour M. "The Decline and Near Fall of the U.S. Army." *Saturday Review of the Society* (Dec. 1972), pp. 58-65.

2152 "Home From Vietnam: For 2.3 Million U.S. Veterans–a New Way of Life." *U.S. News & World Report.* (Feb. 12, 1973), pp. 21-23.

2153 Hottell, J.A., III. "Motivation in Combat." *Army* 20:2 (Feb. 1970), pp. 47-50.

2154 King, Edward L. *The Death of the Army: A Pre-Mortem.* New York: Saturday Review Press, 1972.

2155 Mataxis, T.C. "This Far, No Farther. How the Army Handles Dissenters in Uniform." *Military Review* 50:3 (1970), pp. 74-82.

2156 McClendon, R.O. "Doctors and Dentists, Nurses and Corpsmen in Vietnam." *U.S. Naval Institute Proceedings* 96:5 (May 1970), pp. 278-289.

2157 "Military Morale in America." *Army Quarterly and Defense Journal* (Great Britain) 101:1 (1970), pp. 70-78.

2158 Moore, W.M. *Navy Chaplains in Vietnam, 1954-1964.* Washington, D.C.: Chief of Chaplains, Bureau of Naval Personnel, Department of Navy, 1968.

2159 Moskos, Charles C., Jr. *The American Enlisted Man.* New York: Russell Sage Foundation, 1970.

2160 ——. "A Sociologist Appraises the GI." *Northwestern Report* 3:1 (1967), pp. 2-9.

2161 Nam, Charles B. "Impact of the 'GI Bills' on the Educational Level of the Male Population." *Social Forces* 43:1 (1964), pp. 26-32.

2162 Ognibene, Peter J. "Conscientious Objectors in the Air Force." *New Republic* (Dec. 2, 1972), pp. 15-17.

2163 Palmer, B., Jr. "The American Soldier in Vietnam Has Met the Challenge." *Army* 17:10 (Oct. 1967), pp. 107-123.

2164 Polner, Murray. *No Victory Parades: The Return of the Vietnam Veteran.* New York: Holt, Rinehart and Winston, 1971.

2165 Pressler, L.L. "Civilian Personnel, Vietnam." *Military Review* 47 (Nov. 1967), pp. 39-43.

2166 Sherman, E.F. "Bureaucracy Adrift: Anti-War Dissent within the U.S. Military." *Nation* 212 (Mar. 1, 1971), pp. 265-275.

2167 Toms, J.E. "Justice in the Battle Zone." *U.S. Naval Institute Proceedings* 95 (June 1969), pp. 52-57.

2168 U.S. Senate. Committee on Government Operations. Hearings; *Fraud and Corruption in Management of Military Club Systems.* 92d Cong., 1st Sess., 1969.

2169 White, Cmdr. Jack M. "Seven Days in July [racial confrontation]." *U.S. Naval Institute Proceedings* 98:1 (Jan. 1972), pp. 37-41.

2170 Woolley, H.T., and L.H. Beecher. "Drug Abuse: Out in the Open." *U.S. Naval Institute Proceedings* 97:11 (Nov. 1971), pp. 18-35.

2171 Zinberg, N.E. "G.I.'s and O.J.'s in Vietnam." *New York Times Magazine* (Dec. 5, 1971), p. 37.

VI / DOMESTIC IMPACT OF WAR

A / General

2172 Appleton, Sheldon. "The Public, the Polls, and the War." *Vietnam Perspectives* 1:4 (May 1966), pp. 3-13.

2173 Armor, D.J., et al. "Professors' Attitudes toward the Vietnam War." *Public Opinion Quarterly* 31 (Summer 1967), pp. 159-175.

2174 Bolitzer, Bernard. "For the Immediate Withdrawal of American Troops." *New Politics* 4 (Winter 1965), pp. 18-24.

2175 Brody, Richard A. "How the Vietnam War May Affect the Election (1968)," *Trans-action* 5:10 (1968), pp. 16-23.

2176 Brogan, Denis. "Americans and the War in Vietnam." *Listener* 75 (Apr. 7, 1966), pp. 493-495, 509.

2177 Brown, R.M. "The Church and Vietnam." *Commonweal* 87:2 (1967), pp. 52-54.

2178 ——. "Vietnam: Crisis of Conscience." *Catholic World* 206 (Oct. 1967), pp. 5-10.

2179 Browne, R.S. "The Freedom Movement and the War in Vietnam." *Freedom-Ways* 5 (Fall 1965), pp. 467-480.

2180 Brzezinski, Zbigniew. "Peace, Morality and Vietnam." *New Leader* 48:8 (1965), pp. 8-9.

2181 Burnham, W.D. "Vietnam and the Voter." *Commonweal* 84 (Sept. 30, 1966), pp. 635-637.

2182 Caine, P.D. "The United States in Korea and Vietnam: A Study in Public Opinion." *Air University Review* 20:1 (1968), pp. 49-55.

2183 "The Consequences of the War." *Saturday Review of the Society* (Dec. 1972), pp. 28-83.

2184 "The Current American Mood: Its Consciousness of Vietnam." *Round Table* 220 (1965), pp. 342-347.

2185 Finn, James. "The Debate on Vietnam." *Catholic World* 203 (May 1966), pp. 76-80.

2186 Friedman, A., and Henry S. Commager. "Debate on Vietnam Policy." *Massachusetts Review* 7 (Spring 1966), pp. 407-419.

2187 Halberstam, David. "The Vast Backfire of Activism." *Saturday Review of the Society* (Dec. 1972), pp. 28-32.

2188 Harris, W.H. "Morality, Moralism and Vietnam." *Christian Century* 82 (Sept. 22, 1965), pp. 1155-1157.

2189 Heckscher, August. "Democracy and Foreign Policy: The Case of Vietnam." *American Scholar* 35:4 (1966), pp. 613-620.

2190 Hinckle, Warren. "MSU: The University on the Make." *Ramparts* 4 (Apr. 1966), pp. 11-22.

2191 Howe, I. "When Grave Issues Like Vietnam Are up to Debate, the Writer Can't Keep to His Attic." *New York Times Magazine* (Dec. 5, 1965), p. 43.

2192 Iglitzin, L.P. "Democracy and the Radical Challenge." *Midwest Quarterly* 12:1 (1970), pp. 59-77.

2193 Kissin, S.F. "Why the U.S. Deserves Our Support." *Venture* 19 (Mar. 1967), pp. 19-22.

2194 Landau, D. "Behind the Policy Makers: RAND and the Vietnam War." *Ramparts* 11 (Nov. 1972), pp. 26-37.

2195 Lane, Mark. *Conversations with Americans.* New York: Simon and Schuster, 1970.

2196 Larson, Allan. "Politics, Social Change, and the Conflict of Generations." *Midwest Quarterly* 11:2 (1970), pp. 123-137.

2197 Lifton, Robert Jay. "The 'Gook Syndrome' and 'Numbed Warfare.' " *Saturday Review of the Society* (Dec. 1972), pp. 66-72.

2198 Lowry, C.W. "American Intellectual and U.S. Vietnam Policy." *World Affairs* 128 (Apr/June 1965), pp. 21-27.

2199 McCoy, A.W. *The Politics of Heroin in Southeast Asia.* New York: Harper & Row, 1972.

2200 Mueller, J.E. "Trends in Popular Support for the Wars in Korea and Vietnam." *American Political Science Review* 65:2 (1971), pp. 358-375.

2201 Neuhaus, R.J. "The War, the Churches, and Civil Religion." *Annals of the American Academy of Political and Social Science* 387 (1970), pp. 128-140.

2202 Nuveen, John. "Vietnam: The Neglected Debate." *Christian Century* 84 (Mar. 29, 1967), pp. 399-403.

2203 Perkins, Dexter. "Dissent in Time of War (1789 to the Present)." *Virginia Quarterly Review* 47 (Spring 1971), pp. 161-174.

2204 Ramsey, Paul. "Is Vietnam a Just War?" *Dialog* 6 (Winter 1967), pp. 19-29.

2205 ——. "Vietnam: Dissent from Dissent." *Christian Century* 83 (July 20, 1966), pp. 909-913.

2206 Robinson, J.P., and S.G. Jacobson. "American Public Opinion about Vietnam." Peace Research Society (International) *Papers* 10 (1968), pp. 63-79.

2207 Roche, J.P. "The Liberals and Vietnam." *New Leader* 48:9 (1965), pp. 16-20.

2208 ——. "A Professor Votes *for* Mr. Johnson." *New York Times Magazine* (Oct. 24, 1965), p. 45.

2209 Shoup, David M. "The New American Militarism." *Atlantic Monthly* (Apr. 1969), pp. 51-56.

2210 Smylie, J.H. "American Religious Bodies, Just War, and Vietnam." *Journal of Church and State* 11:3 (1969), pp. 383-408.

2211 Stahnke, P.K. "The New Left and Its Implications for Strategy in the Seventies." *Naval War College Review* 22:1 (1969), pp. 20-42.

2212 "The State of the Vietnam Protest." *War/Peace Report* 7 (June/July 1967), pp. 14-15.

2213 Thomas, Norman. "Let the President Call for Immediate Cease Fire." *New Politics* 4 (Winter 1965), pp. 4-11.

2214 Van der Kroef, J.M. (American Opinion on the Vietnam War). *Contemporary Review:* "I: The Doves." 206:1193 (1965), pp. 295-299; "II: The Hawks." 207:1194 (1965), pp. 22-25.

2215 Verba, Sidney, et al. "Public Opinion and the War in Vietnam." *American Political Science Review* 61 (June 1967), pp. 317-333.

2216 Weaver, G.R. *The American Public and Vietnam: An In-Depth Study of the American People in Times of International Conflict.* Unpublished PhD thesis, American University, 1970.

2217 Windmiller, Marshall. "U.S. Public Opinion and the Vietnam War." *Review of International Affairs* (Belgrade) 18:403 (Jan. 20, 1967), pp. 5-7.

2218 Wogman, Philip. "A Moral Reassessment of Our War in Vietnam." *Christian Century* 84 (Jan. 4, 1967), pp. 7-9.

2219 Wood, W.W. "The Betrayed: Our Men in Uniform Want to Win in Vietnam." *American Opinion* 12 (Jan. 1969), pp. 1-16.

2220 Woolf, Cecil, and John Bagguley, eds. *Authors Take Sides on Vietnam: Two Questions on the War in Vietnam Answered by the Authors of Several Nations.* London: Owen, 1967.

B / Peace Movement

2221 American Friends Service Committee. *La Tragédie vietnamienne vue par des Quakers américans: propositions nouvelles pour la paix.* Paris: les Éditions du Pavillon, 1967.

2222 Beisner, R.L. "1898 and 1968: The Anti-Imperialists and the Doves." *Political Science Quarterly* 85:2 (June 1970), pp. 187-216.

2223 Berrigan, Daniel. *Night Flight to Hanoi: War Diary with 11 Poems.* New York: Macmillan, 1968.

2224 Berrigan, Philip. *Prison Journals of a Priest Revolutionary.* New York: Holt, Rinehart & Winston, 1970.

2225 Dane, Barbara, comp. *The Vietnam Songbook.* New York: The Guardian, Distributed by Monthly Review Press, 1969.

2226 Dellinger, Dave. "Resistance: Vietnam and America." *Liberation* 12:8 (1967), pp. 3-7.

2227 Duncan, David Douglas. *I Protest!* New York: New American Library, 1968.

2228 ——. *War without Heroes.* New York: Harper & Row, 1970.

2229 Duncan, Donald. *The New Legions.* London: Gollancz, 1967.

2230 Foner, Philip Sheldon. *American Labor and the Indochina War: The Growth of Union Opposition.* New York: International Publishers, 1971.

2231 Gannon, Thomas M. "A Report on the Vietnam Moratorium." *America* 121:41 (1969), pp. 380-383.

2232 *GI's Speak Out against the War: The Case of the Ft. Johnson 8.* New York: Pathfinders Press, 1970.

2233 Gottlieb, Gidon. "Vietnam and Civil Disobedience." *1967 Annual Survey of American Law* (1967), pp. 699-716.

2234 Guttmann, Allen. "Protest against the War in Vietnam." *Annals of the American Academy of Political and Social Sciences* 382 (1969), pp. 56-63.

2235 Hahn, Harlan. "Correlates of Public Sentiments about War: Local Referenda on the Vietnam Issue." *American Political Science Review* (Dec. 1970).

2236 Harries, Owen. "After the Moratorium." *Quadrant, 65* 14:3 (1970), pp. 40-43.

2237 Mander, John. "Letter from New York." *Encounter* (Great Britain) 34:1 (1970), pp. 3-10.

2238 McWilliams, C. "Opportunities and Dangers: Growing Public and Church Anti-Vietnamese War Attitude." *Nation* 214 (June 5, 1972), pp. 706-708.

2239 McWilliams, W.C. "Civilian Disobedience and Contemporary Constitutionalism: The American Case." *Comparative Politics* 1:2 (1969), pp. 211-227.

2240 Melman, S., ed. *In the Name of America.* New York: E.P. Dutton, 1968.

2241 Miller, A.H. *Perceptions and Recommendations of the Vietnam Peace Movement: A Case Study of Activists in Pittsburgh.* PhD thesis, University of Pittsburgh, 1969.

2242 Mongillo, Larry. "Ellsberg at Stanford: Performing the New Morality." *New Guard* 12:5 (June 1972), pp. 8-9.

2243 Murdock, Steve. "Labor for Peace: The Unions Find Consensus." *Nation* 215:1 (July 10, 1972), pp. 11-14.

2244 Muste, A.J. "Last Words: Report on a Visit to North Vietnam." *Liberation* 11:11 (1967), pp. 8-11.

2245 Nelson, J., and R.J. Ostrow. *The FBI and the Berrigans: The Making of a Conspiracy.* New York: Coward, McCann and Geoghegan, 1972.

2246 Rose, R.C. "Busted Flat in Washington, Waiting: Clergy and Laymen Concerned Demonstration." *Christian Century* 89 (May 31, 1972), pp. 625-626.

2247 Rosenburg, Milton, et al. *Vietnam and the Silent Majority: The Dove's Guide.* New York: Harper and Row, 1970.

2248 Sainteny, Jean. *Histoire d'une paix manquée.* Paris: Fayard, nouvelle édition, 1967.

2249 Spock, Benjamin M. *Dr. Spock on Vietnam.* New York: Dell, 1968.

2250 Steinfels, P. "Once again into the Streets." *Commonweal* 96 (May 26, 1972), p. 279.

2251 "Theater Goes to War: Anti-War Plays. . . ." *America* 116 (May 20, 1967), pp. 759-761.

2252 *Trials of the Resistance.* New York: Vintage, 1970.

2253 "The Vietnam Protest Movement." *Dissent* 13 (Jan/Feb 1966), pp. 7-9.

2254 Welch, E.H. "What Did You Write about the War, Daddy?" *Wilson Library Bulletin* 46 (June 1972), pp. 912-917.

2255 Wilson, R.B. "The Arrogance of Constitutional Power." *Colorado Quarterly* 16:3 (1968), pp. 267-285.

2256 Woodside, Norma Sue. *Up against the War.* New York: Tower Publications, 1970.

2257 Woodward, Beverly. "Vietnam and the Law: The Theory and Practice of Civil Challenge." *Commentary* 46:5 (1968), pp. 75-86.

C / Student Protest

2258 Altbach, P.G. "Commitment and Powerlessness on the American Campus: The Case of the Graduate Student." *Liberal Education* 56:4 (1970), pp. 562-582.

2259 Asbury, B.A., et al. "The Role of Campus Ministers in Protest and Dissent." *Liberal Education* 56:2 (1970), pp. 317-338.

2260 Asinof, Eliot. *Craig and Joan: Two Lives for Peace.* New York: Viking, 1971.

2261 Bitner, John W. "ROTC: The Universities' Stake in National Defense." *Liberal Education* 56:3 (1970), pp. 454-457.

2262 Brogan, D.W. "The Student Revolt." *Encounter* (Great Britain) 31:178 (1968), pp. 20-25.

2263 Brooks, T.R. "Voice of the New Campus 'Underclass.' " *New York Times Magazine* (Nov. 7, 1965), p. 25.

2264 Casey, Thomas A. "Some Reflections on Student Rights." *Catholic Education Review* 66:5 (1968), pp. 297-306.

2265 Clecak, Peter. "The Snare of Preparation." *American Scholar* 38:4 (1969), pp. 657-667.

2266 *Crisis at Columbia: Report of the Fact-Finding Commission Appointed to Investigate the Disturbances at Columbia University in April and May 1968.* New York: Vintage, 1968.

2267 "Dispute Over the Gas Sprayed on Protestors." *San Francisco Chronicle,* May 22, 1969.

2268 Divale, W.T., with James Joseph. *I Lived inside the Campus Revolution.* New York: College Notes & Texts, 1970.

2269 Eszterhas, Joe, and M.D. Roberts. *Confrontation at Kent State: 13 Seconds.* New York: College Notes & Texts, 1970.

2270 Ferguson, John. "Student Protest and Power in the United States." *British Journal of Education Studies* 18:1 (1970), pp. 32-41.

2271 Flacks, Richard. "The Liberated Generation." *Journal of Social Issues* 23 (1967), pp. 52-75.

2272 Glick, Edward B. "ROTC: From Riot to Reason." *Air Force and Space Digest* 53:10 (1970), pp. 70-73.

2273 Harris, Janet. *Students in Revolt.* New York: McGraw-Hill, 1970.

2274 Hesburgh, Theodore M. "Comments on Campus Unrest." *Social Science* 44:4 (1969), pp. 195-199.

2275 Hurwitz, Ken. *Marching Nowhere.* New York: W.W. Norton, 1971.

2276 Jacobs, Paul, and Saul Landan. *The New Radicals.* New York: Vintage, 1966.

2277 Joy, Ted. "Espionage at Kent State." *Nation* 216:5 (Jan. 29, 1973), pp. 144-148.

2278 Kateb, George. "The Campus and Its Critics." *Commentary* 47:4 (1969), pp. 33-39.

2279 Katz, J. *The Student Activist.* Washington, D.C.: U.S. Office of Education, 1967.

2280 Kazin, Michael. "Some Notes on S.D.S." *American Scholar* 38:4 (1969), pp. 644-655.

2281 Kelman, Steven J. "Youth and Foreign Policy: Youth of the 'New Left' and Their Opposition to United States Policies in the Vietnamese War." *Foreign Affairs* (Apr. 1970), pp. 414-426.

2282 Kryske, L.M. "NROTC at UCLA: the Colors Still Fly." *U.S. Naval Institute Proceedings* 97:12 (Dec. 1971), pp. 18-25.

2283 Laqueur, Walter. "Reflections on Youth Movements." *Commentary* 47:6 (1969), pp. 33-41.

2284 Lipset, S.M. "Rebellion on Campus." *American Educator* 4:9 (1968), pp. 28-31.

2285 ——, ed. *Student Politics.* New York: Basic Books, 1967.

2286 Lubell, S. "That Generation Gap." *The Public Interest* (Fall 1968), pp. 52-61.

2287 Mailer, Norman. *Miami and the Siege of Chicago.* New York: Signet, 1968.

2288 McNamara, R.J. "Students and Power: A Fordham Reflection." *Thought* 43:169 (1968), pp. 202-210.

2289 Menashe, Louis, ed. *Berkeley Teach-In: Vietnam.* Folkway Records, 2 LP Records: FD 5765.

2290 ——, and Ronald Radosh, eds. *Teach-Ins USA: Reports, Opinions, Documents.* New York: Praeger, 1967.

2291 Parsons, J.S. "Students in Conflict." *SAIS Review* 10:2 (Winter 1966), pp. 20-26.

2292 Peterson, R.E. *The Scope of Organized Student Protest in 1967-68.* Princeton: Educational Testing Service, 1968.

2293 Rabinowitz, Dorothy. "Power in the Academy: A Reminiscence and a Parable." *Commentary* 47:6 (1969), pp. 42-49.

2294 Rader, Dotson. *I Ain't Marchin' Anymore!* New York: McKay, 1969.

2295 Schurmann, Franz. "The NLF Asks the American Left: Where Are You Now That We Really Need You?" *Ramparts* 8 (Aug. 1969), pp. 14-22.

2296 Scott, J.W., and Mohamed El-Assad. "Multiversity, University Size, University Quality and Student Protest: An Empirical Study." *American Sociology Review* 34:5 (1969), pp. 702-709.

2297 Skolnick, Jerome. "Student Protest." *AAUP Bulletin* 55:3 (1969), pp. 309-326.

2298 Skolnick, Jerome H., ed. *The Politics of Protest: A Task Force Report Submitted to the National Commission on the Causes and Prevention of Violence.* New York: Simon & Schuster, 1970.

2299 Slek, Merry. "Styles of Handling Student Demonstrations." *Bulletin of the Atomic Scientists* 25:6 (1969), pp. 36-38.

2300 "Special Issue on the American University and Student Protest." *American Behavioral Scientist* 11 (May-June, 1968).

2301 Stavis, Ben. *We Were the Campaign: New Hampshire to Chicago for McCarthy.* Boston: Beacon, 1969.

2302 Strait, Roger. "We Can Become Responsible." *Journal: Division of Higher Education, United Church of Christ* 9:4 (1971), pp. 4-11.

2303 Trachtenberg, Alan. "Culture and Rebellion: Dilemmas of Radical Teachers." *Dissent* 16:6 (1969), pp. 497-504.

2304 Turner, Floyd. "The Student Movement as a Force for Educational Change." *Liberal Education* 56:1 (1970), pp. 39-50.

2305 U.S. Senate. Committee on the Judiciary. Hearings; *The Anti-Vietnam Agitation and the Teach-in Movement; The Problem of Communist Infiltration and Exploitation.* 89th Cong., 1st Sess., 1965.

2306 "Vietnam Critics in Perspective." *Communist Affairs* 4 (May/June 1966), pp. 7-9.

2307 *We Accuse: The Vietnam Day Protest in Berkeley, California.* Berkeley, California: The Diablo Press, 1965.

2308 Westly, D., and R.G. Braungart. "Class and Politics in the Family Backgrounds of Student Political Activists." *American Sociological Review* 31 (1966), pp. 690-692.

D / Draft Protest

2309 Alden, Cmdr. J.D. "National Strength through National Service." *U.S. Naval Institute Proceedings* 95:7 (1969), pp. 68-78.

2310 American Friends Service Committee. *The Draft?* New York: Hill and Wang, 1968.

2311 Barnett, Correlli. "On the Raising of Armies." *Horizon* 10:3 (1968), pp. 40-47.

2312 Cain, E.R. "Conscientious Objection in France, Great Britain and the United States." *Comparative Politics* 2:2 (1970), pp. 275-307.

2313 Carper, Jean. *Bitter Greetings: The Scandal of the Military Draft.* New York: Grossman, 1967.

2314 D'Amato, A.A. "War Crimes and Vietnam: The 'Nuremberg Defense' and the Military Service Resister." *California Law Review* 57 (Nov. 1969), pp. 1055-1110.

2315 Finn, J. *A Conflict of Loyalties: The Case for Selective Conscientious Objection.* New York: Pegasus, 1968.

2316 Flacks, Richard, et al. "On the Draft." In R. Perucci, and M. Pilisuk, eds., *The Triple Revolution.* Boston: Little, Brown, 1968.

2317 Gaylin, Willard. *In the Service of Their Country: War Resisters in Prison.* New York: Viking, 1970.

2318 Hoagland, Edward. "The Draft Card Gesture." *Commentary* 45:2 (1968), pp. 77-79.

2319 Killmer, Richard, Robert S. Leaky, and Deborah S. Wiley. *They Can't Go Home Again: The Story of America's Political Refugees.* Philadelphia: United Church Press, 1971.

2320 Levine, M.H., and R. Serge Denisoff."Draft Susceptibility and Vietnam War Attitudes: A Research Note." *Youth and Society* 4:2 (Dec. 1972), pp. 169-176.

2321 Lynd, Alice. *We Won't Go: Personal Accounts of War Objectors.* Boston: Beacon, 1968.

2322 Sander, Jacquin. *The Draft and the Vietnam War.* New York: Walker, 1966.

2323 Tarr, Curtis W. "The Obligation to Serve." *Air University Review* 23:5 (1972), pp. 2-11.

2324 "War Resisters: Notes from Prison." *Peace and Change* 1:1 (Fall 1972), pp. 79-81.

E / Media: Reporting the War

2325 Arlen, Michael J. *Living-Room War.* New York: Viking, 1969.

2326 Aronson, James "The Media and the Message." In *The Senator Gravel Edition: The Pentagon Papers, Critical Essays.* Vol. 5. Boston: Beacon, 1972.

2327 "As Newsmen See the Vietnam War." *War/Peace Report* 8 (Mar. 1968), pp. 6-11.

2328 Bain, C.A. "Viet Cong Propaganda Abroad." *Foreign Service Journal* (Feb. 27, 1966), pp. 22, 79-82.

2329 Baldwin, Hanson W. "The Information War in Saigon." *Reporter* 34 (Feb. 24, 1966), pp. 29-31.

2330 Blanchard, Ralph. "The Newsman in Vietnam." *U.S. Naval Institute Proceedings* 95 (Feb. 1969), pp. 50-57.

2331 Braestrup, Peter. "Covering the Vietnam War." *Nieman Reports* 23 (Dec. 1969), pp. 8-13.

2332 Browne, M.W. "Viet Nam Reporting: Three Years of Crisis." *Columbia Journalism Review* 3:3 (1964), pp. 4-9.

2333 Cleary, Col. T.J., Jr. "Aid and Comfort to the Enemy." *Military Review* 48:8 (1968), pp. 51-55.

2334 Clews, John C. *Communist Propaganda Techniques.* New York: Praeger, 1964.

2335 Compton, Neil. "Consensus Television." *Commentary* 40:4 (1965), pp. 67-72.

2336 Goodman, G.J.W. "Our Man in Saigon [David Halberstam]." *Esquire* 61:1 (1964), pp. 57-60, 144-146.

2337 Halberstam, David. "Getting the Story in Vietnam." *Commentary* 39:1 (1965), pp. 30-34.

2338 Hunter, William H. "The War in Vietnam, Luce Version." *New Republic* (Mar. 23, 1963), pp. 15-17.

2339 Jaeggi, Urs T.V., et al. *Der Vietnamkrieg und die Presse.* Zurich: EVA-Verlag, 1965.

2340 Johnson, D.B. "Vietnam: Report Card on the Press Corps at War." *Journalism Quarterly* 46 (Spring 1969), pp. 9-19.

2341 Karnow, Stanley. "The Newsmen's War in Vietnam." *Nieman Reports* 17:4 (Dec. 1963), pp. 3-8.

2342 Kirk, Gerry. "Heads They Win . . . Tails We Lose: TV and the War." *New Guard* 12:10 (Dec. 1972), pp. 8-10.

2343 Lucas, John G. *Dateline Vietnam.* New York: Crown Publication, 1966.

2344 Marshall, S.L.A. "Press Failure in Vietnam." *New Leader* 49 (Oct. 10, 1966), pp. 3-5.

2345 McDougall, D. "The Australian Press Coverage of the Vietnam War in 1965." *Australian Outlook* 20 (Dec. 1966), pp. 303-310.

2346 Polsby, N.W. "Political Science and the Press: Notes on the Coverage of a Public Opinion Survey on the Vietnam War." *Western Political Quarterly* 22 (Mar. 1969), pp. 47-60.

2347 "Press Sees Vietnam [Tet] Offensive as U.S. Defeat." *Current Digest of the Soviet Press* 20:6 (Feb. 28, 1968), pp. 3-6.

2348 "Reporting Vietnam: Eight Articles." *New Leader* 49 (Nov. 21, 1966), pp. 3-16.

2349 Rigg, Col. R.B. "How Not to Report a War." *Military Review* 49:6 (1969), pp. 14-24.

2350 Stone, I.F. "Vietnam: An Exercise in Self-Delusion." *New York Review of Books* 9 (Apr. 22, 1965), pp. 4-6.

2351 Turnbull, G.S., Jr. "Reporting of the War in Indo-China: A Critique." *Journalism Quarterly* 34 (Winter 1957), pp. 87-89.

2352 U.S. House of Representatives. Committee on Government Operations. Hearings; *U.S. Government Information Policies and Practices: The Pentagon Papers.* 92d Cong., 1st Sess., 1971.

2353 U.S. Senate. Committee on Foreign Relations. Hearings; *News Policies in Vietnam.* [August 17, 31, 1966] 89th Cong., 2d Sess., 1966.

2354 "A Viet Nam Register: Journalism and a Year in the War." *Columbia Journalism Review* 6:4 (1967/68), pp. 4-13.

2355 Yeh, Hui. "A Television Cameraman in South Vietnam." *China Reconstructs* (Peking) 15:6 (1966), pp. 8-11.

F / Effects on U.S. Economy

2356 Bowen, William. "The Vietnam War: A Cost Accounting." *Fortune* 73 (Apr. 1966), pp. 119-123.

2357 Chamber of Commerce of the United States of America. *After Vietnam: A Report of the Ad Hoc Committee on the Economic Impact of Peace After Vietnam.* Washington, D.C.: 1968.

2358 Cohen, B.J. *Vietnam, The Impact on American Business.* Princeton: Department of Economics, Princeton University, Dec. 1969.

2359 Cook, Fred J. "Greedy War." *Nation* 215:6 (Sept. 11, 1972), pp. 177-179.

2360 Dowd, D.F. "Political Economy of War." *Nation* 212 (June 28, 1971), pp. 811-815.

2361 Dudley, L., and P. Passell. "The War in Vietnam and the U.S. Balance of Payments." *Review of Economics and Statistics* 50 (Nov. 1968), pp. 437-442.

2362 Lee, D.B., Jr., and J.W. Dyckman. "Economic Impact of the Vietnam War: A Primer." *Journal of the American Institute of Planners* 36:5 (1970), pp. 298-309.

2263 Lekachman, Robert. "The Cost in National Treasure." *Saturday Review of the Society* (Dec. 1972), pp. 44-48.

2364 U.S. Arms Control and Disarmament Agency. *The Economic Impact of Reductions in Defense Spending.* Washington, D.C.: U.S. Government Printing Office, July 1972.

2365 U.S. Congress. Joint Economic Committee. Report; *Economic Effect of Vietnam Spending; Together with Supplementary Views.* [July 7, 1967] 90th Cong., 1st Sess., 1967.

2366 U.S. Library of Congress. *Impact of the Vietnam War.* [Prepared for the Committee on Foreign Relations, U.S. Senate] 92d Cong., 1st Sess., 1971.

2367 U.S. Senate. Committee on Foreign Relations. Hearings; *Impact of the War in Southeast Asia on the U.S. Economy.* [Apr-Aug 1970] 91st Cong., 2d Sess., 1970.

INDEX *Prepared by Frances R. Burns*